Margaret McMillan

Margaret McMillan
Portrait of a Pioneer

Elizabeth Bradburn

Routledge
London and New York

Dedicated to the memory of my mother whose humanity, integrity and indomitable spirit are a constant challenge to me

First published in 1989 by Routledge
11 New Fetter Lane, London EC4P 4EE
29 West 35th Street, New York NY 10001

© 1989 Elizabeth Bradburn

Set in 10/11pt Times by Hope Services Ltd, Abingdon, Oxon
and printed in Great Britain by T.J. Press (Padstow) Ltd,
Padstow, Cornwall

British Library Cataloguing in Publication Data

Bradburn, Elizabeth
  Margaret McMillan : portrait of a pioneer.
  1. England. Nursery education. McMillan,
  Margaret, 1860–1931. Biographies
  I. Title
  372'.216'0924

ISBN 0 415 01254 6

Dwell in the past and you lose one eye – forget the past and you lose both.

(Solzhenitsyn)

Contents

Preface

I never had the privilege of meeting Margaret McMillan in person. But after reading her books, lecturing on her experiments and speaking with many of her old students and staff, I increasingly felt that there must be much more about this unusual woman than had been revealed in the extant literature. There seemed to be some unexplained element in her work. So I decided to retrace her footsteps, in the hope that I might be able to unravel part of this mystery.

Dr A. Mansbridge's biography, *Margaret McMillan Prophet and Pioneer* – published in 1932, the year after her death – was a close friend's vivid, personal account of her work and teaching. He depicted Margaret as a woman with mystical qualities who had greatly influenced 'the education of children at home and abroad, both before and during the years of school life'.

D'Arcy Cresswell's memoir, *Margaret McMillan* which appeared in 1948, was the work of a New Zealand poet who reproduced in his own way the facts which Mansbridge had collected.

Towards the end of the 1950s, when members of the Nursery School Association decided to mark the centenary of Margaret's birth, G. A. N. Lowndes undertook to collate the many newly collected appreciations of those who had known her in Deptford. Completed in a few weeks in 1960, his compilation entitled *Margaret McMillan 'The Children's Champion'* contained much original material and was described as 'a voluntary tribute to a woman who was as remarkable as she was lovable'.

My first attempt at writing about her in 1976 was just a short survey of her nursery school and College, but in this biography I have tried to co-ordinate the work of previous writers as well as extend our knowledge of a great woman.

As a pivotal figure in the history of early childhood education, Margaret McMillan's practical experiments have naturally been the subject of much writing. But considerably less attention has been given to the driving force behind them and to the woman who succeeded in translating moral indignation into intelligent, effective action. So I wanted to make an attempt to go some way towards filling that gap, largely because I believe that the character, attitudes and goals of teachers are of fundamental importance in the educational process.

I also wished to present a more ordered account of the different events of her life than already exists, and produce an 'easy-to-read' narrative, free from technical jargon, which the layman, as well as the professional educator, might find helpful.

As I was unable to find any comprehensive list of Margaret McMillan's newspaper articles and pamphlets I set out to make a fresh collection and collation of these, little knowing what a Herculean task I had undertaken. That assignment, together with my endeavours to record the memories of her former students while they were still available, proved to be more time-consuming than I had anticipated; it stretched over a seven-year period.

However, now that the nursery school is a recognised part of our country's educational system, perhaps it is important that educators in particular should appreciate from what small beginnings it has grown, and understand the personal decisions and sacrifices it demanded of its founders.

In the light of current discussions on the urgent need for urban renewal, the provision of more nursery education and more initial and in-service training courses for nursery school teachers, a review of Margaret McMillan's work in a congested inner-city area may be opportune. At a time when a change in attitudes and lifestyles is being called for to enable our interdependent world to survive, perhaps a reappraisal of her bold attack on the causes and consequences of poverty is also timely.

Wherever possible I have tried to let Margaret speak directly to the reader and let her and her contemporaries describe how she tried to care for the disadvantaged and needy. After the story of her life draws to a close there are two additional chapters in the nature of an afterword. Chapter 24 contains a brief discussion on the subject of the book, my approach to the material and some personal observations. Chapter 25, primarily addressed to teachers, parents, school governors and administrators, specifies certain areas of concern within the field of early childhood education today which urgently require attention.

If any readers find fresh hope and inspiration in this book, it will have amply served its purpose.

E. Bradburn
Liverpool, 1988

Acknowledgements

It is with much pleasure that I now offer my sincere thanks to all those who helped in the preparation of this book.

I gladly record my gratitude to the Leverhulme Research Awards Committee for the Emeritus Fellowship which enabled me to complete the research for this publication.

My thanks are due too to the National Christian Education Council for permission to quote extracts from my previous book – *Margaret McMillan: Framework and Expansion of Nursery Education*. I am also grateful to the authors and publishers of the books listed in the bibliography.

Furthermore, I am indebted to numerous librarians, archivists, historians and photographers in Britain, Switzerland and America who willingly entered into the search for the original sources of information I required and were relentless in their pursuit of them.

It would be difficult to mention by name all the friends who read the text and made valuable suggestions, but special reference must be made to the contributions of Harry Addison, Alan Faunce and Margaret Forman. Apart from undertaking such tedious tasks as proof-reading, they read the manuscript more than once and made many constructive criticisms.

Finally, I wish to express my thanks to all the typists who worked on the various drafts, especially Mrs P. Monk who, from the formative stages of the book, gave liberal secretarial help as well as much encouragement.

Major Life Events and Publications

1860	Born in Westchester County, New York.
1865	Death of her father. Left America, arrived in Inverness, Scotland, with her mother and sister Rachel.
1870–6	Educated at High School and Royal Academy, Inverness.
1878	Studied music in Germany at Frankfurt-on-Main.
1879	Employed as a governess in Edinburgh.
1881–3	Studied languages in Switzerland, taught English in Geneva and Lausanne.
1883–9	Returned to Britain, took various posts as a governess, the last at Ludlow, Shropshire.
1889	Lived with her sister Rachel in Bloomsbury, London, and did voluntary work for the Labour Movement.
1889–92	Employed as companion to Lady Meux of Park Lane, London.
1893	Became founder-member of Independent Labour Party (ILP). Accepted invitation from Bradford Socialists to work there voluntarily; Rachel accompanied her.
1893–4	Rachel left Bradford to train as a sanitary inspector and afterwards worked for Kent County Council.
1894	Margaret elected as ILP representative on the Bradford School Board.
1901	Publication of *Early Childhood*, Swan Sonnenschein.
1902	Resigned from Bradford School Board. Went to live with Rachel in Bromley, Kent.
1904	Appointed by the London County Council as a manager of a group of schools in Deptford, London. Publication of *Education Through the Imagination*, Dent.

1907   Elected as Member of the National Administrative Council of the ILP.
Publication of *Labour and Childhood*, Swan Sonnenschein.

1908   Opened a Health Clinic in Bow, London.

1910   Opened a Treatment Centre in Deptford.

1911   Given the use of 353 Evelyn Street, Deptford; used the garden as an open-air night camp for girls and play area for children under five years.
Opened a night camp for boys in St Nicholas' graveyard.

1913   Rented the Stowage site from the London County Council.

1914   Opened an open-air nursery school on the Stowage site, then a Training Centre.

1917   Death of Rachel.
Margaret invested with the Order of CBE.
Publication of *The Camp School*, George Allen and Unwin.

1919   Publication of *The Nursery School*, Dent.

1923   Elected as President of the Nursery School Association (now the British Association for Early Childhood Education), until 1929.

1927   Publication of *The Life of Rachel McMillan*, Dent.

1930   Founded the Rachel McMillan Training College for Teachers. Invested with the Order of CH.
Publication of *The Nursery School*, Dent.

1931   Died in Harrow-on-the-Hill, Middlesex, and buried in Brockley Cemetery, London.

Chapter one

Introduction

Margaret McMillan's life was full of paradox: a Scot who loved her native heath, she spent most of her time in the industrial areas of northern England and East London; born into a middle-class family, she became a colleague of Keir Hardie and founder-member of the Independent Labour Party; deeply spiritual, she was the intensely practical founder of school medical inspection and open-air nursery schools; unmarried, she often said, 'All children are mine.' Trained as a governess, she sought to make good health and education available to the children of the urban slums and in so doing changed the course of educational history.

Outraged by the living and working conditions of the poor in Victorian England, Margaret McMillan threw herself whole-heartedly into the crusade for a better society and found fulfilment in the struggle. She was described as a woman radiant with conviction, and as 'the woman whom no difficulty could daunt'.[1]

She was one of a group of remarkable, well-educated women with high ideals and strongly developed social consciences. Florence Nightingale, Beatrice Webb, Katharine Bruce Glasier, the Pankhursts, are just a few of those who, like Margaret, cut loose from their middle-class backgrounds to fight for the commonweal. Referring to her work in Yorkshire in the 1890s, G. A. N. Lowndes, one of her biographers, saw her as the 'Albert Schweitzer of the Bradford slums'.[2] From her 50s to the end of her life in 1931, she might have been called the Mother Teresa of the Deptford slums.

Margaret's life helped to dispel the myth that the ordinary person could do little or nothing to counteract the social evils of an age. Bishop Gore recognised this accomplishment when he said:

History is full of examples of how much can be done even by one person in removing the burdens which drag our humanity down. Let us think only of two women. What a vast and permanent

1

work Constance Smith did for women in factories and Margaret McMillan for our sickly school children. In each case, we wonder to see how wide-spreading and permanent a remedy could proceed out of a single life.[3]

Margaret was a legend in her own lifetime, and one around whom anecdotes inevitably gathered. But those close to her knew she could never be dismissed lightly; there were hidden depths to her character. Albert Mansbridge, her first biographer and founder of the Workers' Educational Association, recalled that he once asked his friend John Lewis Paton, the educationist and writer, who he thought were the three greatest persons he, Mansbridge, had ever known. Paton 'answered at once: "Charles Gore, Margaret McMillan, and my father." He was right.'[4]

Her influence was not confined to a few individuals, or to her own country. She had a profound effect on educational practice world-wide. Lady Astor, the first woman to sit in the House of Commons, wrote:

> Margaret McMillan was a genius in her way, and it is largely owing to her efforts that nearly every civilized country realizes that it is just as important to begin with children before they are five as it is after that age.[5]

Although intensely busy with the various establishments she founded, Margaret never became entirely bound by them; she had many outside interests. She readily agreed to serve on committees, speak at political meetings, open schools and clinics, and give lectures for those who had only meagre claims on her.

In addition to those activities, her pen was constantly busy with articles, reports and books which were designed to arouse public opinion on a number of issues. The mere list of her books and articles suggests one person's life-work, apart from her practical experiments. Yet, despite all her different involvements, she was never too busy to care for individuals.

Michael Sadler, one time Vice-chancellor of Leeds University, said of Margaret and her sister Rachel, who worked closely with her:

> Their work has been seminal. Both . . . have given their lives for the future of England. As years go on, the significance of their
> . work will become clear. They have pointed the way . . .
> Compassion, courage, persistency, generous thrift, and the thoughtful adjustment of means to ends are the qualities called for by the finest kinds of social reform. These the two sisters have practised.[6]

Margaret McMillan, sometimes referred to as an 'untiring pioneer', belonged to a long line of forerunners who at the end of life could sing:

> We today's procession heading,
> We the route for travel clearing,
> Pioneers! O Pioneers.[7]

Chapter two

Childhood Influences

Margaret McMillan's earliest years were idyllic. Born of good Highland stock on 19 July 1860, in Westchester County, New York, she was fortunate in her forbears. Both of her parents came from families well known for their integrity and social concern and both grew up in Inverness-shire, Scotland.

Her father, James McMillan, was a member of the Clan MacMillan of MacMillan whose family crest displayed a two-handed sword symbolising the obligation of successive generations to defend the unfortunate. This idea was reinforced by the Virgilian motto encompassing the sword – 'Miseris succerrere disco' – which Margaret always translated as 'I learn to succour the helpless.' That was the tradition which she inherited.

James, the youngest of ten children, was reared on his father's farm which was set in an area of great scenic beauty in Glen Urquhart, near to Loch Ness. Describing the district Margaret said: 'It had a mysterious, romantic loveliness, . . . The dark hills stand round in mystic silence . . . and this peculiar listening silence is felt, too, in the valleys and along the banks of the dark clear loch.'[1]

Like many of his clan, James McMillan had a strong sense of justice. Even in his youth he questioned the moral right of landlords to charge crofters high rents and give them little security of tenure. His decision to emigrate to America in his early 20s was both a revolt against what he saw as a semi-feudal system in Scotland and a declaration of intent to make a better life for himself on the other side of the Atlantic.

In America he found work about ten miles north of New York first as a landscape gardener and tender of vines, then as an estate manager. He visited his family in Scotland regularly, but after the death of both of his parents decided to settle in the United States permanently. While the New World gave him a livelihood, the old world provided him with a wife. On one of his return visits to Scotland he fell in love with Jane Cameron of Dochfour, near Inverness. They were married on 3 March 1858, and set out for America the very next day.

Like the McMillans, the Camerons were originally farmers. They were strict Presbyterians – renowned for their moral rectitude and active benevolence. Robert Cameron, Jane's father, being a factor at the Dochfour estate, was able to provide adequately for his family; though he was not wealthy, as a land agent he was comfortably off.

Born near to Tomnahurich (the hill of the fairies), Jane spent most of her early years in Dochfour. Speaking of that area Margaret said: 'The air is soft like a caress in summer; far off, the valleys nestle under the green and purple hills, the hills that listen as no other hills listen and wait in this world.'[2] Jane's family and neighbours found it hard to say goodbye to her when she married: 'the country people for miles around grieved because she was going so far away.'[3]

Her mother, Rachel Cameron, never understood how the McMillans could even think of leaving Scotland – the country she loved so dearly. When her new son-in-law as much as hinted that Scotland was in any way inferior to America, she could not conceal her wrath. In a letter dated 31 August 1859, she wrote: 'Let me once more wield my feeble pen to crush and bruise all who dare throw a reproachful glance or word at the institutions or laws of our exemplary country.'[4]

Once in America, Jane wrote home regularly and dutifully to her family, describing in detail their long 15-day journey across the Atlantic and her arrival in the new land. When they reached their home near New York she said, 'the surrounding country is like the old country', and went on to say that it had 'a beautiful appearance'.[5] Although Jane was radiantly happy with James, Scotland was never far from her thoughts. Margaret said of her mother: 'She was always, even in her great happiness, dreaming of the homeland and the home people.'[6]

This blissful couple had three children. Rachel was born at Throgg's Neck, Westchester County, on 25 March 1859, a few weeks after their first wedding anniversary. Margaret arrived 16 months later. The census return for 1860 shows that by then James was the titular head of a fairly large household. Apart from the four McMillans there were eight resident servants including a coachman, several male labourers and two women servants. Soon, however, they moved to a wooden house on a magnificent site near an estuary. Modelled on the lines of Dutch settlers' houses, it was painted a soft greyish-lavender colour. Margaret gives us a picture of its setting:

> Everything is on a vast scale . . . At the back of the house rose a green slope with a winding path leading up between more trees, but which ceased abruptly at the top of the bank, leaving bare and wide to the dazzled eye a wonderful expanse of laughing and dancing water.[7]

This lush countryside seems to have made such a deep impression on her that she made it the setting for a short story printed in *The Clarion* in 1897.[8]

In 1862 Elizabeth, the last child, was born to James and Jane. Soon after, Jane's sister, known to the children as Auntie Maggie, wrote to Margaret saying: 'Just you try if you can beat Rachel at your lessons. I dare say Lizzie will soon eclipse both of you if you don't take care.'[9] But despite frequent family letters, to the McMillan children Scotland seemed a million miles away.

Recalling her childhood in America, where members of different races lived near to them, Margaret said:

> My clear memories begin with the hot time. The wooden house is a mere shelter in summer. It seems less a house than a kind of roofed series of gateways opening on the wide sunlit world. Darkies come and go through the farther gateway and windows. They live all round us, as well as under our roof . . . Ours is a piebald world.[10]

Their parents took the task of rearing children seriously and were very mindful of their daughters' religious education. Mansbridge, Margaret's biographer, describes a typical Sunday in their home:

> James and the girls were sent, on the Sabbath, to an upper room to sing hymns. When the door was shut and the 'impious' noise could not escape to the mother's ears, he taught them nursery rhymes. Thus light and humour had place side by side with religious austerity.[11]

Margaret's first five years were probably the happiest and most carefree of her life. Recalling them she said: 'It is a very happy life. Our parents are modern and American in their ideas . . . They impose no needless restrictions on us . . . and yet we are not left to the mercy of impulse and riot of selfish instinct.'[12] But Margaret's privileged infancy, full of laughter and love, was soon to come to an abrupt end. In 1865, when Americans generally were still mourning the assassination of their beloved President, Abraham

Lincoln, death broke into the McMillan family circle bringing with it a series of traumatic shocks.

On 16 July Elizabeth, Margaret's youngest sister, died in a fierce heat. To devastate the family further, on 21 July James McMillan died. Speaking of her father's death Margaret said:

> Death is so great a mystery that children reject it often as a reality. We asked where he had gone and when he would be back again. Then we were taken to see him. He lay on a great block of ice. His face was beautiful. The water from the melting ice dripped slowly into a tub . . . There followed strange days. Our mother's grief knew no bounds.[13]

James died intestate, but fortunately he had left an inventory of his estate on an unsigned piece of paper. Later, lawyers ascertained that at the time of his death, his gross assets amounted to $4,470 and his residual estate to $3,470, so his widow was not left penniless, as many previous writers have suggested. The sterling equivalent of US$4,470 and $3,470 was £920 and £714 respectively in 1865. The equivalent in purchasing power of the residual sum of £714 in 1865 would be £20,891.64 in 1987.

Yet there were difficulties in settling James' estate, and Jane was left heart-broken at the double bereavement. Then a fresh blow came with the news that Rachel, whose health had always been precarious, was seriously ill. After a full examination the doctor's verdict was that she was unlikely to survive another North American winter. At this point Jane, who was overcome with sorrow, decided that she must uproot her remaining family, go back to Scotland and join her parents, who were now living in Inverness. For Rachel and Margaret, who were aged 5 and 6, it meant exchanging a home life which they had greatly enjoyed for a life with grandparents whom they had never met.

On arriving in Scotland, the McMillans were received into their grandparents' home at Hawthorn Cottage on the old Edinburgh Road. This solid stone house, situated in one of the town's best residential suburbs, had a dour atmosphere inside, in stark contrast to the lavender-painted wooden house and the joyous, affectionate home which they had left behind; nevertheless, the Scottish home commanded their deep respect.

When they first met their grandfather he was a handsome, white-haired, undemonstrative and silent man. Though Margaret recalled that his affection towards them was not openly expressed, she later came to agree with her mother's assessment of him as the 'one support and bulwark' of their 'otherwise unprotected lives'.[14] Some 40 years later, she dedicated her book *Labour and*

Childhood to him with these words: 'To the memory of my grandfather who was a father to me and whose gentle and chivalrous character first taught me to have faith in humanity.'[15]

Their grandmother was a forceful character who, at the age of 16, ran away from home to marry her beloved Robert. Reviewing their first meeting Margaret said:

> She was not much over 50 at that time. She was shocked by our red mourning and put us into black at once, and she looked disapprovingly at our high boots. Small of stature, she had a strong profile, heavy iron-grey hair and very bright, keen, sparkling eyes.[16]

For Margaret's mother life in her parents' home, where she had to take a back seat, was disagreeable. She could not afford a home of her own, but was able to make a financial contribution to the family's outgoings. She felt welcome, yet knew she was little more than an appendage to the household. Margaret thought: 'It was as if she had done something wrong in becoming a widow' and, despite her occasional efforts to be cheerful, she remained dressed in deep mourning and 'more often she appeared depressed and alone'.[17]

Her daughters, too, were sometimes very unhappy in their new home. They found the sudden change from America to Scotland quite bewildering. They both realised, as Margaret said, that a great love which had made their lives so full of joy had passed away.

Some of the sisters' happiest hours were spent away from the family, when they managed to escape either to the attic, where they were allowed to browse in old family books, or to the garden. The love of nature, which one senses in Margaret's descriptions of her American home, may have been developed in the large walled garden which surrounded the house in Inverness. Speaking of it as a grown-up she said: 'I remember most vividly spring and summer . . . the wall bright with japonica . . . and the flowers in my garden, where I worked on Sabbath morning in utter forgetfulness of the sacred day and looked for judgement and wrath to come . . .'[18] This love of gardens runs like a thread through her life and later was to make her long that all city children should enjoy them too.

Even at an early age Margaret seems to have reflected on some of the deeper questions of life such as suffering and the unequal distribution of wealth. She said:

> I was puzzled mainly by God and Heaven, and Hell, and Death, and Sin. But I was also puzzled to know why some people were

rich and others poor . . . Like most children, however, I gave up puzzling at last and only hoped I might become very rich.[19]

One of the things she suffered from as a child was deafness, which came on at the age of three following an attack of scarlet fever. Although, fortunately, at 14 this cleared without any treatment, according to her own account she never heard her father's voice and only her mother's when she was in her teens. This experience must have had a profound effect on her life in the new home as well as at school and have been an additional reason why this period in Scotland was largely unhappy. Nevertheless, instead of indulging in self-pity, Margaret said she was glad that 'the grave problems of life were not all hustled out of sight and hearing . . . The tragic side of things, the swiftness of calamity and change, the sudden plunge from sunshine to shadow, all this was present . . .' Believing that suffering has a creative part to play in character formation she observed 'how various orders of suffering in children do indeed bear unsuspected fruit and it is not all bitter'.[20]

Sundays at the Camerons' home revolved around the church services, Margaret and Rachel attending both the English and Gaelic. Looking back Margaret remarked: 'Though I was deaf I could hear the wailing Gaelic singing. The ministers I looked on as supermen, and, indeed, the Gaelic minister was a very perfect gentleman, courteous and attentive even to deaf little girls.'[21]

The English-speaking Free High Church which the sisters attended was a very lively institution with an ear open to the world's needs. The congregation's benevolence and interest in other countries probably helped to feed and widen the growing minds of the young McMillans.

Arriving in Scotland at a time when education was neither compulsory nor free, the sisters had a better than average schooling because their family valued education. First of all they were sent to the High School where, as in their Sunday School, they were given a grounding in the Christian way of life.

The High School was probably typical of Scottish schools in general. At this time education usually meant straight instruction of the mind. Methods were formal, discipline was strict; children were expected to be industrious, and those who chose to be disobedient or indolent were punished with a strong leather strap – the tawse. Where this school scored over many was in its exceptionally good, well-informed teachers who engendered a love of learning in their pupils.

Margaret believed that children then were 'expected to learn and listen to a great deal of talk from teachers that *was* over their heads'. Her grandmother approved entirely of children sometimes learning things they didn't understand. She maintained that it gave them something to think of as they grew older instead of having 'everything so easy that the average child could have no great mental exercise at all and nothing much to depend upon as storage'.[22]

While admitting that the curriculum was good, Margaret does not appear to have enjoyed her High School days. She had bad memories of strict teachers which remained with her for the whole of her life. She felt a deep sympathy for the unruly boys on whom the masters used the tawse 'with energy and unction'.[23] Even in the year before she died, writing to one of her old school friends, she said:

> I was a deaf child – and on the whole a very unhappy one . . .
> There was a teacher who knocked my hair ribbons off when I
> didn't know what he said. I used to sit and dream of another
> world where Rachel and Mother were with me and it was all
> beautiful . . .

She expressed a wish to tell a certain teacher the truth about himself and the system: 'Reform. Reform. That's what Scotland needs. What memories of suffering and cruelty I have of my native land.'[24]

During their school days there were obvious differences in the sisters. Rachel was fair, Margaret was dark with jet-black ringlets, and tougher both physically and mentally than Rachel. They differed in temperament too. One of their school friends remembers how Rachel was a happy, vivacious child whom teachers liked while 'Margaret was a very earnest serious student who was generally found "parading the playgrounds with one or two like-minded, no doubt discussing some subjects far beyond their years".'[25] Margaret was physically strong and excitable. In a letter to Lady Astor she wrote: 'Once when I was eight I was asked to my first party. I was so glad that I got ill and couldn't go.'[26] She had beautiful dark eyes and a fine rich voice and was surrounded by an air of asceticism. One who knew her wrote:

> Even in her childhood people noticed and commented on her
> withdrawn, other-worldish air. This was perhaps partly
> occasioned by the deafness from which she suffered . . . And
> even when she regained her hearing, she never quite lost the
> habit of living apart.[27]

In 1874 the sisters left the High School. Their family decided that Margaret, who was now 14, should continue her education as a day girl at the Inverness Royal Academy, while Rachel, who was 15, was to become boarder at a school in Coventry owned by distant relatives who offered her a free place there. So when their school terms began they had their first experience of being separated from each other for months at a time.

Clearly the McMillans were fortunate to have relatives who, at this period, took the education of girls seriously. Their mother in particular, although of only limited means, was determined that her daughters should have a sound education. Margaret tells how, even when they were at the High School, she spent generously on their training, paying for them to have 'coaching as well as schoolwork and private teaching for music and other subjects'.

But why, one wonders, was Rachel and not Margaret sent to school in Coventry? As money was not plentiful, it is understandable that Mrs McMillan would be glad to be relieved of the expense of paying for one daughter's education, and possibly she had no say as to which one was to be educated free. Had she had any choice in the matter, it might have been sensible for her to suggest that Margaret took the place in Coventry, as she would have been less afraid than Rachel of going away from home. Also the departure of Margaret, with her independent spirit, might have lessened the growing tension within the family. She was less submissive than Rachel who, according to Margaret, 'was always trying to please and help everyone – which was an impossible task'.[28] Their mother may have thought that the Midlands' climate would be less severe for Rachel than that of the Highlands. In addition, the school had excellent facilities for physical education.

Anyhow, as arranged, Margaret attended the Inverness Academy which had been founded in 1792 for the education of the upper classes. Here too, as in most Scottish schools, religious instruction was taken seriously and she would be given a sound, Bible-based religious education. She probably had this in mind when, later in life, in an election campaign, she answered a critic, who jeeringly remarked that it was a great pity she had no religion, by saying: 'It was assumed that she had never read the Bible – she, a Scotswoman (laughter)! She had read the Bible, and she had taught the Bible, she believed, with much greater thoroughness than any clergyman in Bradford.'[29]

Whilst Margaret sometimes defended the Academy's reputation, underneath she was critical of many aspects of the school. She felt that girls at the Academy 'were trained to be ridiculous snobs', and that her school life made her 'a rebel and also a reformer'.[30] There was certainly open rivalry, such as snowball fights, between those at a nearby Dr Bell's school and those at the Academy. The prevailing attitudes towards education seemed to be more serious at the Academy than in some schools. Typical of the many entries in the log books of Dr Bell's school, which were unlikely to appear in those of the Academy, were: 'Attendance considerably lower on account of Sanger's Circus. Attendance lower than usual on account of horse racing and games. Miss Annabella McL., pupil teacher, who has been snowed up in Strathmore since Christmas, returned to work.'[31]

What Margaret probably rebelled against most during her years at the Academy was being separated from her sister during term-time. Rachel's absence left her, an energetic teenager, alone at home with a group of elderly, Gaelic-speaking adults. But after three years this situation came to an unexpected end when deep sorrow invaded the family again.

At the beginning of April 1877 their grandfather, who was 74, became ill, grew steadily weaker, and then died. Worse still, three months later their mother, who was only 49, developed hernia trouble. After an illness lasting barely four days, she too passed away on 14 July.

The effect of this on Rachel, who had hoped to do so much to make her mother happy, was devastating, as Margaret reports: 'Rachel had made so many plans to help and gladden her . . . all in vain. This was the end – death! . . . She lost her faith and attended church to avoid argument, but it no longer held any true meaning for her.'[32]

Margaret, who did not write much about her own feelings, must have been deeply grieved too. This was the fourth time in twelve years that the sisters experienced the death of near relatives. Having lost both parents and still being only in their late teens, they now had few really close relatives in whom they could confide.

Mrs McMillan, like her husband, died intestate, but her estate was valued at £372. The smallness of the sum may partly explain why Margaret said her mother's position within the family was becoming increasingly difficult. That there was any money at all was entirely due to her frugality. Margaret recalled, many years later, how as a child she had had to wear Rachel's clothes.

After the funerals, some of Margaret's uncles came to the conclusion that at 70 their widowed mother needed, as well as deserved, a full-time nurse-companion. So they asked Rachel to shoulder this burden.

Had Rachel returned to Coventry her grandmother would have been left alone at Hawthorn Cottage with Margaret whom she did not particularly like, as one of Margaret's letters to a younger friend indicates:

Do you know I remember the actual day on which you were born. I remember what I did on that day. I got into trouble with my grandmother who was not always pleased with me and who as I got older liked me less and less.[33]

There is little evidence to indicate how Rachel felt about not going back to school, or how much choice she had in the matter, but we know that she took full responsibility for looking after her old grandmother. This meant that, instead of continuing her education, training for a profession and enjoying the companionship of her peers, she was forced to spend many years of her girlhood nursing an elderly relative.

Chapter three

Embarking on a Career 1878–89

When Margaret considered a career she said she wanted to become a finishing governess. So Grandmother Cameron who, along with Uncle Donald, acted as guardian to her granddaughters, decided that she should be sent to Frankfurt-on-Main for a year, to study music and learn German.

Because of the ideas swirling around the continent at this time, Margaret would naturally have been exposed to new philosophical, political and economic theories, including those of Karl Marx. Many avant-garde French writers, such as Zola, were attempting to shift the thinking of the complacent by exposing the crude lifestyle of low-paid workers; many painters too were vigorously expressing bold, unorthodox views. It is likely that in this climate Margaret would have re-examined some of the Christian ideas of her early upbringing.

After completing her training, she returned to Britain, obtained a post as a governess with a family called Drummond in Edinburgh, and continued her education there. The Drummond home itself was a cultural centre, being a regular meeting place for some of the city's intellectual élite. Like Mrs Drummond, many of the visitors were in no doubt of Margaret's 'great intellectual gifts and the width of her reading'.[1]

Her generous blend of earnestness and impishness and the way her mind was eagerly breaking out into new fields, can be seen in a letter she wrote to Robert, one of her Edinburgh cousins, who regularly borrowed books for her:

June 15th

My Dear Robert,
   I am very sorry I could not get to see you all last week, but I will be in on Saturday. I cannot however get away for Friday. Mrs D. comes back tonight. I hope she will not scold me. Privately I confess 'I have done many things I ought not to have

done' and I am just going to do another *viz – study* Voltaire, Zola, Flaubert and other sinners. I will, however, begin with the arch-evil one – Voltaire. Can you get him for me before Saturday???

Said a good old leddy to me last night, 'My Dear – if there be anything good, pure, holy, etc. think on that, and avoid the very appearance of evil'. Now I pardon her her brains for her good heart, but isn't that rubbish? How are we to shut our holy eyes on things that affect and sway us whether we will or not? And if we deal with theologians and philanthropists only, what will we do with pessimists and atheists who (tell it not to Aunt) are often the best lot? I'm going to wade into a sink of iniquity to see if there isn't something to be picked up there: in the limpid stream of integrity where I find myself, I find many hard things that hurt my feet, yet never enrich me.

Love to Aunt and all.

> I remain
> Your faithful cousin,
> Maggie.

P.S. I don't mind sending a kiss to Uncle D – in a letter![2]

The most far-reaching event of Margaret's time in Edinburgh was her falling passionately in love. Whilst the details were submerged in Victorian propriety and no personal letters survive, those who knew her felt that the disturbing consequences remained with her for years. Albert Mansbridge, who knew Margaret intimately, said that, although she was conscious of this tempestuous affair all her life, she rarely referred to it. He believed that she 'must have yearned for children of her own' and wrote, 'Margaret the conqueror is an inspiration to all women, hindered in their normal expression, to conquer by love and by loving serve.'[3]

Whether that love affair accounts for her relatively short stay in Edinburgh, or whether a genuine desire to continue her education elsewhere impelled her to leave, we do not know. But in 1881 Margaret left for Switzerland. First she went to Geneva – Rousseau's birthplace – to a school she said was 'filled with girls from 17 to 22 years old', where she taught English and studied languages.

This experience extended her intellectually and socially. She often spoke of 'the glowing enthusiasm for education and living science' that she had found in Geneva amongst her fellow students who were 'exiles, revolutionary refugees' from Russia and

Germany and dedicated 'to the struggle for freedom against every form of oppression and superstition'.[4]

Two students in particular influenced Margaret's thinking. One, a Russian revolutionary called Vera, advised Margaret not to concentrate on teaching the rich but to work for the poor as 'it is not only a privilege, it is the only real work possible'.[5] The other friend was a much-travelled American girl who knew all about the Highland Clearances although she had never actually been to Scotland. Like her father Margaret reacted strongly against any kind of injustice, and her friend's account of the unfair way some Scottish landlords had turned cottars off their land to provide deer hunters with sport grieved her. Thinking over the many conversations she had with these two girls Margaret reported later, 'I came back much enlightened to my native land.'[6] Years later, when she began to embrace socialist theories about the brotherhood of man, snatches of these conversations with the American girl came flooding back into her consciousness.

A thought-provoking letter from Rachel, received about this time, proved to be another seminal event in Margaret's life. At a time when Margaret's emotional life was in such a turbulent state that she found it difficult to control her own nature, Rachel wrote to her about a power which had come into her life and transformed it. Margaret described the incident in this way:

> I was sitting in a garden at Les Grottes, Geneva, one September evening, when I got a letter from Rachel which puzzled me. It described an experience of which I had no understanding and which I had no power to interpret. Something had happened to Rachel, something that had never happened to me – a sudden inrush of new consciousness. Later I learned that this thing had come to many, that it was no uncommon experience, though it was new to me; a swift realisation of life where she had thought there was vacancy. Watchful love, strange intelligence, a throbbing companionship near, invisible, with power to confer a joy beyond expression. Joy, great joy. An adventure such as love is, but a greater adventure, and a keener joy than human love confers.
>
> I sat in the summer dusk near a pond in the garden, and could make nothing of this. I knew of only one kind of love that can come to a beautiful girl. I did not know that there is another, a love more ecstatic and wonderful, that can find us in youth and hold us captive to the end.[7]

This deep spiritual experience, which Rachel recorded in her diary, occurred during the time when her mother's death had made her cynical, if not bitter. But after this event her outlook was completely changed. While the outer circumstances, which compelled her to look after her old grandmother in the limited confines of the home, remained the same, her attitude to the task changed and she became conscious of a new inner freedom. Once liberated from her gnawing negativism, she felt a strong urge to find a great creative mission. Rachel was now aware that, while will-power, time and work had not healed her grief-stricken heart, God had. But Margaret, still driven by her emotions, was unable to understand this. She found her sister's letter so bewildering that she tossed it aside, yet could not forget it entirely.

After finishing her studies in Geneva, where she became fluent in French, Margaret went on to Lausanne, but she could not settle down there. So, after only a short stay, she decided to return to Scotland where she was fortunate enough to secure several posts as a governess, but was very restless and found little satisfaction in anything she undertook. Confiding in her friend, Mrs Sutcliffe, she said: 'I could keep no situation, everyone thought I would be a failure. My Uncle thought I should get married. I see now that that would have been in all probability a failure.'[8]

Records are scanty about the next few years. Added to her emotional problems was the realisation that the future had no shape or form. But fortunately her life soon took an upward turn.

Her last post as a governess was with a young family in Ludlow, Shropshire. There she tutored the children of the Rector, the Reverend Edward ffarington Clayton, in languages and music. Amidst the spiritual climate of that family, like Rachel, she had a dynamic religious experience, and a new, transforming friendship with God began.

This renewed relationship is the key to an understanding of the rest of her life; the social work in which she later became involved was cradled in it. In replying to a letter from Mrs Sutcliffe, who persistently asked her for the facts about her life because she wanted to write a play about it, Margaret tried to describe this spiritual awakening:

> Then it came – the real event. Dear it is never an earthly event at all . . . one night – well *it* came. I know what are called the Invisible Powers, that they are near us all, but reach us I think only after suffering and prayer . . . I don't understand much. Can explain nothing – only that beyond these voices there are others and the others matter most. And the ordinary person can be great, powerful – all powerful if he can get tuned to be the

Instrument of the Unseen. I got only such a little tuned, so very little . . . I would say nothing only you make me, dearie.[9]

Living in the atmosphere of the Rectory, attending the church services and the daily family prayers, must have been conducive, if not directly contributory to that experience. The following appreciation of the Rector by one of his parishioners gives us a portrait of Margaret's employer:

> To few priests it is permitted to guide the spiritual destinies of a single town for over forty years, and fewer still have the courage and selflessness to decline preferment in order that they may finish the work which God gave them to do . . . of him it could truly be said 'he lived what he preached'.[10]

The Rectory, as well as being a spiritual beacon, was also a lively welfare centre. There Margaret saw a wealthy, privileged family taking responsibility for a neighbourhood. Ludlow was largely indebted to the Rector for its dispensary and cottage hospital. In addition he gave food to the hungry. Perhaps his greatest monument, however, were the Church Schools. The cause of education was always dear to his heart.

Margaret arrived in Ludlow a self-willed individualist, a frustrated idealist who had been crossed in love, but she discovered a Power while living with the Claytons, that healed her torn heart and spoke to her at the deepest level of her personality. Writing to Mrs Sutcliffe on one occasion she said: 'Not until we are brought low does the courage awaken which arms itself with secret forces. Secret forces! It is by these that we do not merely go down into the dark places, but go *through*.'[11] After her religious experience in Ludlow, much of her own emotional tumult subsided and she developed spiritual insight and a new love for people. Describing her in later life Mansbridge said:

> To understand her it is necessary to regard her as one who was so deeply rooted in things spiritual as to be indifferent to all else. Yet such indifference, paradoxically enough, endowed her with passionate longing and untiring energy – things temporal must be in harmony with things eternal.[12]

Chapter four

From Ludlow to Bloomsbury 1889–92

While Margaret was away from home working as a governess, Rachel was looking after their grandmother. After her husband's death, Mrs Cameron had to live with a granddaughter to whom hitherto she had not been particularly close. However, 'now that she was flung back on Rachel for companionship and service, she faced the new situation with courage and tolerance'.[1]

Fortunately, during Rachel's years in Inverness, there were four major events which altered the whole course of her life, and subsequently affected Margaret too. Had it not been for several unexpected turns in Rachel's life, Margaret's might have flowed in a completely different direction.

The first of these important incidents was the profound religious experience which she described in the letter Margaret received in Geneva. After this, her old cynicism having disappeared, she began to find a deep satisfaction in the many different aspects of homemaking. Her efficiency astounded the doctors who claimed that 'never before had mere nursing achieved so much' making her grandmother's life 'a happy and even an exhilarating experience to the end'.[2]

The second generative influence came in 1885, after Rachel read W. T. Stead's article on juvenile prostitution in the *Pall Mall Gazette*. There Stead revealed how children of 13 and upwards were enticed into houses of ill-fame as well as bought for anything between five and twenty pounds. Child prostitution was said to prevail in 'no city in Europe to so large an extent' as in London.[3] Commenting on this, one historian said that the general public: 'though still capable of weeping over the plight of little girls in three-volume novels, seemed curiously unmoved by . . . the traffic in living girls.'[4] Eventually, as a result of the uproar caused by Stead's articles, the government was forced to raise the age of consent to 16 and bring in legislation to protect women.

Stead then urged the public to take preventive action to brighten the lot of the workers. He argued for: 'improved dwellings, for more air, for other playgrounds than the street, for more widely extended education, for free libraries, for more baths.'[5] Rachel, though not free at this point to volunteer for any kind of social work, was at least aware now of one large area of social need. At school she had dreamed of taking part in some great mission which would benefit humanity; here was one sphere of service which beckoned her.

The third major influence on her life was socialism. As a slight diversion from housekeeping, she made occasional visits to Edinburgh to stay with relatives who were in touch with a lively group of socialists which included John Gilray who introduced her to socialist papers. According to Margaret, Rachel became 'a diligent attender at Socialist meetings'.[6]

In addition to public meetings, there were small private gatherings of socialists where members studied *Das Kapital*. Dr John Glasse – the well-known minister of Greyfriars – preached socialism, but constantly emphasised that this did not necessarily imply opposition to Christianity.

Rachel's interest in socialist views steadily grew as an extract from a letter to one of her Edinburgh cousins reveals:

> Hawthorn Cottage,
> 24 March 1887
>
> My Dear Cousin,
> I am sending with this letter some of Mr. Gilray's pamphlets, etc., etc., on Socialism. I am very glad to have had them, and could never have collected them for myself, or got anyone else ready or able to do so for me. I think that, very soon, when these teachings and ideas are better known, people generally will declare themselves Socialists. They are 'bound to do it' if they think at all. I instinctively felt they were good people, and now I believe they are the true disciples and followers of Christ . . .
>
> Your affectionate cousin,
> Rachel McMillan[7]

Many years later, when Margaret was reflecting on her own introduction to socialism, she definitely attributed her early beginnings to Rachel's influence on her, together with the discussions she had with her American school friend in Switzerland. She said Rachel was studying strange books and she herself got hold of Marx's *Das Kapital* and 'began to study it as a new Bible'.

The fourth event to change Rachel's future was the death of her grandmother in July 1888. The net residue of her estate amounted to £1,200. After making bequests to numerous relatives, she left legacies of £100 to Rachel and £25 to Margaret. At the end of her testament she wrote:

> I desire to record that I have endeavoured to divide my means as fairly and equally among my children and grandchildren, who have all been good and kind to me, as I could, having regard to what they have received in my lifetime, and what I have received from them.

This sentence may contain the reason why Rachel was given more than Margaret.

Once Rachel recovered from this bereavement she realised that she was free for the first time to plan her future. She turned down offers of help from relatives declaring that 'she must make her own way – must face the world alone'. Margaret recalled: 'She was not at all dismayed as yet by the fact that she had very small means, and no technical training for any trade or profession whatsoever.'[8] But the ideal of a dedicated life never left her.

Considering Rachel's change of heart, her knowledge of Stead's fight to end child prostitution and the Christian Socialism she met in Edinburgh, it was not surprising that, when free, she sought means of fighting exploitation and helping to create a more just society. Believing that London was a den of iniquity she decided to serve there and began by taking a post as a junior superintendent in a working girls' home in Bloomsbury at a salary of £20 per annum. There she first tried to express her Christian Socialism.

At this point Margaret was still working at the Rectory in Ludlow, but a number of factors made her increasingly unsure that her future lay there. Implicit in the socialist literature which Rachel lent her and other books she read, was the idea that if 'the brotherhood of man in a world at peace' were to become a reality, then drastic social remedies would have to be applied. Her uncertainty about staying on in a comfortable job was increased when she recalled the conversation she had had years previously with her school friend Vera, in Geneva, about governesses teaching in rich families. Vera's injunction to 'work for the poor', was a recurring challenge to Margaret.

Following her experience in Ludlow she longed to know how to live effectively and to tackle some of the blatant social injustices of her day. She never wanted to enlist in a bitter class war. Her deep desire was to influence members of all parties, to work not with violence but with love to bring social change.

Reflecting on her belief that ordinary persons 'can be great' if 'tuned to be the Instrument of the Unseen', her mind turned towards the adventure of finding her own peculiar destiny within the framework of God's design for the world. The idea of relinquishing her secure post at the Rectory to become available for some as yet unrevealed creative task became increasingly attractive. In front of her she saw a wide landscape, but no clearly defined footpaths.

Propelled by a strong urge to find her true calling, Margaret left Ludlow and went to live with Rachel at the hostel in Bloomsbury, which was a typical Victorian working girls' home. Some of the occupants were out of work, others held poorly paid jobs. The Head of this home was a pious woman of about 50 who, Margaret said:

> had slipped, without knowing it, into a life of self-indulgence
> . . . Being religious she read prayers on summer mornings in the
> draughty drawing-room, and always gave us religious advice
> when she talked to us at all – which was seldom. She had tea,
> and cushions, and a warm atmosphere in her sanctum. 'If you
> want to keep me, you must take care of me,' she said.[9]

Once Margaret had settled into this hostel, she and Rachel, seeking people with whom they might work, attended lectures organised by different socialist groups. In a dusty room in the Strand they listened to Hyndman of the Social Democratic Foundation, whose pleas included higher education for all, free meals, the abolition of Christian teaching and the introduction of secular education in schools. Then they were introduced to William Morris, who invited them to Kelmscott House. After discussing aspects of socialism with them, he showed them his furnishings. Whilst engaged in serious political argument with the Morris family, Margaret's aesthetic sensibilities were recording the beauty around her. 'Outside' she wrote, 'the Thames shone in the soft afternoon light. The elms rustled in the wind and voices came floating in through the open windows. The carpet shone in the tempered light of the room like a great gem.'[10]

Among other socialists whom the sisters met were members of the intellectual wing of the Labour Movement – the Fabian Society – people such as Bernard Shaw, Annie Besant, Sidney and Beatrice Webb. They knew anarchists too, such as Prince Kropotkin – a refugee from the Czarist regime – and Louise Michel from the Paris Commune. Speaking of some of their socialist associates, Margaret said they realised that in them they met 'anti-Christianity of a virulent type'.

But not all of the socialists they met were anti-Christian. They got to know Keir Hardie, who openly said that 'the Christianity of Christ' was 'the chief inspiration and driving force' of his life. They knew George Lansbury, who often said publicly that you may work for a change in the system and achieve it but, unless you change the hearts of men, you are defeated in your aim. Amongst their other Christian Socialist friends was Paul Campbell, editor of *The Christian Socialist* who, in 1889, published the first article Margaret wrote, 'A Sign of the Times'.[11]

Sometimes, back at the hostel, the sisters had a frank exchange of views about the leading personalities of the different socialist groups. Margaret felt that William Morris 'had nothing of Hyndman's fire and storm, nothing of Hardie's mysticism'. She believed 'you could put his information in your pocket'. When she criticised Prince Kropotkin, Rachel, who knew some of his writings, always defended him; she specially liked to hear him speak.

By degrees the McMillans moved from being spectators to workers for the socialist movement. They began to address meetings, but at first only attracted a handful of 'homeless men and women and street loafers'. Sometimes they supported the dockers' leader Ben Tillett at his meetings, and derived encouragement from union members who, growing weary in their struggle for a rise in wages, said 'things looked 'ealthier now with young lydies abaht'.

They met some of the workers whose lifestyle they had studied – men who were the subject of many economic theories. But they were amongst the minority in the country who worried about social conditions; the majority viewed them with complacency. However, after 1889 when Charles Booth[12] circulated the findings of his massive surveys on the life of the people of London, the upper classes had to admit that workers needed help. The McMillans came to believe that the sufferings of the labouring classes could be alleviated only by action on socialist lines.

Thinking about the low quality of life of the poor compared with her own privileged upbringing, Margaret volunteered to teach singing in the evenings to factory girls in Whitechapel, an area to which many social workers gravitated. A few years prior to Margaret's arrival in Whitechapel, Arnold Toynbee took lodgings there to work amongst the poor. Members of the Salvation Army too worked hard in Whitechapel, for the needs there were manifestly great.

When Margaret started her voluntary work she already possessed some of the qualities of an effective social worker; others she only acquired by bitter experience. She certainly loved the people she was trying to help and believed in their ability to rise, but had little understanding of the general background of slum dwellers. So it is not surprising that her first attempt at enriching the lives of others proved to be a failure, as her own account of her work in Whitechapel shows.

The girls, ranging in age from fifteen to thirty or more, led me a dreadful life . . . They came after a long day's work in the factory. They came as I soon found, merely for a lark . . . Shouts, laughter, sudden questions and gravity, then cat-calls. My chair was a pitfall nearly always. Sometimes there were pins in it. Sometimes a leg was loose, and often it fell for no obvious reason . . . the girls would start two songs together, or put in street-song choruses . . .

Rose, a ringleader, . . . put her elbows on her knees and looked at me, and a gleam of pity struck across her anxiety. 'What d'ye come down here for anyway?' she said softly. 'Wot's yer gime?' A number of girls collected to stare at me. 'Ye're losing yer chances, y'know,' said Rose gravely, 'a-coming down here, ain't yer? A-jawin' to us same as the old women as gives us treats. Why, ain't yer a young 'un yerself? Lors a mussy, ain't yer got a chap?' There was a strange pause. Everyone was kind and they had begun to look at me from a new point of view.

Alice, a very anaemic girl, . . . now fixed her pale eyes on me. 'Ye ain't bad-looking, you know,' she said. 'Not 'arf. She looks queer, o' course,' she went on, appealing to the company, ''er 'air done so comical and that! and no year-rings, nor nothing, but she ain't bad-looking!' (Chorus of 'Not 'er!') 'She's fair good-looking. Might be! She's losin' all 'er chances.' . . .

'We ain't goin' to learn no more,' said Rose firmly. 'Not hus! Them people as come abaht a-'elping of us with 'ymns, and jawin' us, and a-getting up tea-fights – well – their buns is alright, but they ain't got the 'ang of US, see? Ye're a young 'un! What's your gime? This here coming down to us is comical. Get a chap for yerself, my gal: that's what you got to do. We ain't going to learn your stuff. W'y ain't yer got a proper fringe, same as mine? Chuck it,' said Rose, looking at me keenly with her dark eyes. Then doubt and misgiving surged in, tainting the new friendliness a little.

'She's a toff, SHE is,' cried Alice suddenly. 'She and her 'airs!' It was time to go . . . I stumbled down the ladder and escaped into the dark street. One or two fishshops were open too . . . The air reeked with mingled smells, and through it all the rain poured.[13]

As Margaret made her way home to Bloomsbury that night, it was like returning from a voyage of discovery. She fully realised now that her outlook and expectations were entirely different from those of the girls she had tried to teach. In addition, she understood for the first time that these working-class girls had a culture all their own. They were proud of it, were determined to cling to it and had no intention of exchanging it for something which a stranger deemed to be better.

Margaret had yet to learn that neighbourhood squalor, so repellent to outsiders, was taken for granted by slum dwellers. This was their home and criticism of it was deeply resented. They viewed visitors intent on reform dubiously. Social workers, however well-meaning, had to wait until by general consent they were accepted into the group.

Other aspects of the working-class culture in Whitechapel were new to Margaret too. There, in the main, traditional music was scoffed at; poetry was debunked. It was the exception, rather than the rule, for girls to return to any kind of formal education once they left school.

To them, to get married was *de rigueur*; to remain single was to have failed to reach a highly esteemed state. While Margaret endeavoured to interest the girls in ennobling arts, they were trying to tell her that in so doing she was missing her chances of 'catching a fella', possibly of elevation to a married woman's status. Whilst she found their outlook puzzling, they found hers bizarre in the extreme.

At this time, Margaret did not know that the pranks of these factory girls were not necessarily related to her lack of teaching skill. She was unaware that they were passing through perhaps their one and only carefree period. The pre-marital stage for them was often, as Rowntree's research showed, a brief interlude between two separate sections of a dreary, poverty-stricken existence.[14] In the cyclical pattern of poverty which he identified, Rowntree showed that, in between the grinding poverty into which many were born, and the poverty to which most of them returned on marrying and trying to raise a family, a short, rosier spell was often interposed. Then, because of the number of unmarried workers contributing to the home, the family moved, albeit temporarily, above the breadline. Probably some of these girls were just at this stage and happily making the most of it. Added to that, there was a comradeship amongst them, born of hardship shared, which was laced with a natural, raucous humour. Margaret, with her different language and dress, would be a ready target for their spontaneous witticisms and practical jokes.

These factory girls were puzzled by Margaret's visits to Whitechapel. As she left she must have felt like an exile – an outsider looking in on a society to which she did not belong. Reviewing her unsuccessful efforts, she declared: 'I had failed utterly in my first attempt to step outside my own life and its cares. The East End did not want me. It had no use for my feeble powers and vain offerings.'[15]

Chapter five

Park Lane Decision 1892

Margaret never allowed initial failures to deflect her from pursuing her main purposes. She often laughed about them and used them to entertain her friends. She once told a Bradford audience how, after giving a talk on hygiene to working girls, she questioned them to ascertain what they had retained, saying: 'Why is it necessary to keep our houses spotlessly clean?' only to get the shattering reply, 'Because company might drop in at any moment.'

After working voluntarily in Whitechapel, Margaret decided that she must now start to earn a living. Sometimes she was able to make a little by writing articles for papers.[1] These provide us with useful indications of her thinking on current socialist issues and show how she used the press to influence the public. In 'A Sign of the Times' she criticised church leaders who encouraged the poor to have patience with their conditions rather than fight for social justice. She thought the churches ought to enlist the wealthy in the fight against poverty and send them away 'sorrowing from their comfortable pews'.

In her article 'The Church and Socialism' she continued her argument that the Church was doing little to improve the lot of the toiling masses. She set out the aims of socialism as being: 'the ultimate extinction of the evil of poverty', the ending of 'tyranny and injustice' and the establishment of 'equitable laws . . . for the well-being and protection of all'.

Margaret had many thoughts on liberty and longed for rich and poor to find inner freedom. She wanted the working man to be free 'to listen to the higher impulse of his own nature', to become conscious that he had 'a Kingdom within' and 'a law which is exclusively and essentially his own to obey'.

In her article 'Evolution and Revolution', she seemed to be at pains to shift the thinking of some readers about the term 'revolution'. She suggested that men often confused events accompanying revolution with revolution itself and said:

> These terrible events are the result, not of Revolution, but of a
> disease in the heart and at the root of the Social System . . .
> Injustice and Oppression must be acknowledged before the
> class-hatred they give rise to can be dealt with.

Soon Margaret began to feel the need for more than the precarious
income she could earn by writing. As she was not an accomplished
journalist, the newspapers could afford to pay her only small fees,
so after a while she decided to visit agencies to seek regular work
again as a governess. Thus began what she later described as one
of the most colourful periods of her life.

She obtained several interviews, but when she explained that
she was a socialist she found her interviewers lost interest in her.

> Employers treated me as if I was a distant object. One sat at a
> table and took down all I said on tablets just as if it were the Day
> of Judgment. Another looked at me over her pince-nez and
> asked me if I were a churchwoman.[2]

After many abortive encounters, Margaret went back to one
agency and was told rather hesitantly that a titled lady required a
governess for an adopted child. But an air of mystery surrounded
the half-hearted way the information was proffered. Then, as if
trying to inspire confidence, the agent added 'They say she has a
kind heart.' By now Margaret needed work so badly that she took
the particulars – Lady Meux, 41 Park Lane – and made her way to
that address. Describing her journey there she said it was good to
go to the West End, as 'a feeling of revolt against poverty and all
its works' burned within her. Park Lane 'was a new and welcome
change'.

Before reaching 41 Park Lane, she was unaware that it was the
home of the wealthy brewer and baronet, Sir Henry Bruce Meux,
whose other possessions included Theobald's park (a massive
country estate in Hertfordshire), Sheen House at East Sheen,
another estate valued at a million pounds in Wiltshire, a house in
Brighton, as well as a chateau at Sucy-en-Brie near Paris.

The Park Lane house had a butler, maids, and all the
appurtenances that wealthy Victorians considered a necessary part
of civilised life. On arrival, Margaret was ushered into a little
morning-room which she described as 'all lined with plush – a
warm, still nest, bathed in a soft glow of firelight reflected from the
golden lines on leathern chairs and the heavy silver things that
loaded the writing table'.[3]

At the time Margaret was a tallish woman with a dignified
carriage. Her dress was plain but not shabby. Even as a girl clothes

meant little to her. Her casual wind-swept appearance – more in keeping with the Highlands than the West End – was a startling contrast to that of Lady Meux who interviewed her. She was a beautiful, well-preserved woman, given to decking herself out in the finest plumage and well known for her 'ropes of pearls'.

Thinking of her first impression of this woman, along with the agent's puzzling comments, Margaret said: 'This was the woman who was "kind"! . . . I saw already that there was something else. Over and above her strange kindness, she was under some kind of shadow.'[4]

The nature of that shadow was unknown to Margaret but Lady Meux, despite her title and fabulous wealth, was undoubtedly burdened by something. She had been a pantomime girl at the Surrey Music Hall and a barmaid at the Horseshoe Tavern, next door to the Meux's brewery in Tottenham Court Road. Yet, when her husband died she became one of the richest women in England with an income of about £50,000 per annum. It was written of her that: 'Hers is one of the most picturesque of the rags-to-riches or whore-house to manor-house sagas.'[5] She came to be on intimate terms with Sir Henry at the Casino de Venise in Holborn which was 'frequented by a variety of young men . . . and by a large number of amateur and professional prostitutes'.[6]

Sir Henry's liaison with her was a social scandal. The stigma attached to her kind of lifestyle was hard to remove. When they married and Sir Henry gave her £20,000 a year, indignation rose inside and outside the family. Society women snubbed her. Broaching this subject she said to Margaret:

> I'm a woman not received . . . Men come here, distinguished men, but not their women. I am outside . . . It's only right to tell you, that it isn't a good thing for you to come here. You might not get another post.[7]

Once Lady Meux started the interview, Margaret in her customary fashion declared her socialist interests. The rest of the story is best told in her own words:

> 'You don't mean THAT,' she said. 'You – how can you be a Socialist, and also – a – well – a governess?'
> 'I was afraid you wouldn't like it,' I said, with rising hope. 'People don't, and I thought I would find it a difficulty always. I hope you do not find it one.'
> She rang for tea and began to pour out a cup for me, looking almost happy . . . Then I remembered my business here and I asked hurriedly about the vacant post.

'Oh, I don't want you as the child's governess,' said Lady X. 'I want you, if you come at all, to come to me for myself. I've got a lot of letters to write, and I don't spell very well . . .'

'Are YOU a Socialist?' I asked. 'I – a Socialist? Look at my rings!' replied Lady X. She held out her hands, which were loaded with diamonds . . .

'Neither will you be a Socialist,' she said, 'when you have been with ME for a while!' At this I woke up as from a dream . . . I intimated that, being with her, or anyone else, would make no difference to my convictions, that the system under which we lived was in my opinion wrong (I was young), that the poor had risen again and again, but that the change that was now coming was no mere rising!

And here I stumbled, but went on to mention Hyndman and Marx, and many others . . . 'You ARE amusing,' she said. 'To come here and say all that to ME! All my friends are Tories, of course! They wouldn't dare to be anything else here.'[8]

Margaret's Scottish charm and ability to talk vividly on many topics made her instantly likeable to most people and not least to Lady Meux who invited Margaret to luncheon the next day. During the meal she offered Margaret the job at what to seemed to her a large salary and she promptly accepted it.

What Margaret did not understand then was that her new employer took a proprietary view of all her staff; she expected to rule every part of their public and private lives. Once installed, Lady Meux said to her, 'Socialism is a creed for down-and-outs. You will abandon it at once. Besides it's irreligious.' Furthermore, she decided that Margaret should become an actress, so her image would have to be changed. At once she replaced most of Margaret's clothes. She bought her 'dresses, coats, hats, cloaks, gloves, laces and other things in profusion' including a diamond and sapphire brooch and other jewellery.

Recalling this time Margaret said:

I began to appear at the docks and at the Democratic Club in expensive and beautiful clothes that amazed and delighted the comrades (though one or two began to say I was a capitalist, or even a traitor). Rachel, too, was not a little vexed by this departure. She liked to see me in pretty clothes, but she wanted me to buy them myself.[9]

Margaret was caught up in a whirl of activity now and her life changed dramatically. The whole experience was breath-taking. Exciting days in town were followed by weekends at the country mansion set in 70 acres of beautiful parkland. There Lady Meux entertained lavishly, inviting guests to enjoy the swimming pool, the Turkish bath, a racquet court, a roller-skating rink, and a menagerie. She kept native and foreign birds on an island in the river at the bottom of her garden and emus and zebras in the grounds. Recalling her visits there Margaret said:

> We went to her country house and saw the fields and woods. Our clothes would not let us see them well; very uncomfortable clothes, tight bodices, whale-boned up the neck, and squeezed in at the waist, long skirts, tight boots, pinned-on hats and stiffly-dressed hair.[10]

At the town house Margaret's horizons were extended by contact with the many visitors who constantly swept in and out. Many of these were wealthy businessmen, some of whom had shares in Meux's brewery. Wallis Budge, a friend of Sir Henry's, who later became keeper of certain Egyptian collections at the British Museum, admired the boundless enthusiasm Margaret had for her work. He said: 'Her zeal and energy at that time nearly burnt her up . . . when we could make her forget her work she was a delightful and charming woman. We all liked her very much.' Some particularly admired the stand she made for her ideals in 'an atmosphere of dense materiality'.[11]

Margaret received excellent tuition for a stage career and, as a promising pupil, was expected to have spectacular success. Although later she was to use her voice for purposes other than those planned by her employer, she was always grateful for the lessons in deep breathing, singing and voice-production she received at this time.

Despite all the material advantages of the post, Margaret soon began to doubt whether she should stay there for long. Life with Lady Meux was rarely on an even keel. She was eccentric, emotionally unstable, oscillating often between sympathy and impatience with people and causes. Margaret felt that her own life had lapsed into a daily attempt to satisfy the whims of a dubious dilettante. Lady Meux's poverty of spirit was a matter of real concern to Margaret, who wanted her employer to find a purpose bigger than that of merely amassing wealth.

When she was first engaged as a companion, she was able to argue with her employer in a friendly fashion, but this soon gave way to stormy confrontation as their values were so fundamentally different. Margaret was more concerned about 'being' than 'having'; she yearned for a more equitable division of the nation's wealth whereas Lady Meux prized private property so much that she was terribly afraid of being deprived of any of it. She grew increasingly difficult to live with and entertain. Margaret declared: 'Nothing could long hide the fact that all sources of amusement had been used up. And Lady Meux's powers were wasted in remorse, regret and suspicion.'[12]

Notwithstanding Lady Meux's open opposition to her politics, Margaret continued to attend socialist meetings with Rachel. Early Fabian meetings took place at Percy Hall off Tottenham Court Road. Other meetings were held in cafés and private houses; many of them were more like social occasions than business sessions, especially those at Morris's home, where he and Edward Aveling read poems and Bernard Shaw played piano duets with Annie Besant.

Although at the end of these meetings Margaret returned to the affluence of the West End, the life of the poor was never far from her thoughts. She frequently wrestled with two questions: how to help the rich to see wealth as a means to an end and not an end in itself and how to remove from society the poverty and hopelessness which ruined the lives of so many workers?

On May Day 1892, Margaret made a speech on a socialist platform in Hyde Park. Lady Meux was furious when she heard about it and presented her with an ultimatum. 'It's dreadful of you,' said Lady X, 'You're going about with dreadful people. You speak in the Park . . . How can you do it?' Margaret said 'You knew . . .' 'Knew! I didn't believe it . . . well, that's the end' said Lady X. Later she became more tragic. 'I'm not of the stuff that traitors are made of!' And still later: 'Decide or go.' Finally Lady X who was 'ready to die for Park Lane' repeated 'Go! You may blot me out of your memory.'[13]

Now Margaret was forced to choose between socialism and the possibility of inheriting a considerable fortune from Lady Meux. Balanced on the horns of this dilemma, Margaret decided to turn her back on comfort and security. The challenge of working for the downtrodden and helping to right some of the social wrongs of the age proved stronger than the lure of fame and affluence. So she crossed the Rubicon, left Park Lane and once more took a leap into the unknown.

Doubtless the news of Margaret's decision to renounce personal advantage would be received with amazement mixed with scepticism by some of her newly-acquired acquaintances. But to choose socialist principles in preference to material gain or popularity, though costly, was not an exceptional occurrence among early socialists. Personal sacrifice was accepted as normal amongst the men and women of all classes who worked in the Labour

Movement. At that time, sincere socialists gave their time, talents and money for the sake of the cause; not infrequently, they lost jobs, houses and some of their treasured friends because of their views.

Writing from the inside of the Labour Movement about its pioneering days, Elton listed a number of men who suffered and gave sacrificially for the cause. Speaking of George Lansbury, a mill-hand in the East End at thirty shillings a week, he said:

> Each Saturday when work is over he takes the train for the provinces, harangues a Socialist meeting on Saturday night, and three more on the Sunday. Nobody pays him and the meetings are frequently riotous. The railway returns him to London in the small hours of Monday morning, usually between three and five. He walks back through the silent streets to Bow and reaches home in time for the day's work in the mill.[14]

Keir Hardie, another of Margaret's friends, also encountered men who offered him bribes, but, though penniless, he refused them and consistently made that stand throughout his career.[15]

F. W. Jowett, a partner in a small wool business, was amongst those who lost friends because of his socialist principles, especially when he put the welfare of workers before the profits of mill owners. His biographer, Fenner Brockway, said of him: 'He had . . . the greatness which in disappointment as well as popularity, remained content in the service of principle.'[16]

After Margaret left Lady Meux's employment because of her principles, their relationship was strained but not broken. Both she and Rachel kept in touch with Lady Meux for many years but it was she who tried to sever their friendship. Soon after the General Election in 1906, when the Labour Party secured the return of 29 MPs, she said to Margaret, 'You help them, I will see you no more.'[17] Even so, Margaret seems to have remembered her with affection and had almost telepathic knowledge of her as a letter to a friend written in January 1911, a few months after Lady Meux's death, shows:

> I was in America when Lady Meux died. In the last week I was so unhappy. I was always thinking of her. She was dying all that week. She hated my views . . . She said the Budget was killing her and that I was helping.[18]

Although saddened by the estrangement between her and her employer, Margaret never, throughout the rest of her life, showed any signs of regretting the decision she made in Park Lane, although for many years she was keenly aware of the consequences of it.

Chapter six

A New Political Party 1892–3

Having lost her paid employment in Park Lane, Margaret joined
Rachel again at the Bloomsbury hostel. To try to earn her own
keep she wrote articles for socialist papers and gave lectures;
though she received no more than a pittance for either of these,
she hated taking any payment. Money never meant much to
Margaret; she only wanted enough to enable her to live frugally
and prevent her from becoming a drain on Rachel's resources. So
she spent most of her time working voluntarily for the Labour
Movement; she had yet to find her own distinctive calling.

Margaret was one of many in London who helped to create the
demand for a national Independent Labour Party (ILP), and was
part of the fermentation Fenner Brockway described in his
biography of Jowett:

> In Manchester, London and many more centres Socialists were
> forming themselves into groups to secure independent Labour
> representation in Town Councils and in Parliament. Keir Hardie
> was addressing large meetings urging the need for the workers
> to form their own Party and using his weekly paper '*The Miner*'
> to popularise the new idea. In 1892 the Scottish Labour Party
> was formed in Glasgow, and by this time local Independent
> Labour Parties had sprung up in many places.[1]

Speaking of Margaret's contribution to the agitation, K. Bruce
Glasier wrote:

> For five years before the I.L.P. was born, Margaret McMillan
> was working in London strengthening all that was best in the
> nascent Labour movement there . . . Margaret had found her
> way to all sorts of workmen's clubs. She had spoken for the
> Fabian Society too . . . she attended the meeting in the old
> London Democratic Club where . . . the name of the
> Independent Labour Party [was sent out] as a rallying cry for all
> the scattered groups of workers in Britain.[2]

34

Recalling this period some years later, Margaret indicated that she was dissatisfied with her life in London; speaking of what she really wanted to do she wrote:

> I had now finished two trainings – a training for a 'finishing governess' (as we were called then) and the hard training to be an actress, but I no longer wished to be an actress or a governess. My earnest desire and purpose was to cast away from these orders of service and to devote myself to the new party that was born in Bradford.[3]

The 'new party' to which she referred was the national Independent Labour Party formed in Bradford in January 1893. Its chief architect, Keir Hardie, called it a 'Labour alliance' – a loose federation of socialist groups and trade unions. He was by now a Member of Parliament for South-West Ham and in his address to his constituents before his election campaign in 1892 he had described the Labour Movement as 'the outcome of the quickening of the public conscience towards the toiling masses and the extremes of wealth and poverty which at present exist'. His aim was to turn a social movement into a political force and he injected his own philosophy into it. His thinking provides a key to an understanding of why Margaret wanted to devote herself to 'the new party'.

Unlike many of those who had hitherto led the Labour Movement, Hardie was through and through a working man, reared in a home which knew the direst poverty. At the age of 10 he had gone down the coal mine as a 'trapper' and worked as a coalminer for more than twelve years, so he knew the lot of working men from the inside. Brought up an atheist, at the age of 23 he found a genuine Christian faith. At the same time he met socialism. His faith and his socialism were fused in a passionately held philosophy informed by Christian values. For many years this was to give the British Labour Party a unique character among the growing socialist parties of Europe. He once wrote that 'the agitator with a touch of the seer' was the ideal leader for a movement of social reform. The phrase described him exactly. He was more than a politician. He was a prophet.

His philosophy found an immediate echo in Margaret's own thinking; she saw in the Labour Movement an instrument which could be used to create a better society.

Contemporaries said that Keir Hardie regularly paid Margaret what, for him, was the rare compliment of rising when she entered a room and saying 'I'm glad tae see you Maggie.' It was said that they were close friends – kindred spirits – who shared the same longing for a new society expressing a new set of values based on Christianity. Hardie described himself as 'an agitator'; Margaret spoke of herself as 'a rebel and also a reformer'. Her character resembled Hardie's too. Mansbridge called her a 'Prophet and a Pioneer', while J. B. Priestley referred to her as a 'burning pioneer and prophet of Socialism'. Although she and Hardie were different in social and economic background, and education, they reached socialism by similar routes.

Both of them had been fed from the same sources – especially the writings of Thomas Carlyle and John Ruskin. Like Hardie, Margaret followed the promptings of conscience, no matter what it cost; and like him she was aware of an inner voice directing her, sometimes in surprising directions. Mansbridge claimed

> There was aim in her life – the creation of a society that would make beautiful life possible for all. She harmonized the teaching of Christ, William Morris and Karl Marx in a powerful synthesis of her own, which satisfied the needs of her ardent nature.[4]

That judgement, if true, indicates that she was not aware of the profound ideological contradictions which lurked, as yet hardly visible, at the heart of the Labour alliance.

However, being in agreement with the underlying philosophy of the ILP as outlined by Hardie and with the aims of the new party, Margaret became a founder-member, although she was unable to be at the inaugural meeting. During the ensuing months she sought to further its objectives in her work in London, but, as she said herself, her dearest wish was to work alongside members of the Labour Movement in Bradford. Although Margaret could not envisage how that dream could ever come true, she had already taken the first step towards its realisation when in the spring of 1892 she accepted an invitation to lecture at Bradford's Labour Church. In socialist circles an invitation to speak in Bradford carried with it a certain prestige, as can be gathered from Cross's biography of Philip Snowden. Recalling how Snowden at first only spoke in local halls and clubs, he went on to say: 'Then he accepted a much bigger challenge by going to Bradford itself to address the Labour Church in Peckover Street. Bradford, birthplace of the I.L.P., was the veritable Rome of Socialism.'[5]

It was not entirely surprising that this honour should be conferred on Margaret, since excellent reports of her speeches in Hyde Park had already reached Yorkshire. Many knew her as an outstanding orator and admired her because of her ability, directness and abhorrence of humbug. Margaret's Bradford speech was a great success; it so impressed the listeners that an even more exciting invitation soon followed.

A deputation from the Labour Church went to London to ask her to work full-time for the socialist cause in Bradford. Labour Churches – there were 25 of these in the early days of the ILP – acted as centres of propaganda for the Labour Movement. There socialism was often presented as an ethical gospel and Labour songs were sung to old chapel tunes. As there was a crying need for speakers who could inspire and instruct members of the growing Movement, it was obvious to many that Margaret would be a great asset to Bradford. She was a speaker who could appeal to the heart and the intellect.

Unfortunately, the invitation committee did not offer Margaret any salary; they may have imagined that, because at this time she was well-dressed, probably in clothes given to her by Lady Meux, she had a private income, but this was not the case. Nevertheless, the possibility of working with dedicated socialists in Yorkshire so gripped Margaret that it never occurred to her to ask whether there was even a small pot of gold at the end of the rainbow. She just resolved to discuss the invitation with Rachel.

Many believed that socialists in the north were more successful in spreading their ideas than their counterparts in the south and this may have influenced Margaret's thinking. Villiers wrote:

> It seems to me almost impossible to get so closely into touch with the minds of the bulk of the London workers as the Independent Labour Party has already done with those of the manufacturing districts. There are scores of public meetings, addressed by such men as Philip Snowden, in the towns of Lancashire and Yorkshire every year, which number anything from two to five thousand . . . A lecture by Mr. Snowden, in a provincial town, is an event of some importance . . . The people who hear it are a sufficient proportion of the local population to reappear in little groups next morning in every workshop in the town; and are sufficiently delighted with what they have heard to ensure that the principal topic on Monday among the working classes, after Saturday's football match, shall be Sunday's Socialist lecture. Of course nothing of the sort is possible in London. Even the largest audience would be scattered hopelessly next morning among workmates who had never heard of the meeting.[6]

According to another writer – Price[7] – Margaret believed that in the north there was a truer interpretation of socialism than in the south, and that the thinking of F. W. Jowett, Arthur Priestman and other Yorkshire ILP members was nearer to the heart of the Labour Movement than that of the London intellectuals. The Yorkshire members certainly were an enthusiastic, diverse group. Mansbridge said they were

> so varied in experience and equipment as to make a
> combination which would have been remarkable in any place at
> any time. In addition to working men and women, trained and
> experienced in reform movements, there were manufacturers
> and literary men.[8]

Margaret had little time for mere theorists; she appreciated the down-to-earth, well-informed, practical men that Yorkshire produced and felt that in Bradford socialism had been so stripped of embellishments that its true form could be seen. She wrote:

> London is brilliant. London is the Brain of the World. But I love
> to think of Bradford. For there labour was shorn of all that is
> ugly and debasing. One saw it as in morning light, half-freed,
> active and giving promise of what it will be one day when
> divorced entirely from ignorance and failure.[9]

After pondering the Bradford invitation the sisters felt sure that Margaret should accept it. Then, to Margaret's surprise and delight, Rachel decided to go to Yorkshire with her and throw in her lot too with the socialists there.

Chapter seven

Bradford 1893–4

When the McMillans reached Bradford in November 1893, they found a county borough beginning to emerge from the grip of bitterness consequent on the 19-week lock-out at Lister's woollen mill in 1890–1. By then, alongside the residual hard feelings and despair, there was a touch of expectancy, the dawn of fresh hope. Members of the newly-formed Independent Labour Party were asserting that injustice and deprivation were not inevitable; they were spreading the idea that workers could strive to end exploitation and create a wholly different society where justice reigned. People's spirits were lifted by reports that the new party intended to make the wretched living and working conditions of labourers paramount questions in British politics.

The sisters were soon to become aware of the sterling qualities of the Yorkshire folk that J. B. Priestley described:

In the West Riding, as in other parts of the industrial North, you see what the Industrial Revolution did to the country and to the people . . . You knew that most of the wealth had been produced by the people who went . . . early in the morning, to huge dark mills from those miserable, dingy little streets 'back o't' mill'. It was their nimble fingers, tired eyes and aching backs that really produced the mansions and grouse-moors and yachts and hot-houses, the silks and peaches and cigars and old brandies, that were enjoyed far from the dingy little streets and dark mills . . . Even when I was a boy at school, I knew then that something was most damnably wrong, that we were not within sight yet of social justice.

I knew something else, too . . . It was that these industrial workers, exiled from the sun and the fields, condemned to spend their time between houses like barracks and factories like fortresses, people who could never speak quietly because they were so used to screaming and shouting above the din of their machines, were yet among the salt of the earth. They ought to have been sluts and brutes, but they were not – they were decent and kind, humorous and hopeful, often responding eagerly to any faint gleam of beauty – a song, a sunset, a handful of wild flowers – that touched and illuminated their lives.[1]

The McMillans, eager to work with these wholesome people, arrived in Bradford one wet, blustery Saturday night and went straight to their lodgings at 49 Hanover Square, Manningham Lane. Describing that night, Margaret said:

We saw . . . in the Market Place, the shining statue of Oastler with two black and bowed little mill-workers standing at his knee, which Lord Shaftesbury unveiled in 1869 and it stood there, a tragic avowal of things that went on in 1893.[2]

Later, when she took up the task of alleviating the conditions of poor children, friends said that Margaret always felt Shaftesbury's spirit about her.

The next morning the sisters set off as soon as they could for the Labour Institute. This disused church in Peckover Street, which the socialists rented, served a threefold purpose: it acted as the headquarters of the Independent Labour Party; it was an indoor meeting place for socialists, and a place where socialist songs were popularised. It became a centre to which hundreds journeyed each Sunday as well as during the week.

Williams[3] conveys through the writings of early socialists something of the unrestrained enthusiasm and unconquerable courage that pervaded the Labour Movement in the early days. He reports:

The Sunday meetings of the I.L.P. held in a thousand halls suggested religious revival meetings rather than political demonstrations. The fervour of the great audiences that assembled in centres like Glasgow, Bradford, Leeds, Huddersfield, Birmingham and Bristol was quite beyond precedent in British political history. Men who had grown old in years had their youthful enthusiasms renewed under the glow and warmth of a new spiritual fellowship. They were born again: they joyfully walked many miles to listen to a favourite speaker; they sang Labour hymns: and they gave to the new social faith an intensity of devotion which lifted it far above the older political organizations of the day.[4]

Snowden tells us that,

Working men who had toiled all day at arduous work went out

at nights into the streets to preach in their simple way the new gospel of emancipation. Men who had never before attempted public speaking were given courage and the gift of effective oratory by the new passion for social justice which consumed them . . . Vocal unions were formed which accompanied cycling corps into the country at week-ends and audiences were gathered on village greens by the singing of choirs; then short and simple addresses on socialism were given. On their country jaunts the cyclists distributed leaflets and pasted slips on gates, and sometimes stuck them on cows, bearing such slogans as 'Socialism the Hope of the World' and 'Workers of the World Unite'.[5]

According to Williams, it was not only from the quality of its leadership that the ILP gained its power. 'It came from the faith and devotion of thousands of ordinary men and women.' Typical of many of these was Johnny Coe. 'I've read about these old martyrs who went to the stake for their religion', he said, 'but since I became converted to socialism I can understand it. I'd be willing to go to the stake for my socialism.'[6]

Snowden, who in the early days of the Labour Movement never travelled less than a hundred miles a week to preach the socialist gospel, said during a break from his strenuous activities: 'For a while I have left the storm and stress . . . How often my friends tell me how hard my life must be. How little they know of its rapturous compensations!'[7] Writing of him Cross said:

It was hard work . . . Snowden would limp for miles from railway station to meeting hall . . . he and the party were too poor to afford cabs. After the meeting he would gather with the leading local comrades at somebody's fireside, drinking cups of tea, smoking his clay pipe and talking with them far into the night . . . The little band of itinerant lecturers . . . was the link which held the party together.[8]

On arrival at the Labour Institute, Margaret and Rachel stepped into this religious fervour and found a most unusual cross-section of people. Members of the Social Democratic Federation and the Independent Labour Party, Swedenborgians, Chartists and Secularists were there, along with those who bore no label but came out of interest or curiosity. Here was a group of people who, while holding disparate views, were united by the hope of a new society and by their common socialist commitment. Margaret said you could feel that hope surging through the meeting 'as you might feel the moorland wind in the streets'. This motley collection of people at the Labour Institute met first for a religious service and afterwards for a lecture followed by home-made teas served in the roomy cellar.

Margaret never forgot the ecstatic welcome she and Rachel received, how they were 'swept into the warm glow of socialist comradeship' and experienced a great feeling of solidarity as if belonging to a vast army. Describing some of the characters who greeted them at the Institute she said:

> The centre of the group was 'G. Doobleyou Smith' . . . He was the treasurer and had been counting the money. He pushed aside the pyramids of pence and shillings on the table and rose to shake hands, his face expanded and glowing with smiles of welcome. A chorus of welcome from the people assembled made the little room ring. Edward Hartley, very witty, had a shop; Arthur Priestman, dark-eyed, serene, a member of the Society of Friends; George Spencer, old and stout, but powerfully built and very calm, with a sense of his responsibilities as a chairman; F. W. Jowett, and half a dozen women, hearty and hot from the preparation of the cellars as tea-rooms: this was the company that welcomed us . . . they were a new order of people to us from the first.
>
> I had to speak . . . Then the . . . religious service began. It departed from all the customs of other churches . . . The Swedenborgians repeated the Lord's Prayer with the chairman, but the Social Democratic Federationers did nothing of the kind. The old chapelgoers, or some of them, enjoyed the hymns, but the Secularists did not enjoy them – thought they were mere weakness and held their books anyhow. The lecture was the thing . . . They had made plans for us, they said. 'We've got it all ready.' This was good hearing, for our own plans were indefinite enough. Out of the mist we had come into what seemed a new morning . . . It was enough to sit in the midst of this company and feel that they had been waiting for us all our lives – waiting while we were little, waiting while we were at home or abroad, waiting while I trained to go on 'the boards', waiting while we lived bewildered and adrift in London, waiting till . . . at last [we] knew that our wanderings were over.[9]

These Bradford socialists were full of verve and abandon. Margaret said that looking back she could not but see that 'the life of all the new comrades was the life of the early Christians'. Katharine, Bruce Glasier's wife, also remembered the total involvement of the members together with their 'sacrifice of home and friends, of bank balance and careers – nay, of health itself' and how they made it with a 'reckless cheerfulness that today would seem all but insane'.[10]

Margaret, learning from her failure in Whitechapel, started her new work for the party by first studying the area and its residents. Later she spoke on waste ground, street corners, in clubs as well as in the Labour Church. Hundreds walked for miles to hear her. Many were moved to tears by her oratory, and the applause at the end was deafening. Once, when asked about her eloquence, she said that it did not come from her own power but that the words were put into her mouth. Jowett said of her:

> She was an eloquent and attractive speaker, in great demand not only for Bradford meetings, but for meetings in other towns. It was a hard life, relieved only by the friendly gatherings around firesides in the ordinary homes of ordinary working people. In spite of the inconvenience of travel, often including dreary waits in cold weather on wind-swept station platforms, Margaret felt it as a new and creative experience giving purpose to her life.[11]

However inconvenient it was for Margaret to get to the meetings, she went even if the only means of transport was a milk cart. A Mr R. Meats recalls:

> A few of the comrades thought well to take her to Bulwell, a mining district four miles from Nottingham. Miss McMillan was well content to ride in a coal cart belonging to a comrade, Mr. Tom Culley, and a rare cheer the Bulwell miners gave her when she alighted from her uncomfortable seat.[12]

In the early days, these meetings mostly took place in the open air. Often a chair was borrowed from a nearby cottage for the speaker who gave an address from it to a handful of listeners and afterwards made an uncomfortable journey home. Looking back on these years Margaret said:

> The life of the working classes was no longer a secret or a thing remote or a creation of the imagination. It was a close and thrilling reality. Here were the people who made the new movement – the women and the men who had lived without hope, but had now conceived a great and wonderful hope. We shared the life of crowded kitchens or living-room . . . We got to know too, in their own homes, the factory 'hands', saw the children go to work early, and were roused, like the rest of the household, by the 'knocker up' . . . Occasionally, but not often, we were invited to a well-to-do home and were reminded of a world we had half forgotten.[13]

Katharine B. Glasier recalls how she first met Margaret in Bradford in a small white-washed bedroom in a Bradford worker's home:

Margaret was ill with a relaxed throat and Rachel was anxiously nursing her . . . Margaret was soon sitting up when she should have been lying down – her dark eyes flashing, the cheeks flushed, her shoulders charged with power; urging, protesting. 'Of course! We all hate the poverty – and the riches of capitalist society. But the real poverty goes deeper than wages. It is in the starved, cramped, diseased bodies and minds; the eyes that do not see; the ears that do not hear; how can we change them?'[14]

By degrees the movement grew and hope rose. Recalling those days Margaret reported:

Chapel people joined us and local preachers. Many who left the chapel and some who remained in it joined the new party. We had friends in the Whitmanites at Bolton, in the Secularists at Leicester, and also in Spiritualist groups in various towns and villages. The leader, as far as platform work was concerned, was Keir Hardie, though there were others – such as Bruce Glasier – who did a colossal amount of propaganda. And the party quickly got a new literature of its own suited to the needs and tastes of North-country people.[15]

Thinking of the change she saw in some workers Margaret reported that:

More than a few began to read good poetry and the older classics; Ruskin and Whitman and Carlyle silently appeared on many new-made shelves . . . Women began to prop books against their looms. They dreamed new dreams . . . There was a feeling – almost a certainty – that soon the hard life of the poor would be changed, and the worker would share with the student and the well-to-do. Anything might happen, since so much had happened already.[16]

While Margaret spent much of her time away lecturing, Rachel often stayed in Bradford. Arriving home tired one Monday after speaking in Barrow, Margaret found that, during her absence, Rachel had been considering the future of the Movement as well as their penurious state. Speaking about their financial situation Rachel said: 'You won't earn anything. I must earn money. I am going to train for a sanitary inspectorship.' Margaret was amazed and puzzled as to how Rachel could achieve this ambition. But Rachel insisted that this was her next step and her face was radiant. She said she would study in London and live at the Bloomsbury hostel whilst working for her examinations.

The sisters talked at great length about this; separation was not an attractive proposition to either of them. However, following her inner conviction, Rachel went first to Liverpool, to do social work, and later to London to take up her studies there. After qualifying as a sanitary inspector in 1895, she became a peripatetic teacher of hygiene for the Kent County Council.

Margaret, now alone in Bradford, threw herself totally into work for the party and managed to stay solvent by speaking and writing. Despite the quality and popularity of her lectures, close-fisted Yorkshiremen usually limited her fees to five shillings per session plus a small travel allowance. Recalling his experiences as a lecturer for the ILP at this time, Jowett mentions the bare remuneration speakers received:

> Only when speaking away from home was there any allowance even for expenses. The allowance was 5/– for expenses and the bare cost of the railway ticket. When the cost of stamps and stationery, contributions to collections and necessary food on long journeys are taken into account, it will be realised that the amount left no margin for unforeseen expenses.[17]

Margaret fared as well as most lecturers, but even then she earned little. In a letter to a friend many years later she said: 'I never could earn a living, nor help my dearest ones at all, always a burden and a failure. And yet I can get money for poor children.'[18]

The sums she earned by writing were small too; she could only live modestly on them. Her articles 'Drink in Labour Clubs',[19] 'Music in Labour Clubs and Elsewhere'[20] and 'Women of the I.L.P.'[21] were all written at this time. Thinking of her and the frugal existence of early socialist workers, J. B. Priestley wrote in his Foreword to D'Arcy Cresswell's memoir of Margaret:

> In those days embarking on a career of this sort, you were sustained by an inner fire and by little else. You existed on tea and stale buns, dressed in shabby old clothes, and wondered where the rent was coming from. It was much worse for a woman than it was for a man. But, if you fought like a tigress, you got things done, little things that soon led to bigger things.[22]

However, in the summer of 1894 Margaret's life took an unexpected turn. She was invited to become an ILP candidate in the forthcoming School Board elections and agreed to be nominated for the East Ward.

Once Margaret signalled her intention to run for a place, the party's enthusiasm knew no bounds. Members mobilised every available agent at once to ensure her success. A manifesto was drawn up and meetings quickly arranged. In fact, the preparation was so thorough that members of other political parties began to fear the formidable opposition they had in Margaret and the other ILP candidates. The Liberal paper even admitted that the ILP manifesto was so good, especially on educational and religious topics, that the Liberals 'could wish for nothing better than that it might be adopted in substance by Liberal candidates!'

When the campaigning began, Margaret sought every possible means of putting her views on education before the electorate. It is in some of these speeches and articles that glimpses of her early views can best be caught. Addressing the Bradford Sunday Society at the Temperance Hall on 'Education False and True', she referred to mothers as the chief educators. In her article entitled 'To All Overworked Mothers',[23] she outlined her vision for the education of women and argued that they should be taught to understand science and politics, so that they could answer their children's questions. In another of her election speeches she maintained that those who taught young children needed more skill than those who taught seniors. She said it was 'a relic of barbarism' that in schools 'the very youngest children should be relegated to pupil-teachers, themselves perhaps only the merest children'.[24]

Often Margaret held several open air meetings in a day. Charlie Hunt, the self-appointed bellman for the socialist movement, willingly walked miles to announce her meetings. Although he started his work at 6 am, he belled for two hours before that to help Margaret's election campaign. Charlie was devoted to her and never forgot how sensitive she was to his feelings when he worked with her one Saturday afternoon.

> I belled and she spoke. They all came out in their clogs and mill brats, and mill skirts, and listened to her. They did not like it when she spoke against the half-timers working in the mills at ten years of age. However, we got a good hearing. On the way home in the tram, she said, 'Charlie you look sad.' I told her I had just got to know that my young sister had T.B. Margaret McMillan said she would like to help, but had no money. She would write to Lady Evaline. This lady sent £7 to pay for treatment for my sister, and Margaret McMillan sent her own doctor. I shall never forget her, or her great kindness to me.[25]

With Charlie's vigorous belling and Margaret's fine reputation as a speaker, the meetings were invariably well attended, but even so many spectators doubted whether she would be successful. On election day, despite many gloomy predictions, she polled 12,489 votes, and gained a seat by a very narrow majority. Speaking of this Margaret said:

> On the evening of the election I went to Bowling Back Club to see my constituents. We were all very much depressed, because, as one comrade said, it was too bad to have only one out of three elected and her only a woman. 'You don't even know the history of the Board,' said a Liberal lady, sighing . . . But there were other voices. 'You'll do champion, Margaret,' cried a weaver comrade very heartily.[26]

On 6 December 1894, Margaret attended her first meeting of the School Board and was elected to the Education Committee, the School Attendance and School Management Committees. It is as a member of this School Board that she emerges as a notable social reformer. Brockway speaking of her time in Bradford said:

> Margaret was almost the perfect harmony of idealist and practical reformer. There was a mysticism in her thought which made her writing and speech difficult to grasp at times, but it found expression in a character of rare beauty and service and in a contribution to child nurture which has made a deep mark on educational progress.[27]

Had she died at 32, it is possible that the governess turned companion would have passed away virtually unknown, but at 34 Margaret McMillan walked into the nation's life and thereafter remained at the heart of much educational reform.

Chapter eight

On the Bradford School Board 1894–1901

Although essentially a political movement, the ILP was interested in more than politics; it created an enthusiasm for education among its members. So once elected to the School Board, Margaret found herself working in a new context where, though still involved in the fight for better wealth distribution, she was more directly concerned with alleviating the consequences of poverty and enriching the lives of the victims of poverty.

Taking her official duties on the School Board seriously, she made regular visits to schools and began to see the need for many educational reforms. Although Bradford had a reputation for being progressive in education, Margaret soon became aware of the gaps in its provision.

To begin with the majority of school buildings were ugly. They were set in depressing, treeless streets, intersected by passages giving access to the houses' privy middens. The small, soot-covered back-to-back houses which had been flung up in close proximity to mills during the Industrial Revolution had no through draught for ventilation. They had one room upstairs, one down, and a windowless cellar where coal was kept.

School buildings themselves were drab and unlikely to appeal to anyone, like Margaret, who embraced William Morris's ideas on beauty. Nationwide, most nineteenth-century schools were ill-proportioned; classrooms were badly ventilated, inadequately heated, poorly lit and over-crowded. Bradford's Board schools were no exception; their spatial, visual, thermal and aural environments stood in stark contrast to the schoolrooms Margaret had worked in as a governess. Of one Bradford school she said:

> The school in which I am specially interested has been in a disgracefully crowded condition ever since I was elected. The poor children are being taught in lobbies, and the blind children are consigned to a room that looks like a dungeon.[1]

As she continued her visits to educational establishments, the conviction grew that most school buildings had multiple deficiencies and that many officials were complacent about them. As she began to tackle the question of poor educational facilities, she met fierce opposition from officials, teachers and parents, as well as members of the general public.

Not only were buildings bad but she felt that the classes were too large. When the Vice-President of the Board maintained that 'some people can teach a class of ninety and do them all justice', Margaret, who could be disturbingly blunt, told him that was nonsense and 'very dangerous nonsense too'.

Throughout the land, schools' curricula were narrow and, when Margaret arrived in Bradford, the stultifying effects of the system of 'payment by results' could still be seen. Commenting on what happened when the children weren't being drilled in the 3 Rs she said:

> The science lessons in our schools are excellent as far as they go;
> but they don't go very far. The language classes (taught in the
> higher schools) are of little value as the teacher is much in the
> same state as the pupil, as regards familiarity with pronunciation
> etc. The needlework is something wonderful to behold; but the
> mothers complain that the girls don't patch well.[2]

Poor as the school buildings and curricula were, when Margaret saw the pale, sickly children sitting in rigid desks for most of the day, she gave priority to the improvement of health for all school children. During her study of socialism she had come to understand that good health was the only capital most working men possessed. Without that their future prospects were grim. She decided that the same was true of children.

Most of the children she saw in schools were dirty as well as being disease-ridden. She felt that 'the lamp of the soul was literally put out in them' and their escape from ignorance was being impeded. Even those children who were not obviously sick had little resistance to disease; compulsory schooling meant compulsory contact with every form of disease. In addition, the lessons themselves demanded effort and some children had little stamina. One doctor said: 'There are children who are delicate without having any disease . . . On some days they are too tired to do anything and must rest.'[3]

Margaret maintained that much ill-health in children was due to poor breathing, foul air, uncleanliness, insufficient exercise and the severe malnourishment which she felt was related to the low wages of their parents. These factors made it difficult for children to benefit from the instruction offered to them, therefore Margaret began to work to remedy the situation.

First, she wrote a pamphlet for parents in very simple language, about infectious diseases and stressed the importance of general cleanliness. Then she fought vigorously for improved ventilation in schools and for correct breathing to be taught. Later she recommended school baths with the result that in 1897, against considerable opposition, Wapping Street School was provided with a swimming bath, together with twelve slipper baths, and Feversham Street School was given one in 1903. Then she advocated the provision of interesting, wholesome school dinners. Writing some years later, she spoke in glowing terms of the meals provided for Bradford's school children.[4]

Margaret could see so much that was crying out for attention and felt she had been elected to the School Board to fight the battle of the slum child. Fortunately, on health matters she soon found an ally in Dr Kerr, the School Medical Officer. (Bradford had a School Medical Officer in 1894, thirteen years before Parliament made medical inspection compulsory.) During one medical inspection, he discovered that, out of the 300 children he examined, 100 had not taken their clothes off for over six months – they were sewn into them. Some Bradford children had curvature of the spine, others had hollow chests, many had rickety legs. Socialists generally knew that the free public libraries were under-used because workers were too hungry and tired to use them profitably, but were slow to see that this was also true of children in school.

The urgent need for improvement in the health of adults and children could be seen in Bradford's high infant mortality rate which in 1893 was 198 per 1,000 live births. But such facts which impelled Margaret to take action often left others unmoved. Her suggested reforms were often rejected at School Board meetings because they might lead to extravagant expenditure. Referring to the disapproval and discouragement she experienced she declared: 'My fellow-members forget my existence, for the most part. And my remarks, when I make any, are listened to, stared at, and allowed to fly into space in the most disconcerting way.'[5]

During a period when few women engaged in public work, Margaret had to fight against prejudice as well as misunderstanding. On committees she often had to stand alone, experiencing not only open opposition to her advanced ideas but the more subtle form of counteraction – the conspiracy of silence. Replying to a letter from Mrs Blatchford, who complained that visitors to her home gladly spoke to her husband, Robert, a prominent socialist journalist, but only addressed her when they wanted another cup of tea, Margaret said: 'I can sympathize with you, I also have found myself continually in company with those who would not speak to me. I used to feel it so much. I truly suffered.'[6]

Considered a persistent faddist, Margaret continued to fight for the benefit of children. One of her colleagues on the Board, Alderman W. Leach, wrote, 'I recall the jeers which greeted her first demand, as a member of the School Board, for school baths: first derision, then anger at her persistence, then examination, and finally proud acceptance.' Speaking of the way Margaret won the support of committee members he said, 'She first stunned them by her boldness, then appealed to their intelligence and finally mesmerised them.'[7]

Often it was her genuine care for people which endeared her to others. Her fight for a rise in the wages of Bradford's caretakers earned her the title 'The Caretakers' Friend'. Once when the question of a rise in their wages came before the Board, they appealed to Margaret for help. She gave them facts about wages in other areas which enabled them to make out a good cause for an increase and they got it. When there were complaints that confidential information had been leaked, Margaret openly admitted what she had done, saying that she felt entitled to do so.[8]

Margaret's care for children included their intellectual growth. In her first year on the School Board she realised what cognitive psychologists are currently saying – that the foundations of intellectual development are laid during the earliest years. She wrote then, 'What is the use of saying "We must begin with children"? Too late. We must begin with the babies.' From this time onwards the all-round development of pre-school children interested her. After reading Séguin's work on handicapped children in France, she began to realise that some effects of early disadvantages might be difficult to retrieve. 'Who', she asked, 'can make good to a child the loss of vital capital by his own progenitors, or re-build the vault of an impoverished brain?'[9]

The half-time system, like ill-health, was to Margaret another despoiler of children's educational opportunities and therefore something to be fought. Despite improvements made by Factory and Education Acts, it was still possible in 1894 for 11-year-olds to attend school for half a day only and work for the other half. Thinking of Margaret's concern about children who, on returning from the mills, fell asleep at their school desks, J. B. Priestley once said, 'What didn't worry Lord Salisbury, Joseph Chamberlain, A. J. Balfour, worried her.' But her fight for these children did not make her popular either with management or labour. Many parents, who themselves started to work at 9 years of age and ploughed their way through a 72-hour week, did not see why their children needed anything different. Conventional wisdom said that the half-time system was crucial to the woollen trade and the national economy.

It was claimed that in 1890 Bradford employed more half-timers than most other boroughs. Lowndes stated:

> In 1894 there were 4,134 half-timers in Bradford's mills . . . The morning 'turn' at the mill was from 6 a.m. to 12.30 p.m. and the wage was 3s. 3d. per week. The afternoon 'turn' at the mill was from 1.15 p.m. to 5.45 p.m. and the wage was 1s. or 1s. 6d. to 2s. 6d. per week . . . These half-timers were exhausted, white and blanched. Very quickly they lost powers of concentration and all interest in school work.[10]

Margaret's attack on the half-time system was typical of her approach to problems generally and possibly reflected her early Fabian training. She first collected facts about it nationally and locally. She read doctors' medical reports and found that one practitioner, after examining 52,000 factory children, said that: 'the great majority had been weakened and crippled seriously by the conditions under which their earliest years were spent, and that all had been affected . . . physically, morally and mentally.'[11] Then she collected the views of teachers. Many of these observed that once children started work their interest in class lessons waned and their mental activity was reduced. Then they acted as a drag on their classmates.

After collecting and sorting all this information Margaret publicised the facts. Moving amongst the textile communities of Lancashire and Yorkshire she thrust the evils of the half-time system and the benefits of education in front of the public. But this was another uphill task. Many workers dubbed full-time education 'new fangled' and Margaret 'impractical if not dangerous'.

The climax of her attack on the half-time system came in 1895 when she led a deputation to Asquith, the Home Secretary, to protest against it. At Westminster, she pleaded for the age limit to be raised forthwith and for the system to be ended altogether in due course. Soon after this the age for half-timers was raised from 11 to 12 years, but the practice lingered on until 1918 and was finally abolished only in 1922. Through her protests and her writings, such as 'Child Labour and the Half-time System', she did much to change the views of officials and the working classes about this system.

Margaret also saw the need to help parents to see their children from a new angle and to raise their expectations of them. Many saw their offspring only as investments, as contributors to the family budget. But she wanted parents to be aware of their children as persons in their own right. Through her articles and speeches she was instrumental in helping parents gain a new vision of themselves and their children and believe that they could all have their lives enriched. Lowndes said that many of those who heard her dreamed dreams, discovered hidden depths within themselves, and 'thereafter led changed lives'.

Her impassioned speeches on education greatly moved her hearers; it was not uncommon for her to address thousands at a time. One eyewitness said:

> When she stood up to speak it seemed that a holy calm pervaded the room. She had a lovely face. One never noticed her dress because her face and quiet and still bearing held one's attention to her last word.[12]

Another, speaking of rallies in St George's Hall, said:

> People walked five or seven or more miles into Bradford to hear the speakers. Long before the scheduled time, the hall was packed with some 4,000 or more people when Margaret McMillan was due to be the speaker. A thrill of expectancy used to surge through the hall. Of all the speakers, it was she who lifted that vast audience to spiritual heights.[13]

Professor Alexander, the eminent philosopher, tells of a crowded meeting held in the Free Trade Hall in Manchester in the nineties.

> As Margaret got up to speak a loud voice rang from the back of the hall: 'Our Maggie'. The whole audience cheered . . . She so manifestly cared for them and for their children. The discerning among them knew her for a prophet.[14]

For the rest of her years in Bradford her specific objectives became the changing of parental attitudes towards the health and education of children, and the creation of a more informed electorate. But, as she remarked, 'the persons most closely concerned in the education of the little John Smiths of England [the parents] . . . are strangely indifferent, indeed apathetic'.[15]

Bradford was a cosmopolitan town. Consequently it had a number of residents who were interested in foreign languages. So, along with others, Margaret saw the possibility of creating a centre where foreign languages could be taught and international contacts fostered. Being a fluent linguist she started to give free lessons in French and German to mill-girls in an old cellar in the evenings. Then in 1894, when the Cercle Français was established, she was chosen as first president.

To interest more adults in education Margaret undertook to give public lectures on a variety of topics which socialist newspapers publicised. *The Labour Leader*,[16] for example, gave advance notice in June 1895 that Margaret was to give a course of lectures in August. Later reports say she gave a series of six addresses entitled 'Studies from the French Revolution'.[17] One report said that 'a very large audience assembled on Sunday night at the Labour Church to hear Miss McMillan give the concluding address'.[18] *The Labour Prophet* stated that Margaret gave a number of addresses on 'Art in the Middle Ages' and said they 'deserved more than the passing notice we can give'.[19] These lectures represent just a few of the many Margaret gave to educate the electorate.

Typical of the many favourable comments on these popular lectures, and the lecturer, was:

> The sensation of the gathering was Miss McMillan's paper on 'Four Great Educational Ideals' . . . Miss McMillan is one of the people of whom the I.L.P. is justly proud . . . But it is not only as an educationist that Miss McMillan ranks high. As a personal influence for clean, high, resolute life she has no second.[20]

The news of Margaret's oratory and integrity spread beyond the Yorkshire boundaries. She was often in demand as a speaker in Scotland, in Lancashire and in the south of England. The public notice of a Glasgow meeting ran like this: 'Miss McMillan, the gifted author of "Handal Stumm", "Early Childhood" etc., lectures in the Albion Halls, Glasgow, tomorrow (Sunday). Those who have listened to her before will be glad of this opportunity to hear her again.'[21]

Margaret appealed to different kinds of audiences. She was as well received in meetings where the frock coat and the top hat were customary as in dockers' meetings. Of a great open-air meeting of workers in Liverpool, it was said:

> She was explaining the power of right thinking in producing beauty out of the most unlikely material . . . I remember how the great multitude strained every nerve to hear what she was saying, whilst their poor brains tried to take in the argument. From the open mouths and bewildered expression on many of the upturned faces it was evident that many of the words conveyed but scant meaning, but it was equally evident that her hearers were being influenced in a wondrous way.[22]

The same thing happened at a gathering of agricultural labourers in Oxfordshire. One man said that she looked 'like an angel on the day of judgement proclaiming mercy to some poor wretches who thought they were about to be damned'.

In addition to speaking to adults, Margaret gave talks to children in the Socialist Sunday School as the following press account shows:

Margaret McMillan gave an interesting, lucid and altogether charming address, telling in a simple and racy manner Hans Andersen's fairy tale about 'The Yellow Duck' . . . The children's interest was completely captured and retained from start to finish.[23]

Margaret reached many ordinary persons through her writings. During her years in Bradford she wrote some hundred articles, several short stories, not a few pamphlets and a number of books. When *The New Party* – a book to which Margaret contributed along with Keir Hardie, Walter Crane and others – was reviewed in *The Clarion*, Margaret's fight to involve women in social reform was emphasised.

To quote again from 'The New Party', this time from the article by that clever woman, MARGARET McMILLAN: 'Women work in mills, workshops, homes and therefore the question of Social Reform concerns them. In the past we were told that they have no business in the area of politics . . . But the wage-struggle has taught woman that she even more than man is influenced by all that takes place in the economic and industrial world.'[24]

Although through her articles and lectures Margaret had a wide outreach, her books reached a smaller public and as a rule were reported less favourably. One critic of *Samson* claimed that Margaret had just missed writing a notable book and he would look forward with interest to her next! *Early Childhood* – which appeared later – got a better commendation:

The book is indeed a little principia on the science and art of education . . . It is a book that should be read by every socialist, and by everyone interested in the welfare of children and in the progress of the race.[25]

Although Margaret was popular in some spheres, life was never a bed of roses for very long. She spent so much time struggling to bring educational issues before the general public that eventually members of the very party which had nominated her for the

School Board began to complain that she spent too little time on politics and too much on education. One newspaper said:

> Her work on the Bradford School Board absorbs her, but it is as great a mistake for Margaret McMillan to hide herself in the dominie's desk as it is for John Burns to bury himself in a London sewer. Ordinary folks can do that work. The giants are national property.[26]

Sometimes people also criticised her lectures saying they did not contain enough socialism. Others, defending her, said she took socialism wherever she went because equality and fraternity emanated from her.

In fact, however preoccupied she might have been with School Board work, she never neglected the party. She gave to that in full measure. One finds her reported as gracing party platforms, attending funerals of party members, sometimes writing their obituaries. 'Tom Maguire – A Remembrance'[27] was typical of many such writings.

Another of her activities was acting in sketches at socialist gatherings – once she took the part of a landlady. Her training for the stage was never lost; it was used in the most unexpected settings with the ordinary rank and file whom she loved to meet socially and who enjoyed meeting her. In these gatherings she must have brought a much-needed touch of glamour and panache to what otherwise might have been pedestrian, suburban social evenings. If it was known that Margaret would be at a function it was crowded out, for she could turn any ordinary tea-party into a rare occasion. She had almost a child-like love of parties and gave many, especially to poor children, although she had limited means.

Margaret worked hard and played hard, but food and sleep gradually became grudged necessities. There was so much to do. And whilst it would be untrue to say that during her time on the School Board she reached all of her goals, or that the increasing improvements in schools were entirely due to her efforts, nevertheless, whilst she was in Bradford many of the innovations she fought for, especially those concerned with the physical improvement of children, began to be introduced. Many class-rooms became more attractive – some being equipped like nursery classes. Methods of teaching became less formal, individual work began to take the place of class lessons. Creativity became increasingly valued so that composition replaced dictation. To help children master the abstract side of mathematics, concrete materials such as shells and bobbins were more frequently used in arithmetic lessons and teachers were encouraged to think of education in terms of children's learning as well as of teachers' teaching. Handwork and nature study improved, visits to parks were introduced and the importance of school journeys became recognised.

Sometimes she was on sub-committees which discussed improvements in the quality of the instruction given in day and evening schools. She was concerned with schemes for the teaching of household management, she was a member of a small working-party studying physical education for pupil teachers and older girls. On a committee which examined the particular difficulties of teachers in elementary schools in inner-city areas, she suggested that their salaries should be raised and made equal to those of teachers in Higher Grade schools for older pupils situated in the best residential suburbs.

At this time Margaret often urged the need to recruit good potential teachers and give them sound initial and in-service training. In her series of articles 'Education in the Primary School',[28] she frequently referred to the quality of primary school teachers. On occasion she herself taught at the pupil-teachers' centre. There she tried to inspire teachers to be always learners, discoverers, craftsmen. In many of her suggestions to them, Froebelian influences can be clearly seen.

As a member of the School Board she visited the famous Froebelian Kindergarten in Kensington, under the direction of Madame Michaelis. Her article 'An English Kindergarten'[29] shows how impressed she was with the cheerful classrooms there, the friendly atmosphere, a free yet ordered programme, the provision of play material such as sand, clay and paint, as well as the more didactic sense-training apparatus. Margaret maintained that children learned through play-experience and accumulated information which could be used later in the 'high mental life'.

Not all teachers who had worked formally under the rigid system of 'payment by results' would take kindly to Margaret's Froebelian ideas. Some of them would naturally feel threatened by her suggestions which implied that long-established practices might change. Most of them probably felt more secure giving straight instruction in the 3 Rs than trying to use informal methods of teaching. Once, when trying to answer teachers' questions about where the 3 Rs would come in if they used freer approaches, she said: 'I am sure I do not know exactly: and it really does not matter so long as they do not come in too early.'

Already the central role of language, and the part played by teachers' questions in the educative process, was being propounded by Margaret. In school she wanted children to have the opportunity of listening and speaking to other children, when most teachers thought it virtuous to have silent classrooms. In her article 'Voice Production in Board Schools'[30] she stressed the need for teachers to have voice training and arranged for her former drama teacher – Mrs Behnke – to give them a course of lectures. Margaret looked forward to the time when grown-ups would 'possess voices full of subtle intonations which would make conversation quite a delightful thing'.

Although she was passionately concerned about practical teaching, she was no mere pragmatist. Apart from studying Froebel's philosophical writings, she read the works of Rousseau, Pestalozzi, Séguin, and other authorities with much interest, sometimes making special journeys to the British Museum in London to consult educational tomes written in foreign languages. Her wide knowledge of current literature, which included books by Lombroso on neurology, Donaldson on the growth of the brain, and many others, can be seen in a long, detailed letter she wrote during her School Board days to a friend who asked for her advice about books on education.[31]

Having studied many different philosophies and methods, she was particularly drawn to the work of Séguin. But it wasn't only his methods which interested her, it was his view that, 'to make the child feel that he is loved, and to make him eager to love in his turn, is the end of our teaching as it has been its beginning'. It was this philosophy which she accepted and worked out in her own inimitable way with different groups of children.

She wrote an account of how she advocated freer methods of teaching, long before Dr Montessori's work was popularised in Britain, to the chagrin of some.

In Belle Vue School, Bradford, in the year 1896, I began, with the headmistress, certain experiments, founded on the principles of Edouard Séguin. The School Board consented to let these experiments go forward, in spite of a good deal of misgiving. A very deliberate training of the basal sense of touch was begun, by means of a scale of materials of textures varying from the smoothest satin to the rough surface of fretted wood. The children touched these with closed eyes; they practised writing on sand and also drawing by touch on low boards and easels. Finally stained canvas was stretched all round the rooms, tables, floor, any surface was made available for writing and drawing, and a colour wheel and scales of coloured paper were introduced, by means of which the graduation and naming of

58

colours went on apace. Needless to say, we had by this time
found that the old furniture was impossible. All forms and desks
were eschewed, and the infant room furnished with tiny chairs
with rounded backs and feather light tables! Delivered from the
notion that utter stillness was a virtue, the children skipped
about the room freely . . . The School Board was alarmed. The
parents also. 'The Board of Education will not pay for this kind
of work' they cried; 'We can't earn grants, we can't win
scholarships by it.'[32]

However, by 1898 newspapers were readily acknowledging the
valuable contribution Margaret had made to education while on
the School Board. Even Tories and Liberals had to agree that she
had skilfully influenced schools' curricula. *The Labour Leader*
said:

The literary reputation of Miss McMillan is well known to our
readers, but it is not perhaps so well known that, as an expert in
physical education, she stands almost unrivalled. Since her
accession to the Board she has been mainly instrumental in
establishing classes for clay modelling, brush painting, etc., and
baths and breathing lessons.[33]

However, after seven years of hard work on the Board Margaret
became unduly tired; constant over-work, insufficient sleep,
irregular meals, took their toll on her. She became mentally and
physically exhausted; her body refused to go on working under
such pressure.

Chapter nine

Leaving Bradford 1901–2

In the autumn of 1901 Margaret was compelled to take a prolonged rest and went to a private nursing home to recover. When Lady Meux heard about this she paid the fees, but Rachel, not wishing her sister to be under any obligation to her, repaid them in full. Then, when Margaret was well enough to leave there but still not fit for work, Rachel arranged for her to take a holiday in the Scottish Highlands. Speaking of this Margaret said: 'I yearned for a sight of the hills and my darling sister sent me up to Oban.' Mansbridge thought that Margaret's mind and body would have given way long before had she not been able to draw on the re-creating power of spiritual impulses.[1] Those, along with Rachel's devoted care, he believed stopped her from having a complete breakdown.

During her stay in Oban, Margaret looked out over the Sound of Mull to the purple hills and ever-changing vistas of the Hebridean islands. Being filled with a deep longing to go there, but not having the fare, she conjured up an ingenious plan to overcome the financial hurdle. She informed the town authorities that if they would pay for her boat passage across, she would write about the tourist attractions of the islands. They agreed to this proposition and forthwith she sailed over to Lochboisdale on South Uist. Later two boys rowed her over a treacherous sea to the remote island of Eriskay, and while they pulled heavily on the oars, she regaled them with stories about London, the Queen and monkeys at the zoo.

As they moved nearer to Eriskay, she made enquiries about where she might stay. Margaret takes up the story:

'There's no inn on the island', said the eldest lad in answer to questions. 'And no one takes in here because the bothies are full of smoke'. 'There is the Presbytery', said the youngest boy, 'Father Allan will tell you what to do.' And indeed, that was

Father Allan's business – to help strangers and be the staff of every islander . . . he came up the path on hearing that there was a visitor . . . Gravely but kindly he bade me welcome, and ordered candles and supper.[2]

She stayed the night there and had deep conversations with the priest.

Father Allan was an able linguist, a renowned folklorist and an orator, but even more important he was a true man of God who was loved throughout the island. Margaret declared: 'Love was around him, quick and constant . . . The children loved him . . . The young men trusted him as a brother, and the old men and women longed for him when the shadow was on them.'[3] When he died she wrote of him:

> But the lives of such men do not fade like smoke. They are
> visible signs of a great transforming power that liberates itself in
> the human heart, a power that rises above self, and becomes a
> part of the larger life.[4]

Thinking of his cultured interests Margaret wondered whether he ever wanted to get away from this distant island. ' "Do you never feel lonely?" said a stranger to him once. "That maybe", he answered, "but that would be one of the smallest of matters to think on for me." '[5]

The atmosphere of peace and certainty in him must have contrasted sharply with Margaret's turbulent spirit. His quiet heart drew conversation from her. She began to tell him her life story and how she had arrived at this stage. She said that at present she was in a fog – the future had no face. Then she blurted out, 'Politics are not enough.' To which Father Allan replied, 'Very true. That is only the Kingdom without. It is by the Kingdom within that the world must be won.' Perhaps, like Keir Hardie, Margaret was beginning to be disenchanted with politics. In 1913 Hardie confessed:

> I often feel sick at heart with politics and all that pertains
> thereof. If I were a thirty years younger man . . . I would,
> methinks, abandon house and home and wife and child, if need
> be . . . to proclaim afresh and anew the full message of the
> Gospel of Jesus of Nazareth.[6]

Father Allan's helper made a good meal for him and his guest, then left for a walk in the moonlight with her fiancé. Watching her go through the door Margaret said to the priest, 'Those dear lovers and the magic night – that must be true romance.' Father Allan commented, 'It is for them. We all have different paths.' To which Margaret replied, 'How strange it is we know that way is not for us.' When the priest enquired about her future Margaret said that on arrival it had seemed obscure but since being in his house it had come to her clearly that she must now join her sister. 'I've been away from her too long. The next thing, we must do together. That is all I know, but it is enough.' 'To see the next step clearly is always enough', said Father Allan. 'Perhaps we could not go on if we saw where it would eventually lead us.' Then the dialogue in the play, *The Legend of Margaret McMillan*, which Mrs Sutcliffe wrote after Margaret related her experiences to her, and which was performed several times at the Bradford Technical College in April 1924, continues in this way:

Margaret	It is strange how I feel about this place. I have never been here before, and yet it feels like coming back. I never knew that it was Eriskay, and yet I have longed for it. It is the answer to something . . . You see I'm trying to find out what I have to do in the world, and all the time Rachel is working steadily on, sending me her hard earned money so that I may continue the quest.
Father Allan	Why are you so sure that there is something for you to do?
Margaret	Father Allan, surely you have sometimes heard voices from some other world than this and behind them other voices, calling, urging you on?
Father Allan	Yes. I have heard them.

Time seemed to stand still that night. It was a memorable evening. They talked on and on, then finally Margaret said: 'I don't suppose you can have any idea of what you have done for me, but I feel you have brought me, so beautifully and simply, to the end of my search.'

Father Allan	Oh, I have done nothing, but there is the unseen world all around us. The veil wears very thin, sometimes.
Margaret	I have talked so much about myself. May I ask you one thing? What made you come back to the island when you had all the world to choose from?
Father Allan	I did not choose . . . I was sent.
Margaret	And what is this strong tide that is sweeping us on?

Father Allan   I don't know. I only know we must go with that
tide.[7]

The morning after this encounter with Father Allan, Margaret
left and went to Skye. A few days later she left the Hebrides. She
was refreshed, but still not fit for work. So, instead of returning to
Bradford, she went to stay with Rachel in London. In November
members of the School Board resolved that 'an expression of the
Board's sympathy with Miss McMillan in her illness be forwarded
to her with the hope that she may soon be restored to health'.[8]
Subsequently the Chairman wrote to Rachel expressing his best
wishes for Margaret's early recovery, not only on his own behalf
but including his wife and children together with hosts of friends.
'It is clear', Mansbridge said, 'that she was regarded with no
common affection.'[9]

Margaret did not attend any more School Board meetings until
the end of February 1902, when she was warmly welcomed. On
her return she immediately threw herself into the work in
Bradford. In September she was one of the speakers at a protest
meeting in Leeds of 100,000 people, designed to show the
government Yorkshire's opposition to certain clauses in the 1902
Education Bill, then before Parliament, and the lack of government
consultation about them. The government proposals which aroused
most hostility were, the one seeking to abolish the 2,559 School
Boards and replace them with 330 Local Education Authorities,
and that proposing that sectarian schools should be a charge on the
rates.

Socialists generally were against the abolition of School Boards,
mainly on the grounds that this would take the control of
education away from people who had been chosen to administer it
because of their special interest in the subject.

Although still far from fully fit, Margaret made an impassioned
speech at the meeting. She condemned the Education Bill largely
because it would rob women of the opportunity of becoming
members of such Boards, when there were already too few doors
open to them to serve on public committees. *The Yorkshire Daily
Observer* reported her as saying:

> When this bill was passed into law, all women would be put on
> one side. Their work was mentioned very little at present; but by
> this bill it was to be wiped out altogether, and the children's
> education would be in the hands of a section who were not
> responsible to the ratepayers.[10]

Towards the end of the meeting a resolution was passed calling on 'the Prime Minister to withdraw the Bill or to dissolve Parliament'.[11] Despite strong opposition from so many people, the Bill was passed with certain amendments and, to Margaret's sorrow, the death knell of School Boards was sounded.

Although to outward appearances Margaret's health had improved, it soon became apparent to her close friends that again the work was becoming too onerous for her. School Board colleagues, the majority of whom were not of her own party, hoped against hope that she would not be forced to relinquish her seat. But early in November she felt compelled to resign from the Board. The committee accepted her resignation regretfully and immediately put on record their high appreciation of her services.[12]

Although realising that she would shortly relinquish her office she struggled on to the bitter end. She attended meetings about the in-service training of teachers; she was present at discussions about a course leading to the advanced Froebel Certificate; she spoke at the Bradford Branch of the Froebel Society, on 'The Child as Artist'. So ended eight full years of unceasing toil on the School Board for the benefit of the children, parents, teachers and citizens of Bradford.

When her resignation was publicly announced friends and foes alike paid tribute to her work. The Chairman of the School Board said, 'She was a pioneer whose influence had been greatly felt in the city. Her ideals were far in advance of the current education of the day.'[13] One of her chief opponents on the Board wrote saying: 'I always considered it a piece of good fortune for the society you represented that they were able to secure the prestige which your well-known abilities and cultivated character brought them.'[14]

Writing from Whitehall about Margaret's time in Bradford, Sir George Kekewich, Permanent Secretary to the Board of Education, remarked that: ' "Bradford had presented the Board with so many new problems . . . that, during the whole of the past eight years, it had been in bad odour with the Board of Education." This, he considered, "did Bradford great credit".'[15]

At one of her farewell parties, Margaret met Joseph Fels,[16] an American millionaire, a Jew who tried to use the wealth he derived from the manufacture of Fels Naphtha Soap, which he said would remove the stains from everything 'except the character of the average politician', for removing the causes of human misery. In Margaret he found a kindred spirit. Describing her husband's first meeting with Margaret, Mrs Fels said: 'In conversation, he discovered that here was a personality with views and ideals of unlimited importance for the well-being of the future generation . . . and worthy of every degree of support.'[17]

Thus began a lifelong friendship with this rich philanthropist whom Margaret described as being 'small, like St. Paul; curious like Nicodemus; impetuous like St. Peter . . . consumed throughout all and above all by burning thirst for righteousness'.[18] It was partly due to his generosity that, after leaving Bradford, she was able to achieve so much for deprived children elsewhere.

Margaret went to Yorkshire with theoretical ideas about the creation of a new society. She left with a clear commitment to shaping the future through the improved health and education of young children – a commitment from which she never retracted. Love for humanity had always been at the heart of her political agitation, and her educational reforms were essentially creative acts of compassion.

Although Bradford had proved a tough assignment, Margaret had grown to love it dearly. Her references to it were always in affectionate terms, such as 'the city of my heart', 'the city of the child'. Consequently, when the inevitable break with it came, she felt it poignantly. But she left behind her many legacies. She had not only benefited the city's children, but had given her party and country a new vision of what could be done when the needs of the poor were given priority.

Chapter ten

The Years Between 1902–5

The beginning of the twentieth century was a period of great social upheaval and unrest. When Edward VII succeeded to the throne in 1901 Britain was still at war with the Boers in South Africa. At home many urgent problems dominated political agenda and called for action by the Conservative government. These included free trade, imperialism, collectivism, state regulation and *laissez-faire*, policies of social welfare, the quest for better wages for workers and the claims of women for emancipation. Read, the historian, commented: 'The Edwardian age was to be marked by a sometimes feverish search for greater "efficiency" in many aspects of national life – military, governmental, commercial and social.'[1]

This quest for 'efficiency' naturally turned attention towards education. Britain was beginning to be out-stripped in trade and industry by other countries. Curtis and Boultwood, in their historical survey of English education, report: 'There was a strong case for the provision of more efficient elementary, secondary and technical education . . . the position of England as a first-class power depended on sea power and school power.'[2]

It was in the context of this drive for 'efficiency' that many of Margaret McMillan's future projects on behalf of deprived children's health and education were to be initiated – though her main concern was not so much wealth creation as the development of a more humane society.

December 1902 found Margaret recuperating in Kent, but intensely interested in the passing of the 1902 Education Act – a landmark in British education which promoted local administration of education and led to a more unified national system. Prior to that educational resources, though scant, as Margaret had seen in Bradford, had been spent largely on elementary education; but now attention was turned towards the needs of older children. For the first time, elementary and higher education were considered together. The new education authorities were now empowered to provide education 'other than elementary' – a term covering secondary and technical schools, training colleges for teachers and adult education.

This wider conception of educational provision was welcomed by the socialists and especially by Margaret, despite her continued opposition to the abolition of School Boards. Before this, secondary education was mainly the prerogative of children whose parents could afford to pay fees. And it always saddened Margaret, who had been widely and expensively educated, that poor children were denied access to education other than elementary. She favoured a university education for every working man's child who could profit by it, but the priority, she believed, was to spend more money on the health and education of young children. To her, that was the most efficient use of educational resources as it would provide a sound foundation for secondary and tertiary education. So she continued to campaign for that through her political party and her writings.

Acting on the inner direction that she had received in Eriskay – that she and Rachel would do their next piece of work together – after leaving Bradford Margaret went to join her sister. Rachel, now a peripatetic teacher of hygiene, resided in the pleasant residential town of Bromley, ten miles south-east of London. She lodged with a Miss Illott, who lived with her maid in a large terraced house at 51 Tweedy Road and Margaret joined her there.

Going to live with Rachel was a venture of faith for Margaret. She was not quite sure how they would get on together after being separated for so long. She wondered if the old affinity between them still existed. Towards the end of her time in Bradford, she had sensed a certain distance in their relationship. Describing this, she said:

> I felt that she was going away from me . . . There are such withdrawals. They are not estrangements. They do not imply desertion . . . She was gathering up her powers to do her own work – a work in which she was no longer a mere helper.[3]

However, on arrival at Rachel's, Margaret received the warmest welcome. She need not have been apprehensive. There were no shadows between them; the old union of hearts still existed.

At first, Margaret's time in Bromley was tedious. There, apart from her sister, few eagerly awaited her arrival. She had no trumpeter. After the adulation she was accustomed to in the north, the south seemed cold and indifferent. She exclaimed: 'Even the Labour Party outside Bradford was cold.' Looking back nostalgically she said:

> The break with Bradford could not be other than painful . . .
> The wild venture of 1893 had become, in 1902 . . . a very
> exhilarating and ever-renewed happiness. London had nothing
> to offer in exchange. A more chill atmosphere could not be
> encountered or imagined.[4]

However, some of her friends both welcomed her back and
made suggestions about her future. One of Joseph Fels's biographers described how in 1903 he attended a reception given in
Margaret's honour:

> The occasion was held to celebrate Miss McMillan's return to
> London after her resignation from the Bradford School Board
> . . . During the course of the reception, Fels offered her
> financial assistance 'if she would conceive and carry out a
> scheme of hygienic centres of larger scope than Bradford had
> been able to allow her'.[5]

But Margaret did not immediately accept Fels's offer. She was still
unsure what she should do.

The only security to which she could cling now was that inner
conviction that her next step was to work with Rachel, along with
the reassurance that Father Allan had given her, that to see the
next step was enough. Describing her feelings she said: 'It was
midwinter. I had no plans and was back in the mist.'[6] She did not
of course realise at this time that she was uneasily sandwiched
between two of the most creative periods of her life. She was only
conscious that one had ended; the other was not yet visible.

During their years apart, both of the sisters had gained first-
hand experience of social conditions which impeded physical and
intellectual growth. As a result, quite independently of each other,
they had both become increasingly aware of the need for a new
kind of education to offset deprivation.

In the course of her work, Rachel saw hundreds of cases of
arrested development. The stunted growth of mothers and
children, together with the urgent need for education in child-
rearing, seemed to meet her in every village. Her classes in
hygiene were attended by women of different age groups and
social backgrounds. On the one hand she saw poor, over-worked
women who had had no preparation for marriage and little
training in child-rearing, struggling to bring up their children in
badly-built houses devoid of facilities. On the other hand, she saw
well-to-do women who had had some education but too few
outlets for their energies. While the poor had too much to do, the
rich had too little. Women in both groups were manifestly

disadvantaged and were under-functioning intellectually. Margaret tells us that Rachel was 'thinking of all this want and waste and of strange repressions. Already she was wondering how the two classes were related, or might be related if the way could be opened.'[7]

When her lectures were over, Rachel often visited homes where she helped children with their homework and gave the adults advice on sick-nursing and reading matter. She saw the dire need for further education for all, but especially for women with young children. As Margaret said: 'In the midst of it all, she realised more and more that fragmentary help was almost useless – that at every stage of childhood and youth the tides must be taken that ensure later success.'[8]

Margaret's work on the Bradford School Board had also led her to see that in education voluntary efforts alone were inadequate. Something more systematic was needed. So, by different routes, both sisters had become aware of the lack of sound educational provision and the unequal chances children had of obtaining firm foundations for elementary education. Consequently, they found to their great joy that they had common interests and much that they wanted to discuss together.

As well as enjoying their own deliberations on social problems, they began to revive old friendships and make new ones. Margaret visited Lady Meux again, but the relationship finally broke down. Neighbours and friends started to visit them. Prince Kropotkin, the Russian anarchist who lived nearby, Hyndman, the Marxist, and Mrs Cobden-Sanderson, the wife of the painter, were just a few of those who began to call on the McMillans. By degrees their home became a centre of conviviality, where agitators and promoters of good causes enjoyed meeting each other. Albert Mansbridge, who often went round to discuss his ideas on adult education, describes a typical gathering: 'There was Joseph Fels . . . the Lansburys, a devoted couple; Margaret Llewellyn Davies, promoting women's suffrage; the Stanton Coits, heading the Ethical Movement; and the Countess of Warwick, ready to encourage any democratic adventure. In reality it was a "salon".'[9]

Margaret's task of trying to keep the peace between the guests could have been no easy one for they usually held different views about the way society should be reformed. Hyndman propounded atheism, the Lansburys, Christian Socialism, and other members of the group took up philosophical stances in between these polar points. Mansbridge remembered speaking there with pride about his ideas of evening classes for workers, but Prince Kropotkin tore them to shreds. 'His contempt of their study of Economics was cutting', Mansbridge said. Kropotkin thought that the workers 'should learn about the Universe, and their place in it'.[10]

Social gatherings and generous hospitality were marked features of socialist comradeship in London as they had been in Bradford. One of Margaret's greatest pleasures was filling her home with friends. She found discussions on the arts, on politics and people, and the mysteries of life, irresistible. Many discovered that she was an unforgettable raconteuse and soon learnt that time spent in her company was something to be savoured.

These regular colloquia unquestionably added interest to the McMillan household, but they also made a dent in the housekeeping money. So Margaret, wishing to make her own contribution to the household purse, decided once more to earn whatever she could by giving public lectures. Before long, considerable work came her way which earned her a small income as well as a good reputation as a speaker. She gave a series of lectures for the Ethical Society, which was the southern equivalent of the Labour Churches. Dr Stanton Coit – a friend of Joseph Fels – was the minister of the West London Ethical Society and it was probably through him that Margaret was invited to give these lectures. They were well received as the following press report showed:

> Miss McMillan, who is lecturing in different parts of London on 'Education', is giving a series of splendid lectures to crowded audiences at the Ethical Society's room (Buckingham Street) on 'Education through the Imagination' . . . We are glad to learn that these original and helpful lectures will be embodied in a book, so that those who have not had the advantage of hearing them will still be able to read and study the practical conclusions of this able woman.[11]

Although Margaret addressed members of the Ethical Society, she never embraced their rationalist views, or their disbelief in supernatural powers. She firmly believed in the teaching of Christianity in state schools and was against all efforts to remove it from schools' curricula. Her own deep respect for Bible teaching was reflected in a report of a lecture which she gave about the same time to a group of Scots at the Caledonian Christian Club in London, on 'Life in the City and its Possibilities': her two main themes were the division between 'Life as a Career' and 'Life as a Mission'.[12]

Many of the socialist Sunday Schools taught ethics but not Christianity. Speaking at the Coliseum in Leeds in 1911, where the first Leeds Socialist Sunday School demonstration was held,

Margaret followed the Countess of Warwick who was reported as saying:

Socialist Sunday Schools did not go far enough nor deep enough, because after all no matter how good ethics were, without religion they could not be very inspiring . . . Her experience of ethics without religion was that more often than not they turned young people into prigs and bores.

Continuing the argument Margaret said:

On the free development of the child depended the future of the race. (*Applause*) Through the development of the powers of sympathy as well as the powers of intelligence the children of the future would be able to think and speak and act as brothers . . . If you must not teach dogmas, don't conclude that you must not teach any religion. That you must teach consciously and continually or you will be blighting the young minds under your charge.[13]

As well as lecturing, Margaret started to write again to earn money. A quick glance at even a few of the books, pamphlets and articles which she produced during this period reveals the breadth of her thinking and her sense of urgency.[14]

In addition to lecturing and writing, she found that as her health improved she could gradually increase her voluntary work. She became a member of the Council of the Froebel Society in 1903 and was elected a member of the National Administrative Council of the ILP in 1905, along with Keir Hardie, Ramsay MacDonald, Mrs Pankhurst and other notable socialists.

Occasionally she was able to return to Bradford to officiate at special functions, such as the opening of the baths at Feversham Street School. On that great day in 1903, she performed the opening ceremony with such enthusiasm that she was only prevented from falling into the baths by the prompt action of the Chairman! The golden chain the teachers of Bradford presented to her in recognition of her work in their schools became one of her most treasured possessions.

Sometimes Rachel, trying to build up Margaret's health, arranged for them both to take short holidays. An entry in Bruce Glasier's unpublished diary for 4 September 1903 reads: 'Oban to Glasgow. On boarding the steamer this morning we walked into the arms of Margaret McMillan! She also with Rachel has been on tour . . . Margaret comes home with us.' The entry for the next day reads: 'Margaret leaves early for Belfast.' But even when Margaret was supposed to be on holiday, her mind constantly turned to the social questions which the popular press was forcing on the attention of the public.

In 1904, Margaret received an invitation from the London County Council which proved to be seminal. She was asked to become a Manager of the schools in Alverton Street, Deptford Park and Trundley's Road in Deptford, south-east London. Once she accepted this invitation it was as if the woman and the mission met. Thus began an association with Deptford which lasted until her death.

As a schools' Manager, Margaret soon obtained first-hand evidence about the deplorable lifestyle of those who lived in this London slum. As she walked through Deptford's mean streets on her way to the schools, memory stored what eye and ear had recorded. On the way back to her home in Bromley, she reflected on the conditions and the people she had left behind. They were unforgettable; they became etched on her mind. She was aware that while she could escape to the tree-lined streets of Bromley, Deptford's inhabitants were locked into this depressing habitat which was a national scandal.

Although Britain was at this time prosperous beyond precedent, the living and working conditions in Deptford, as in many other urban areas, were so bad that, judging from Margaret's accounts, a stroll along the perimeter of Hades might have been preferable to a walk through its streets. Recalling what she saw there, she mentioned:

> The stained and tumbling walls, the dark, noisy courts, the crowded rooms, the sodden alleys all hidden behind roaring streets . . . Women who care no more. Girls whose youth is a kind of defiance. Children creeping on the filthy pavement, half-naked, unwashed and covered with sores.[15]

On arriving home, Margaret gave Rachel graphic accounts of her Deptford visits. Speaking of the children's living conditions she said:

> Many children live in one-roomed tenements. From these close-packed chambers where they sleep, the mother, as well as the children, departs in many cases in the morning. Of 110 boys, . . . 44 had a mother at home . . . of the other 66, the mother was dead or at work all day. The nurse could not find anyone 'at home' when she visited their sleeping places.[16]

While some of the mothers could find work, many of the fathers were often unemployed; they were unskilled labourers who only occasionally managed to find casual work.

The impoverished early beginnings and slender chances of future success of these children weighed heavily on both of the McMillans. But, as two middle-aged spinsters having neither money and influence nor power, they wondered how they could tackle these social problems.

As a Fabian, Margaret was familiar with the idea of reorganising society so that all could enjoy a decent life. According to Cole and Postgate, Fabian socialists envisaged 'a heap of reforms to be built by the droppings of a host of successive swallows which would in the end make a Socialist summer'.[17] But in Deptford the victims of injustice were living pitifully and dying prematurely; they could not wait for the 'Socialist summer'. More urgent action was needed than the suggested 'organization of lectures' and the undertaking of 'local investigations or study of local problems'.

The ILP committed itself in conference to 'free primary, secondary and university education' and 'the provision for the sick, disabled, elderly, widows and orphans', but did not seem to have clear ideas as to how their resolutions could be implemented. Dowse[18] maintained that the early socialists were so engrossed in trying to meet public demands for information about the principles and policies of the Labour Movement that they spent too little time thinking through the practical implications of their ideas.

It seemed almost impossible for the sisters on their own to make much of a dent on social wrongs. They discussed incessantly how they could tackle some of the fundamental issues in the country generally and in Deptford in particular. Their old objective – 'a new and nobler race in a new and nobler social order' – remained constant, but they were puzzled about the immediate steps they could take towards reaching it.

By now, Margaret realised that many members of the ILP put most of their faith in Labour representation and parliamentary seats. But she had become disappointed with the performance of many elected representatives. She felt that, although in private some politicians and ILP members made an intellectual assent to what seemed morally right, in public they withdrew from that position when pilloried. There was, for instance, considerable rhetoric about the feeding and medical inspection of poor children but little relevant action. She asserted at an ILP conference in 1905 that 'Every State-aided school should have medical inspection and the whole force of the Party should be concentrated on extorting reforms in regard to elementary instructions.'[19] But she and her sister believed that, 'As no party in London wanted to stand for anything or anybody, this action would have to be entirely our own.'[20]

Margaret and Rachel could see that, behind the human wastage which irked them so, lay ill-health and ignorance. The public conscience needed to be enlivened about these twin evils before a new society could be created.

Having reached this point, the sisters then considered what more they could do to push the need for health and education to the fore. With Rachel's concurrence, Margaret had already agitated for reform, lectured about it, written articles to the press, lobbied MPs, and used every means at her disposal to put the disturbing facts about the physical condition and ignorance of Britain's children in front of the country's policy-makers; but as this had little success, ultimately they decided that they themselves would have to take the necessary initiative. Their first step was to draw up plans for a health centre. Margaret wrote:

> Our next step was to find a friend at the Board of Education. And, indeed, we had one good friend there who was always ready to listen and to sympathise – Sir Robert Morant, the Permanent Secretary at the Board of Education. We sent our scheme to him, and it is probable he read it with some amusement and astonishment. We met him, I think, in a room at the office. He had the draft in his hand . . .
>
> 'It's all right,' he said gravely, but with a smile hidden in his eyes. 'Only remember. There is no Act on the Statute Book that gives any power to a local authority to carry on this kind of work in schools. You did it in Bradford, you know; you didn't know the law; didn't want to know it, I think.' He smiled. 'Well, to whom are you going to appeal to get your health centre?'
>
> I did not answer at once; indeed, I had no answer. The smile went out of Sir Robert's eyes, and he looked at us very kindly. 'I'll get some copies printed. Yes, I'll get them printed,' he said, 'and I'll circulate them – among my inspectors.' . . . 'I shall get it printed,' he said again, looking at the scheme. 'That's all I can do just now.'
>
> So the scheme was printed and treated with all the respect he could have given to a Government document, and there the matter ended.[21]

So the sisters left Morant's office feeling somewhat deflated but with a kind of nagging feeling inside that this health scheme was something they must pursue though they did not see how to proceed.

Later that day, they went out to see Joseph Fels, whose gracious home, Elmswood, at Bickley, was always open to his many friends. During that visit, the sisters were asked what they had been doing lately. Margaret took the scheme from her pocket and showed it. The rest of the remarkable episode is reported by her. Fels said:

'Something to help poor children? Health centre, eh? Start at once. I'll give you five thousand pounds.' This offer almost paralysed me for a moment . . . He told me he had been at our farewell meeting at Bradford, that he had talked to the Bradford people and wanted to help me. That he *would* help willy-nilly . . . We went home through the quiet dusk. It was a clear night, almost like tempered daylight. Along the road, the trees stood as if listening . . . the whole world had passed into a kind of enchanted peace. Rachel did not look elated, or even pleased. She seemed to be thinking, feeling, dreaming, far away, communing with someone, or something, not here, or visible here. Is there real guidance in this world or from another? 'Well!' I said to her, 'Here is money.'[22]

Now that the financial obstacle had been overcome, the next task was to see how the money should be used. Margaret offered her scheme and the money to the London County Council but heard nothing for five months and then wrote to the Chairman. Recalling his response she wrote: 'His astonishment knew no bounds. He lost no time, however, in investigating the matter, and we were at once invited to meet the equally astonished Education Committee (who had never heard of the offer) and put our case.'[23]

The sequel can be found in the LCC's Day Schools Sub-committee Agenda Papers.[24] Joseph Fels attended an LCC meeting on 19 July 1905 to report on his offer, and was asked to put all his suggestions in writing for the committee.

After reading Fels's letter and Margaret's Memorandum, the LCC's Educational Adviser suggested to the Committee that it might be wise to consider what had been done elsewhere before embarking on any new health scheme. So a delegation was sent to Bradford to ascertain what had been done there at Margaret's instigation. Margaret then wrote to Jowett, who would be likely to meet the LCC officials, to suggest what he might say:

I never succeeded in making them carry out things in a thorough way at Bradford . . . they tell me it's all gone wrong there – that the babies are not going down to the baths and that there is no real education for health . . . Tell them [the LCC officials] I wanted trained physiological teachers, not swimming mistresses . . . Tell them that the baby and infant rooms were *intended* to be places of play, in the bath – not to learn swimming or be

bothered with lessons there at all but only to get the pleasure
and impressions that are the beginnings of all capacity to learn.[25]

No report about a delegation visiting Bradford appeared in the
minutes, but it became apparent that the Committee was afraid of
the initial cost and maintenance of Margaret's scheme. She
envisaged that in every school there would be 'one or more
classrooms adapted for training in personal hygiene' together with
'a teacher specially trained and qualified for this work', 'that a
certain number of schools should be grouped together and that a
central bath would be provided with shower-baths at each
school'.[26]

The Committee calculated that a bath embodying Margaret's
suggestions would cost £5,535, and promptly decided that cheaper
ways of providing for the physical needs of children should be
sought. At this time, financial resources were stretched to the full
in education authorities throughout the country. Few had enough
money to meet the rising cost of expanding curricula, the new
equipment being recommended for schools and the demand for
more teachers. After the New Code of 1871 there was a growth of
specific and class subjects outside the 3 Rs. Birchenough gives an
indication of the specific subjects added to the curriculum after the
Code of 1882, when children were tending to stay at school longer.

> In order to encourage more attention to English and elementary
> science and to the practical training of girls, English (literature
> and grammar), physical geography, and a new subject called
> elementary science were added to the list of class subjects and a
> grant was paid for instruction in cookery . . . The list of specific
> subjects was further extended to include agriculture, chemistry,
> sound, light and heat, magnetism and electricity.[27]

Consequently by the time LEAs came into being it was apparent
that the cost of educating children was steadily rising and
Margaret's comprehensive health proposals naturally made the
LCC apprehensive about the expense involved. In addition, it
would appear that the Committee was becoming less sure about
using the £5,000 on one project in Deptford, where Margaret was
a Manager of schools. Fels's biographer maintained that:

> The Education Committee of the London County Council
> treated her ideas as unsound and extravagant romanticisms . . .
> the basic trouble was that the Education adviser, the Executive
> Officer and the Medical Officer were philosophically opposed to
> the conditions set forth by Miss McMillan.[28]

In the end a state of deadlock was reached. Neither Fels nor Margaret were willing to move from their original scheme and the LCC would not budge from their position. Tired of arguing with the Committee and trying to persuade them to accept Margaret's scheme, tired too of their veiled suggestions that the money would be acceptable but not the scheme, in September 1906, Fels finally and irrevocably withdrew his offer to the LCC.

Turning now to the McMillans he said, 'You can have the money. Begin alone. Never mind them.' But Margaret did not take the money; neither did she open a health centre at this point. She was wise enough to see that the physical betterment of children was a many-faceted issue; it wasn't only a health centre that was needed. She foresaw the need for school meals and medical inspection and was already involved in events leading to legislation for their provision.

Chapter eleven

School Meals Victory 1906

'Should the State be permitted to enter the most elemental of all fields of parental responsibility, the provision of meals for children?'[1] This was one of the most contentious issues clamouring for the attention of politicians in the first decade of the twentieth century.

Margaret McMillan's struggle for the systematic feeding of school children by the state reached a climax in 1906, but she first began agitating for the feeding of ill-nourished children when on the Bradford School Board in the 1890s and constantly brought the matter to the notice of members of the ILP. As a result of her co-operation with Robert Blatchford in promoting the Cinderella Club, which served dinners to poor children during winter months, food was provided for thousands of underfed children in the city.

After initiating and being present at the first school medical inspection in 1899 with Dr Kerr, Margaret realised that there must be many more ill-nourished children than had been acknowledged hitherto. No reliable statistics were available of the number of half-starved children in Britain. In London there seemed to have been a hard core of hungry children in the slums for many years. The London School Board's 1889 inquiry into the provision being made for feeding school children, had showed that 12 per cent of the children in its care were regularly in need of food, but less than a half of these received any help from any source. In other large cities the need for some means of feeding children was apparent, but attempts by voluntary agencies to meet it were sporadic and often limited to winter months.

Not only was there a need to give more hungry children food but a more systematic distribution throughout the year was required. Although it was known, and regretted, that many went to school breakfastless and remained hungry throughout the day, this situation was generally accepted as inevitable and most people were glad to leave the voluntary bodies to take responsibility for it.

Ordinary people felt powerless to bring about any improvement. Any individual who decided to bring change would have to say goodbye to popularity and ease, be determined to fight ceaselessly and have the ability to influence Members of Parliament. Margaret's experience on the Bradford School Board prepared her for this role. There she had seen that significant changes could be achieved where a sustained initiative was taken.

She believed that it was the duty of the state to feed hungry children and committed herself to strive to that end. She thought that if the state compelled children to go to school, it should be obliged to feed them. Emphasising this point, she wrote in 1901:

> The State compels the children to work – it makes the demand for sustenance urgent, intolerable. But it does not compel parents to feed their children. Hence it is certain that to some of these hungry little ones free education is less of a boon than an outrage.[2]

Later she was to express the view that money spent on educating half-starved children was money wasted. She believed that poor feeding in the early years drained the mind so that children had difficulty in learning and recalling their lessons.[3] But her ideas were not generally accepted.

While she was considering how to mobilise public opinion and gain support for the systematic provision of school meals paid for by the state, a cluster of factors in which she was not directly involved helped to stimulate interest in the nation's health. The timely convergence of these enabled her to pursue her own ideas in a more favourable climate and created the preconditions for legislation on school meals.

When it became known that between 40 and 60 per cent of the men who volunteered between 1899 and 1902 for military service in the Boer War had been assessed as physically unsuitable, public discussions about the physical deterioration of British citizens were stimulated. Later the combined results of four major reports on health focused attention on ways of improving the health of the nation's future citizens.

First, the Report of the 1902 Inter-departmental Committee on the Employment of School Children[4] exposed the high proportion of children employed before and after school, and commented on the damaging effect long hours of work had on their health and education. It showed that children often arrived at school tired, and unable to 'avail themselves to the full of the education offered by elementary schools'.

The second report, that of the Royal Commission on Physical

Training in Scotland in 1903, in highlighting the extent and degree of physical defects and disabilities in Scottish children, raised queries about English children's health as well. Recognising the close relationship between physical health and poor feeding, the Commission suggested that 'it should be one of the duties of the School Boards and School Managers generally to inquire into cases of apparently insufficient feeding', and that 'they should provide facilities for the provision of suitable food'.[5] Further, it proposed medical inspection mainly as a means of securing information about the state of the national physique.

Thirdly, in 1904, the Duke of Devonshire's Committee on Physical Deterioration made a thorough examination of the question of national physique in England and Wales. The report recommended that municipal and voluntary organisations should combine to feed habitually undernourished children, pointing out that care should be taken to 'maintain the responsibility of the parent in this matter'.[6] In addition, it suggested regular medical inspection of school children, improved lighting, ventilation and physical training in schools.

Fourthly, in 1905, Lord Londonderry, the President of the Board of Education, appointed an Inter-departmental Committee to ascertain what was already being done 'in respect of Medical Inspection of children in public elementary schools', and 'to inquire into the existing arrangements of voluntary agencies for provision of meals to school children'. Furthermore, the Committee was requested to report on 'the possibility of improving the organization of Medical Inspection and Feeding but without any charge upon public funds'.[7]

The Committee's report produced firm evidence of the prevalence of underfeeding. It publicised the extent of the work being done by 350 voluntary agencies and underlined their diverse character and provision.[8] Sheffield, for example, had the children's Breakfast Committee; Birmingham, the School Cheap Dinner Association Society and Liverpool, the Food and Betterment Association.

In addition to the many different organisations which gave meals, school log books revealed that teachers often paid for food for poor children, despite their low wages. (In 1900, the salary of most certificated teachers started at £65 per annum and rose by yearly increments to £120.)

Largely through the findings of all these reports, by 1905 children's health and feeding had become an important subject of debate at government level, in medical circles, church groups, political meetings, at fashionable parties and in working men's clubs; many newspapers carried articles about it too. But the government, though sympathetic towards the children, was disinclined to become involved in the matter. For one thing it was saddled with numerous grave economic problems and its finances were strained; for another, there were demands for money to be spent on a bigger and better navy and there was mounting pressure for social reform such as a system of old age pensions and national insurance. Balfour, the Conservative Prime Minister, made his position clear in declaring that he was not against hungry children receiving food, but that he would not sanction any measure to that end which would increase local taxes. Le Gros Clark, in his history of the School Meals Service, reports that in letters to *The Times* during 1904

> several of the writers complained that the taxpayers were already overburdened and that the provision of free meals would pauperize the families concerned . . . The scheme had many advocates; but there was still in some measure a sense that children ought not to be relieved outside the circle of the family.[9]

The ILP had long been interested in the municipal feeding of children and the Bradford Branch in particular kept this issue alive. In a series of articles on 'Socialism and the Questions of the Hour', the Party's mouthpiece – *The Labour Leader* – often brought the question of school feeding to the fore. In 1904, rejoicing over the amount of publicity the subject had gained in a relatively short time, it announced:

> Only a year or two ago this was considered to be the most revolutionary of all our practical proposals . . . we were all inclined to assume that this was one of the reforms which would have to wait a long time for realization . . . but, lo! to-day, it greets us in the market place, and smiles upon us from the columns of our morning newspapers.[10]

By 1905, such a growing number of trade unionists, politicians, teachers, doctors, officials of voluntary agencies, as well as public-minded individuals like the McMillans, had stiffened their resolve to secure reform, that the government could no longer ignore the nation's ill-nourished school children. There was a growing sense of urgency about the fate of starving children. At long last the political will to tackle the issue realistically was in the process of being roused.

Margaret and Rachel were in the thick of all this ferment and yearned to see how legislation on school meals could be promoted.

Rachel, although working full-time in Kent, was just as committed to the fight for school meals as her sister but could spend less time on it.

Although written evidence is scanty about how Margaret fought for school meals, there can be no doubt that she was greatly involved in the struggle and employed the strategies she learned when working with the ILP in Bradford.

According to Mansbridge from 1902 to 1908 she 'fought strenuously for progressive causes as politician, lecturer and writer'.[11] In all these roles she drew attention to society's responsibility for children's health.

The social gatherings she and Rachel held in their flat in Bromley, and those they attended at the homes of their socialist friends, played a part in spreading information about child health and possibly in shaping policy. Evidence that such matters were discussed informally at these functions can be found in one of Morant's letters to Margaret about medical inspection, where he said 'we have to some extent at least done, what I told you long ago at the Cobden Sandersons' that evening we meant to do'.[12]

Through lecturing to different organisations Margaret formed a network of friendships with many who had political and industrial power and few would escape hearing about her interests. After becoming a lecturer for the Ethical Society in 1903, she was admitted to a circle of Ethical enthusiasts which included politicians such as J. Ramsay MacDonald, who from 1901 to 1904 was a member of the London County Council, became MP for Leicester in 1906, Chairman of the ILP during that same year and Leader of the Labour Party in the House of Commons in 1911. He would undoubtedly have heard her rehearse the arguments for the feeding of school children many times. She also knew many who became prominent in their trade unions.

As the Manager of a number of schools in Deptford, Margaret would naturally meet elected representatives of organisations and local government officials at the committee meetings. At these gatherings she was kept in touch with the facts about half-starved children in the neighbourhood, so that when she addressed others she could speak convincingly about actual cases of hardship. For instance, it was discovered that one boy attending a Deptford school had not had any food for two days.

As well as lobbying political and industrial figures, Margaret influenced others who possessed power. The Countess of Warwick, a socialist though not a member of the ILP, described Margaret as one who had 'most influenced my thoughts in a long life'.[13] She frequently left her mansion, Easton Lodge, set in a 1000-acre park in Essex, to work for the state provision of meals. The writer, Anita Leslie, after reviewing the Countess's involvement in several charitable causes maintained:

> What Daisy Warwick fought hardest for was the feeding of hungry children, and if in assessing her whole life one tries to pick out the time that really matters, then the years 1902 to 1906 . . . are those which win her a laurel crown.[14]

She helped to gather information about starving children and then used her influence with prominent individuals such as Sir John Gorst, a former Vice-President of the Board of Education, to secure legislation on feeding.

In her autobiography, Lady Warwick recalled visiting schools in 1905, then giving the Board of Guardians a report on the poor condition of children which proved to be influential. 'The Guardians passed a resolution in favour of feeding the children, and a report was drawn up and forwarded to the London County Council and to the Board of Education.'[15]

Margaret's own main platform was the ILP. At the Party's local and national meetings she repeatedly drew attention to malnourished children. Many other members too, like F. W. Jowett of Bradford, were eager to pressurise the government to take legislative action on meals. It is significant that one of the two 1905 Bills on school feeding was Labour-inspired.

The mounting pressure from many different quarters at last forced the Conservative government to act. Under The Relief (School Children) Order of 1905, it established a precedent for state aid by ordering Poor Law Guardians to feed needy school children; any cost would be recoverable at the discretion of the Guardians. Unfortunately, this move proved to be counter-productive in that it actually *increased* the number of hungry school children. Gilbert, the historian of national insurance in Britain, said that by 'driving the Guardians into the business of feeding, the Government caused many parents whose children were genuinely undernourished to withdraw them from school dining-rooms for fear of being designated as paupers'.[16] Parental attitudes, together with the harsh official administration of The Relief (School Children) Order, demonstrated that the Poor Law system was ill-suited to helping under-nourished children. A better way must be found.

The outstanding victory of the Liberals in the General Election of January 1906 and the programme of reforms they initiated, despite fierce opposition, were to help Margaret realise some of her cherished ambitions, school meals amongst them. Writing of this time Le Gros Clark said:

> There may have been Liberals in the House and there were certainly many Liberals in the country, who would still have preferred to use the traditional method of granting relief through the Poor Law Guardians. But by the time the new Parliament had assembled early in 1906 the pressure was felt by every Party in the House.[17]

Within three weeks of the new Parliament's opening, W. T. Wilson, the newly elected Labour MP for Westhoughton, introduced the Education (Provision of Meals) Bill to the House of Commons as a Private Member's Bill. This asked that power should be given to Local Education Authorities 'to make such arrangements as may be sanctioned by the Board of Education for attending to the health and physical condition of the children educated in public elementary schools'.

Many of Margaret's old friends supported the Bill including Keir Hardie, Arthur Henderson and James Ramsay MacDonald. The following entry in Bruce Glasier's private diary, at a time when animosity between Hardie and MacDonald was growing, indicates that Margaret kept in touch with Labour MPs during the passage of the School Meals Bill, but even so they did not always come up to her expectations: 'Sunday, 19 July, 1906. Sheffield N.A.C. There is much personal friction between MacDonald and Hardie . . . Miss McMillan speaks rudely to them both – she is fearfully hurt that they did not do as she wanted in the House.'

Debate on the Bill was heated and prolonged. Many MPs argued that state provision of meals would undermine parental responsibility. Others feared that if the government accepted the moral obligation to feed children there was no knowing where its responsibility would end. F. Jowett, giving the ILP view, maintained that voluntary agencies could not adequately feed children, but that the state should.

The Opposition maintained that the Bill constituted 'a vital departure from the principle of limited State activity . . . it took the State into an area that it had hitherto carefully avoided, but one which might logically lead to full protection by society against all hazards of modern life'.[18]

After much controversy the Bill was finally passed, receiving the Royal Assent on 21 December 1906. The new Act empowered Local Authorities to pay for meals on school days for all needy school children within their areas, but restricted expenditure to the sum of a halfpenny rate. Circular 552, issued by the Board on

1 January 1907, explained that the Act was not obligatory and imposed no duty. Its object was to ensure 'that children attending public elementary schools should no longer be prevented by insufficiency of suitable food from profiting by the education offered'[19] and it gave LEAs authority to provide premises and facilities to assist the work of voluntary organisations.

Documentation about Margaret's actual involvement with the passage of the School Meals Bill through Parliament is scarce. She may have written little about it because, as well as being engaged with this Bill, she was at the same time embroiled in the struggle for medical inspection of school children and in agitating for a health centre in Deptford. But her influence on the ILP and on their adopting school feeding as a main plank of their policy is unquestioned. McBriar writing in *Fabian Socialism and English Politics 1884–1918* stated:

> In the main the education policy of the Labour Party was formulated for it by the I.L.P. and particularly by Margaret McMillan . . . So far as Parliamentary action was concerned, the Labour Party devoted itself chiefly to pressing for the provision by the State of free meals for school children.[20]

Although the achievement of this reform owed much to Labour Party pressure, its passage through Parliament (along with other reforms) was made possible by Liberal support. Barker, in his study of the Labour Party, shows that often it merely stated policies 'which had long been current amongst many liberals', policies which socialists could not claim as 'their exclusive property'.[21] Yet it was Labour MPs who were responsible not only for introducing the Provision of Meals Bill but also for much of the impetus that got it through Parliament. When the victory finally came Jowett hailed it as 'a red letter day in the annals of socialist politics'. Commenting on the success of the new enthusiastic Labour group in Parliament, after the Bill's second reading, he said: 'To secure within 3 weeks of the opening of the new parliament, the admission of a principle which . . . the entire Liberal and Tory Press has endeavoured to scotch, either by scrupulous or unscrupulous opposition . . . is extremely interesting.'[22]

Perhaps the sustained fight for school meals and medical inspection which started in Bradford when Margaret was there in the 1890s lies behind Mansbridge's claim that 'It was largely due to her efforts that the Education (Provision of Meals) Act was in 1906 placed on the Statute Book, and the question of meals for needy school children finally settled.'[23] Palin in his booklet on feeding children in Bradford wrote: 'The genesis of the movement that led up to the question of Child Feeding being brought within the range of practical politics must be placed to the credit of Mr. Robert Blatchford and Miss Margaret McMillan.'[24]

When the Act was due to come into force many Jeremiahs prophesied that now the state was able to give financial assistance to the working classes, parents would stop trying to feed their children; they would expect the state to do it and so the demand for meals would increase dramatically. In practice none of these predictions came true. Describing the situation in Bradford, Palin wrote: 'When circumstances improve, parents are the first to report to the Committee and are often most grateful for what has been done for them, and are anxious to make way for the children of those less fortunate than themselves.'[25] Some members of the electorate forecast that in future demands from LEAs for government grants for school feeding programmes would escalate. But in fact relatively few applied for support as they were reluctant to implement the Act. In 1909 only 113 out of 328 Authorities had appointed school canteen committees and even by 1911/12 only 131 were operating schemes. Le Gros Clark reported:

> The number of children being fed rose gradually, but not spectacularly. For example, in London (which probably showed the steepest rate of growth) there were about 29,000 children provided for weekly in 1906; in 1911 the figures reached 41,000. Most of the country areas paid little regard to the Act.[26]

The Act had numerous critics. Dicey, the distinguished jurist, voiced the opinion of many when he said that the government was encouraging culpable parents instead of punishing them. He did not think it morally right that

> a father who lets his child starve, and then fails to pay the price legally due from him for a meal given to the child at the expense of the ratepayers, should under the Act of 1906, retain the right of voting for a Member of Parliament.[27]

Even some Labour supporters criticised the new Act; they felt it should have compelled Local Authorities to provide meals, it should not have limited rate-aid to the amount that a halfpenny rate would raise, nor left the time of feeding flexible so that some Authorities could give breakfasts, and others provide mid-day meals.

Despite its many limitations, Margaret was one who recognised the Act as a major triumph. Once it was on the statute book, she began to consider how she could help its full implementation and decided she must use her pen to keep this matter to the fore. In her article 'Free Meals: How the Bill Works' she cited her experience, as a Manager of schools in Deptford, to illustrate how the London County Council seemed keener to get out of its obligations than fulfil them. 'The very first thing we discovered as managers', she said, 'was that the City Council did not mean to adopt it as a measure for feeding the hungry.'[28]

From her Deptford experience, she realised that Local Authorities would need prodding to use their powers and that teachers might need to be shown what could be achieved under the new regulations. Otherwise a feeding centre might develop into what she called, 'a mere stoking place for the famishing' – a canteen rather than a dining hall. In her article 'School Dinners To-day', she gave a glowing account of the varied meals Bradford offered, the room where children ate and the atmosphere in it.

'Do come to the dining-room where 150 children are going to have dinner' she said. 'Love, not what we call charity, presides at it. The tables are spread with snowy cloths and bright with flowers and there are many tables, just as at aristocratic parties where guests dine in groups . . . the food is delicious.'[29]

Writing on the need for school meals, she claimed that many scholarship holders in secondary schools hadn't the stamina to continue their studies because they were malnourished. 'What is to become of my small professor?' she wrote of one underfed child, 'luck may be on his side. It's just possible he'll squeeze through somehow.'[30]

In 1909 she wrote a pamphlet with her friend Mrs Cobden Sanderson, to implore Local Authorities to seize their new opportunity to feed children well and take the opportunity to provide a gracious service. Mrs Cobden Sanderson highlighted the poor conditions under which many children were being fed.

Margaret emphasised the need to give more thought to the food provided and declared that it was a mistake to think that because children were hungry they would eat anything. She argued:

An opportunity is now offered to raise the physique of the whole nation. To put children off in future with any kind of weak soup, to offer them any order of 'filling' pudding, to feed them with jam and starchy bread, will now mean the flinging aside of this opportunity.[31]

In the same pamphlet Margaret mentioned the social aspect of meals and pointed out that good conversation could enrich school meals. She maintained that children in wealthy families frequently had visitors in their homes and heard stimulating adult conversation, whereas the slum child was often denied this pleasure. In a later pamphlet she stressed the educational opportunities that school meals afforded teachers. Doctors reported that some children never chewed food, they merely swallowed it 'as a letter is sent down a pillar box'. She thought children could be trained to eat properly, and that the taste for good food could be developed. School meals, she said, provided an opportunity for: 'the re-education of a basal sense taste. Re-education, because, in the case of thousands, the natural and healthy taste in food has been ruined.'[32]

While fighting for school meals, Margaret also advocated training in housekeeping for parents; she knew that malnutrition was sometimes caused by ignorance and irresponsibility and that some young babies were offered 'sausages, red herrings and pickles' whilst others had to exist on 'picking a bit of whatever we have'.

As a socialist however Margaret believed that the major underlying cause of malnutrition was poverty. Where surveys existed this view was substantiated. The following extract from a report of the home circumstances of school children in Derby in 1907, gives a picture of the underlying poverty in the homes of many half-starved children.

> Father out of work, 45 per cent; father ill or disabled, 15 per cent; father away in search of work, 6 per cent; no father and other relatives poor, 15 per cent; one or both parents drunken, 5 per cent; . . . cases where in the opinion of the committee the income, although very small, might have been sufficient to give the children more food, 13 per cent.[33]

Margaret believed that when the socialist transformation of society had been achieved, poverty would be alleviated, if not eliminated. Meantime her hope was that a substantial increase in family income would encourage parents to feed their own children adequately. However, while wages were low, her immediate objective was at least one good meal a day for every child, provided by the state.

In retrospect it can be seen that the campaign for school meals, in which Margaret and her ILP colleagues played a central part, had more far-reaching consequences than they realised at the time. For it was during the debates which preceded the Act that many politicians came to believe that the state should have a due sense of responsibility for the welfare of its needy citizens. Gilbert, the social historian, maintained that the 1906 Act on feeding was more than a law which relieved hungry and sick children; along with the Education (Administrative Provisions) Act of 1907 which established medical inspection it 'marked the beginning of the construction of the Welfare State'.[34]

Chapter twelve

Mother of School Medical Inspection 1907

Once the 1906 Education (Provision of Meals) Act was on the statute book, Margaret devoted more time to the battle for medical inspection. During the campaign for school meals, the Inter-departmental reports and the Parliamentary debates had made the need for a uniform system to cater for children's health increasingly plain. But the government's delay in promoting school medical inspection alarmed her.

Several times Margaret had seen medical inspection affirmed in principle then legislation to secure it deferred. Birrell, the President of the Board of Education, included a clause about it in his Education Bill, but this was dropped in December 1906. Margaret was bitterly disappointed by that; she knew the high incidence of incipient disease school doctors found in Bradford, and how much public ignorance still existed about the state of children's health. In one of her articles she asked: ' "How are the citizens of to-morrow? Well or ill?" These are questions that are not asked, even in teachers' examination papers . . . There are means, special means of finding the true answer in school.'[1]

Fortunately, despite the government's dilatory attitude, many doctors, teachers and welfare workers had begun to see the importance of child health and early diagnosis of defects. Margaret, along with these allies, was determined that the state should be made to accept responsibility for the health of young children. Mansbridge declared that in her first years in London she: 'never ceased to press for the Medical Inspection of School Children . . . She bombarded the Press, pleaded whenever she could get an audience. "Get a Medical Department," "Sweep out disease." '[2]

She kept issues concerning child health to the fore at numerous conferences. Two of the most influential of these were the North of England Education Conference, held in January 1907 in Bradford, and the International Congress on School Hygiene, held in August of the same year in London. At both of these gatherings, she made informed contributions and deliberately tried to interest others in medical inspection.

At the North of England Education Conference, doctors described the results of surveys on the health of school children in their cities. Dr Arkle, Medical Officer of Health for Liverpool, claimed that doctors often found it difficult to examine children quickly and thoroughly because of their unsuitable clothing. Describing the examination of one eleven-year-old girl he said: 'After loosening the dress, three bodices and a pair of corsets, I arrived down to another old velvet dress which fastened at the back. At this point I gave up.' Arguing that too much clothing or too little contributed to ill-health in children he said:

> It seemed as if many of the children on obtaining a new garment put it on over the old ones, and, in fact, carried all their property on their backs. In such cases, when one arrived at the skin it was always found to be in a condition of unwholesome perspiration, although the weather was cold. On the other hand, a great number of the children were shockingly underclad. One little girl had an ingenious costume which looked quite smart until analysed. It consisted of a very thin chemise – a footman's old red waistcoat folded tightly round her and fastened with a piece of string, and a blue overall, with straps over the shoulders. It looked like a very neat dress, but was shamefully inadequate . . . Another curious fact was that large numbers of the children were absolutely stitched into their clothes.

He had found that children were fleabitten and verminous. They were starved, dwarfed, deformed, in need of spectacles and yet 'gave one the impression that, with better chances, they would make a fine race of men but at present they have no chance'. He felt that if the physical side of children was not attended to 'you might as well throw the money expended in educating them into the sea'.[3]

At the same conference, Dr Crowley, School Medical Officer of Health for Bradford, reported on the examination of 2,000 children in his area and commented on the underfeeding, dietary deficiencies, dirty bodies, lousy heads and poor clothing he found, but suggested that 'to punish children for the neglect of parents is very short-sighted policy'.[4]

After these papers had been read, Margaret pointed out that 'there was a geography of disease and also a sociology of disease'. Not only did one find particular diseases affecting particular areas, but also different diseases affecting different classes of society. She then expressed the hope that in the ensuing discussion the old argument that to provide medical inspection and treatment 'might destroy parental responsibility' would not be advanced again; she proposed that it might be better to find out how much parental responsibility there was to be destroyed and added: 'Parental responsibility was almost nil among large masses of the population of large cities, not because the people were wicked or unnatural, but because they were ignorant.'[5] Developing this point, another speaker remarked: 'Someone ought to be appointed to go round to see that young mothers really understood this new business that had come to them.'

During a lively discussion, T. P. Sykes, President of the National Union of Teachers, spoke of the effect on children's health of the crowded conditions and poor ventilation in some schools. He maintained that primary school children only had half the space and cubic feet of air that secondary school children had.[6]

Stimulated by the conference, Margaret began to disseminate the main ideas discussed and to turn her mind again to legislation. She suspected that, even if a bill on Medical Inspection was passed, many local authorities would need to be pressurised into implementing it. So in preparation for this, she started to collect facts about the physical condition of school children. Then she worked through all the channels open to her to awaken interest in the subject. National and local ILP meetings gave her many opportunities to keep the matter before the public as well as to discuss it with influential individuals.

At the 1907 Annual ILP Conference held on 1 and 2 April in Derby, Ramsay MacDonald presided over a meeting of 'Elected Persons and others interested' where Margaret read a paper on medical inspection. Later her main points were printed in the Conference Report, 'for the guidance of our members elected to educational authorities'.[7]

A few months after this conference, Margaret addressed a private meeting of the ILP held at Clifford's Inn, London; Keir Hardie was in the chair and much to her surprise Robert Morant, Permanent Secretary at the Board of Education, bustled into the gathering. Characteristically, she took the opportunity of speaking to him personally about child health and, though hampered by red tape, he promised to support her work. Margaret followed up that discussion with a letter. An extract from Morant's reply appears below.

26.vi.'07

Dear Miss McMillan,

I am very glad indeed to get your letter. I wanted to write to you after our talk, but hesitated to trouble you with a letter.

I wanted to say that I hoped I had not seemed discourteous in contradicting so curtly and speaking frankly as I frequently did last Friday. But I see from your letter that I need not write this, for you have taken all of it in good part . . . But *between us*, we shall do something I am sure, if we can avoid raising public hubbub against our efforts. But I found it an immense help to have had a talk with you. I trust we may have many more together.

Sincerely yours,
R. L. Morant

Gilbert, the social historian, maintains that Morant was in favour of medical inspection but that he wanted to avoid what he called a 'public hubbub' about it because he knew that it would be a costly innovation. He knew that once doctors inspected school children they would uncover such a mass of disease and defect that no government would be able to resist the subsequent demands for treatment. Consequently 'his main concern was to produce his measure for the health of children quietly, bury it among a mass of other details and get it passed without debate'.[8] While Morant was working quietly and diplomatically in the background, Margaret was busy forcing the general public to take note of the condition of sick children.

The International Congress on School Hygiene, held from 5–12 August 1907, at the Imperial Institute, London, gave Margaret another opportunity to focus attention on child health. Once the Congress was announced she used *The Labour Leader* to urge people to attend. She wrote:

From every quarter of the globe . . . men of international fame will speak the last word of science on every question concerning the life of the rising generation . . . I hope, Labour Members of Parliament and Labour members of local committees, I.L.P.-ers, Clarionets, Fabians, S.D.F.-ers will be gathered together . . . I hope as many Labour delegates and visitors as possible will attend. But in any case we must all try to read the best of the papers.[9]

When it was known that many leading figures from different parts of the continent were planning to come, Margaret wrote to Morant asking him to allow members of his department to attend. His reply reveals the irritation that her persistence sometimes aroused in busy officials.

24.7.'07

Dear Miss McMillan,

I am extremely glad that you have been so good as to write to me, and to write frankly. I thank you very much . . .

So far from our showing 'very little encouragement' to this Congress, we have done far more than we ever said we would do, and have in the last few weeks before the opening been doing a great deal more. We are sending, ourselves, more representatives, and representatives of higher standing than we have ever sent (so far as I know) to any previous Congress, and they will take part, not be muzzled listeners . . . I have honestly been doing my best to help the Congress; and the Government have, honour bright, done all that, under the circumstances, it could do: and have followed the Nuremberg lines to the full, and done *more*.

Again thanking you, I am,

Sincerely yours,
Robert L. Morant

During the Congress, a group of doctors, who were already quietly working for medical inspection, launched their proposals to campaign openly for it; this decision heartened Margaret. As the conference proceeded her own thinking about health was considerably broadened, particularly by the distinguished speakers from overseas. There she met Dr Jessen of Strasbourg, the father of school dentistry, Professor Griesbach, the father of school hygiene, who tried to reform German homes through the school, and Burgerstein, the Austrian writer and student of children, who encouraged parents to study their own offspring. Schuyten, the Dutchman, who had done extensive research on fatigue was there; Gulick of New York was present too. Of him Margaret said: 'He has probably transformed thousands of homes; he has certainly influenced thousands of parents . . . He is the pioneer of baths, gymnasia, roof-gardens, play schools, and all that makes for health.'[10]

At the end of this stimulating Congress Margaret wanted to see something of the European experiments at first hand. She went to Strasbourg to see Dr Jessen's work on the care of teeth; she visited Stuttgart to observe German experiments and meet some of the innovators. As a result of these visits and her subsequent reading, she became even better informed on the subject of child health and more determined to share these new ideas with politicians and others, in the hope that they might be included in future legislation.

Joseph Fels's wife throws a sidelight on Margaret's persistent struggle for medical inspection; she wrote:

> Miss McMillan was working for medical inspection in the schools . . . She prepared a précis and secured the supporting signatures of the most enlightened medical men of London . . . She secured also the support of the then president of the National Union of Teachers. Armed with this document she went to the House of Commons and interviewed her friend, Mr. Jowett, M.P. for West Bradford. Her plan contained three provisions – compulsory inspection, an annual report, and a supervisory board at Whitehall.[11]

Describing her sister's role in the struggle, Margaret recalled a delegation to Parliament led by Sir Victor Horsley, the great brain specialist:

> The atmosphere of the House was chilly . . . the great House can be quite indifferent, distrait, as it were, over a reform that involves the lives and future of millions. But so it is. It was distrait now, when a group of doctors came to put a case for medical inspectors and sent Sir Victor as their spokesman.
>
> The members of the House were ruffled by his speech and conversation. More than ruffled. They were roused, angry . . . so that the deputation went away in haste. Nothing settled, perhaps unsettled rather, and Sir Victor not inclined to go back.
>
> Rachel at once began to make arrangements for a new deputation. She wrote out the *précis* setting forth what we and others believed to be essential at this moment . . . even if the people did not feel any need for them . . . Meantime, Rachel's deputation was a very influential one . . . Mr. J. W. Jowett piloted us through the House. (It was not a very easy thing to do. Once he lost half of us and declared, as if we were sea monsters, that he 'couldn't see top nor tail of them'). Mr. Percy Illingworth stood our friend with the Minister and Mr. Keir Hardie introduced us. Every member of the deputation spoke and made some impression. Rachel did not speak. Yet it was she alone who carried out the whole project . . . It was she who, when all was falling to pieces like a broken chain, forged and re-forged the links, re-collected us all and still held to our purpose.[12]

Soon the campaigners' persistence was rewarded. In February 1907, Reginald McKenna, who had recently replaced Birrell as President of the Board of Education, introduced in Parliament the Education (Administrative Provisions) Act, which gave the reformers part, though not all, they sought. The new Act, which came into operation on 1 January 1908, made the systematic inspection of school children compulsory, and empowered local authorities to raise health standards in school children.

Margaret's battle however was still not over. Although the Act made medical inspection mandatory the medical treatment of sick children was only optional; it was left as a power which the authority might exercise under certain conditions. But the Act did prompt local authorities to make provision for inspection. Whereas before 1907 only a few of them had made any arrangements at all for inspection, towards the end of 1908 all the 328 authorities were endeavouring to do something towards it in public elementary schools.

Reporting on the passing of the Act *The Labour Leader* paid a tribute to Margaret's part in it by saying:

> The agitation for the medical inspection of children, which Miss Margaret McMillan inside and outside 'The Labour Leader' columns did so much to promote, and which was carried into Parliament by the Labour members, bore fruit in one of the provisions of the Education (Administrative Provision) Act passed last session.[13]

Writing of Margaret after her death, Mansbridge said:

> About 1899 she compelled the first recorded medical inspection of schoolchildren at the Usher Street schools. [Bradford] . . . This success, and her subsequent influence with the officials of the Board of Education, made her the undoubted founder of medical inspection in English elementary schools. In creative power and her influence in promoting legislation Miss McMillan undoubtedly affected the education of elementary schoolchildren more than any other person.[14]

Lowndes assessing Margaret's contribution to the health of young children said: 'Margaret McMillan was undoubtedly the mother of school medical inspection and of the treatment clinic. She has a fair claim to the title of "the godmother of school meals".'[15] Gilbert said:

> In many ways the beginnings of the school medical service should date from the election of Margaret McMillan to the Bradford School Board in 1894. The physical condition of students in this northern city was appalling . . . It may be significant that both school feeding and medical inspection received an early and potent impulse from Bradford, and that

both of these movements had around them, as had the I.L.P. itself, an atmosphere and an appeal that invited support of stern, north-country Nonconformist radicals.[16]

In drafting the circulars expressing the principles of the new Act, Morant turned to Margaret for help. The letter below contains his invitation to her to discuss this with him at his office.

28.X.'07

Dear Miss McMillan,
  I wonder if it is telepathy – I have twice in the last three days sat down to write to you, but hesitated to trouble you. I wanted to ask if you would come and see me for a good talk in Whitehall on the inauguration of the Medical Inspection under the new Act, and help me by going through my Draft Circular with me . . . Would it be asking too much to beg you to give me the benefit of your criticisms, and to have, first, a good straight talk on the matter? If you could, and would, come, would 2.30 on Wednesday, the 30th, suit you at my office in Whitehall?
Sincerely yours,
Robert L. Morant

There were three principles behind the Board of Education's Circular (No. 576 issued in November 1907), which Morant drafted with Margaret's help.

First, the narrow purpose was to fit the child to receive and to take advantage of the system of education provided . . .
Secondly, the object was to secure, not merely a physical or anthropometric survey, but the physical improvement and, as a natural corollary, the mental and moral improvement of coming generations. The third principle was that this physical and health supervision was to be provided for *all* the children of school age.[17]

Once the principle of school medical inspection was established Margaret turned her full attention to what had been her long-term goal all along – medical treatment. Morant repeatedly tried to impress on her that while inspection was a compulsory duty on the local authorities, treatment was entirely optional in the Act. But this fell on deaf ears as far as Margaret was concerned. As Mansbridge said, 'She knew as every one else did ultimately that treatment was the unavoidable consequence of inspection.'[18]

This point was not obvious to everybody – as Lowndes pointed out:

The Government and indeed most Members of Parliament seem

to have been quite satisfied that it would only be necessary for the school doctors to examine a child and point out the defects from which he was suffering to send his parents post haste to the family physician. In the event parents did nothing of the kind.[19]

Margaret could see now that her next tasks were to urge the state to provide treatment and press parents to take responsibility for their children's physical condition. At the Annual ILP Conference held in Huddersfield in April 1908, she was reported as saying that although the medical inspection of school children had been secured,

> the next step was treatment . . . School surgeries were needed where the children could have treatment . . . One million pounds were needed . . . It depended largely on the Labour Party to make of practical value the great step which had been taken in the order for children to be medically examined.[20]

Margaret agonised about the pupils in schools who were suffering from debilitating diseases, which affected both their physical well-being and their intellectual performance. Inwardly she railed at the callousness of those who could let children suffer needlessly. She was prepared to go to any lengths herself to help sick and deformed children receive the medical treatment they needed, even if it meant visiting the homes of ailing children and pleading with parents to get the best treatment possible for their offspring.

The following letter from a Deptford parent shows Margaret's genuine concern for children.

> Sir,
> I can Truthfully Tell you in the year 1907 about 24 years ago Miss McMillan came to our House we were living in Creek Rd. at the time and my children attending Creek Rd. School . . . She said I have visted your little boy Charlie in his Class and spoken to him and find he has a Cleft Pallat and do you know he will never speak properly without an operation and will be Handicapped in his Manhood through it. I have come now to get your Consent to have it done. I said I will speak to my Husband and see if he agrees with it. He did not as when the Boy was Born Dr. Russell our own Dr. told me he was Born with A cleft Pallat. I did not know what it ment then so I asked him he said the Roof of the Mouth is Cleft but it is only partly Cleft I said can anything be done for him while he is a Baby he said no, as he gets older and grows the flesh will join together of its own accord. Of course I and my Husband Believed in what he said

and nothing was done for him, when Miss McMillan came to help us it was just the same we would not have it Done we were under the impression the Dr. was Right however she would not take no for an answer she said she knew a Physician and told him all about our Boys Case and he said that was nonsense it would never Cleve together of its own accord. Well she kept coming to our House 3 times a week trying to Persuade us to alter our mind for a whole year we still said not, we were both very much against it, at last she came with A Letter from Dr. Berry A Physician in the Royal Free Hospital Grays Inn Rd. and said I have A letter here for you to take your Boy to Dr. Bury and he will perform the operation when he is fit. Well I thought after her taking that trouble I will take him to the hospital, so I went to the Hospital saw Dr. Berry myself and left him there he was a very Delicate child and they had to keep him there six months before he was strong enough for the operation. But from that time Miss McMillan became the Best friend I ever had personally and also my Boy. I shall never forget her the Day he was operated on she was on the phone all the time it was being Done. She was so worried she said Mrs – if anything happens to your Boy you will blame me for it and I shall expect it. as you and your Husband have been so very much against it you would not have had it done only for me. I said yes we should but however thank God and Miss McMillan it was successful and he is A strong Healthy Man to-day. the father of 6 children but I should never have known Miss McMillan only for him and his affliction. well when he came out of the Hospital after being there 9 months she sent him away Convalesent to A Beautiful Farm Hous in May Land Essex, where he had plenty of Milk from the Cow and New Laid Eggs he came back after 6 months Bonny Healthy and Fat. from that time Miss McMillan never lost sight of us, her and her sister Rachial used to have my Boy at their house to tea every Wednesday. he was ten years old by this time, they lived in George Lane, Lewisham, that would be about 1909. I used to take him there after he came out of school and go Back for him at 8 o'clock it was a 2d ride from our home and she used to come in our home and have A Chat with me at least every 2 or 3 weeks.

Yours Respectfully.[21]

Chapter thirteen

Starting a Health Centre in Bow 1908-10

Once local authorities were given the mandate to provide for medical inspection, Margaret was keen that parents should know of the opportunities available to them. Furthermore, she wanted the electorate to press for medical treatment alongside medical inspection in health centres, as many children of working-class parents were unlikely to get any treatment at all unless it was paid for outside the family. So Margaret was anxious that health centres, providing treatment for children and education for parents, should become popular and get off to the right start. Speaking of her apprehensions she exclaimed:

> What I fear quite frankly, is that this new work will pass into the care of the Local Government Board. Then it will be mere rescue work – not educational work. Then it will mean the care of paupers – not the training of an awakening democracy.[1]

Behind the Board of Education's Circular (576), which set out the duties of local authorities regarding medical inspection, lay several principles which needed to be conveyed to the ordinary man, along with the hope that parents would take increasing responsibility for their children's hygiene. The circular emphasised that, 'It is in the home that both the seed and fruit of public health are to be found.'[2]

To communicate this thinking to the electorate and create a demand for treatment, Margaret wrote innumerable articles. No sooner were initiatives taken anywhere in the country than she reported them. As so often happened, Bradford led the way and Margaret brought its experience to the notice of the public through her articles in *The Labour Leader*.[3]

Margaret and Rachel also sought to promote interest in treatment centres through the ILP. As a member of the National Administrative Council of the Party, and Chairman of the Committee for the Promotion of Children's Physical Welfare (in the ILP's Metropolitan District), Margaret could draw attention to specific issues in committees. As a result of her agitation, ILP representatives decided to seek an interview with the LCC's Day School Committee to put forward the idea that a school treatment centre might be opened in Bow in the east of London, at the Devons Road Infant School. Margaret was a member of the delegation.

The idea received an unenthusiastic response from the LCC's members. They were distrustful of Margaret's schemes, fearful about the cost of implementing them and afraid that they would lead parents to take less responsibility. Consequently they were reluctant to take much action themselves. However, during the discussion they agreed to a treatment centre being established but decided to take minimum responsibility for it.

In publicising the results of the interviews Margaret disclosed:

> The Council has decided to let a room at a nominal rent of one shilling a year to the Committee for the Promotion of the Physical Welfare of school children. It will also forward to the Committee the names of children whom the medical officer considers require treatment, and whose parents have given their consent to such examination or treatment. The Council at this point washes its hands of us and of the parents. It leaves them free, issuing circulars to them to fill up if they desire the treatment, and it leaves us responsible.[4]

As the LCC offered no monetary help for the venture, the Committee for the Promotion of the Physical Welfare of school children, on Margaret's suggestion, decided that a charge of seven shillings and six pence had to be made for each treatment. In the meantime the LCC made an arrangement with certain hospitals to treat school children in their out-patients department at the rate of five shillings per child; but these hospitals, which usually had long waiting-lists, were mostly situated in the centre of the city, where they could only be reached by public transport from Bow. This made treatment at least as expensive as that at Devons Road centre. The fees there, although higher than the hospitals', never covered the costs. Margaret had to seek additional means of financing the centre. But she was governed more by what needed to be done than by her resources. People who saw the value of what she was doing gave money for her projects. Joseph Fels promised to give £400 per annum towards the financing and equipping of the proposed treatment centre. Speaking of him Margaret said:

Our good friend who pretends that his aim in life is to sell soap, but whose real aim is . . . to snatch the young and helpless from the jaws of death and suffering, will watch the little bark to see that the first waves do not overwhelm it. So the little enterprise will go forward.[5]

Two members of the Physical Welfare Committee who were doctors – Dr Eder and Dr Tribe – kindly offered their services for the new treatment centre, and Miss Grant, the headmistress of the Devons Road Infant School, who was a woman of great vision and compassion, gave her full support. She welcomed the centre and proved to be a great friend to the committee. So the venture was launched. But the LCC adamantly refused, apart from letting a room at a nominal rent, to take any further responsibility for the centre. Therefore Margaret, as Chairman of the Health Sub-committee of the Physical Welfare Association, undertook to be fully responsible for it.

Authority for the running of the clinic was vested in the ILP committee, but as a voluntary body, it had no power to enter the school. However, the LCC set up a Children's Care Committee and appointed an excellent nurse – Nurse Pearce – to serve on it. She had the right of entry to schools, offered to become part of the Devons Road team, and to attend sessions at the clinic with the doctors.

When the pupils of Devons Road School arrived for their instruction one foggy day in December 1908, they found that a clinic had been installed in the headmistress's tiny upper room. Thereafter, for two afternoons each week, this new establishment was open to mothers and their sick children. Doubtless the air in Miss Grant's room would be heavy with the foetid smell of dirt and disease after the sessions, but nevertheless she continued to give the clinic her blessing.

The school was located in an area of high social need where many children were 'at risk'. Speaking of the neighbourhood Margaret mentioned: 'the dark slums where "England's babies are creeping", the dark and noisy hovels where they sleep in coiled heaps, the filthy lanes where they play above the noisome drains, and the great, terrible streets.'[6]

Poverty, aggravated by fecklessness, ignorance and disease, manifested itself on every hand. Work was difficult to find and wages were low. Dockers were said to 'fight like dogs' for employment, but even the successful ones earned only about five shillings a day. The wages of most railwaymen were below £1 per week – a few received twenty-four shillings together with 'their brass buttons'. Women tried to supplement their husband's income by doing work in their own homes. Matchbox-making and tailoring occupied many women, but their work was badly paid and their overheads relatively high. Miss Grant alleged that:

the homeworker had to find her own paste, string and cover . . . no fire could be low as a good heat was needed for drying the boxes. I have seen a living room (9 × 9) with the table covered with boxes in the making and the rug with those drying, and by sitting ' 'ard at it' one could earn seven shillings weekly.[7]

When visiting homes teachers found pitiful signs of poverty as Miss Grant recalls: 'We found more than one baby quite nude, propped up between pillows before the fire whilst its one set of clothes was washed and dried.' Another mother said: 'I've got nothing to put on 'er so I keeps 'er in bed.' Frequent deaths added to the harsh existence and created new problems. One woman said, 'You see, I lost two babies and I only 'ad three nightgowns and 'aving to use one each for laying 'em out left me short.'[8]

Despite poor wages the families were large. Many mothers had fourteen, sixteen, eighteen or even twenty children. Reminiscing about the size of families, the headmistress said:

Our record family of one pair of parents was twenty-seven (of whom twenty-four lived), and of these, as in several other instances, an uncle and niece, or an aunt and her nephew, toddled happily together into our infants' school, and more than once the niece or nephew was the elder of the two.[9]

Love between the parents not infrequently grew cold. Miss Grant reports that many widows were better off than wives whose husbands were alive because at least they got the Relief. One remorseful married woman said:

'Really, though praps I oughtn't to say it, I should have been thankful if the Lord 'ad took mine when 'e was so bad last spring. God forgive me for saying such things. I do get so depressed.' Another said, 'All the outings I get is out to the washtub and back again.'[10]

It was into this grim situation that Margaret came with a deep care for the health of the children of Bow. Having obtained the premises, the equipment and the staff, the major battle of winning parents to use the clinic now lay ahead. She naturally wanted to do this sensitively and put a lot of thought into drafting the first invitation to parents. She explained to them the need for treatment for ailments such as discharging ears, throat and eye infections, then graciously invited them to bring their sick children to the centre. Once the attitude of suspicion thawed, the co-operation and affection of parents was won.

On the day that the centre was opened, a very orderly group gathered at the school. One can see in the following report of this event Margaret's imaginative care for people.

> In the narrow corridor there is a crowd of patient mothers (very soon it is hoped arrangements will be made to give them seats, and also to fix the hours of attendance so that they need not be kept waiting). On the floor near the fire sit a crowd of patient little children, every one suffering more or less, but all silent and amazed . . . Young as they are, however, it is already too late to save all from the results of early privation or mishandling.[11]

From these mothers it soon became apparent how much the Bow clinic was needed. Some showed that they had only a scanty knowledge about the causes of ill-health, the names of ailments and parts of the body. Mothers were overheard telling their neighbours that, 'Doctor said she's got indigestion of the lungs', 'pneumonia on the brain'. The headmistress reports: 'Occasionally we suffer from "a congregation of diseases". "Rose is very bad. She's got 'ooping cough, pumonia 'nd bronchitis."' Gradually many old wives' tales and practices based on superstition manifested themselves. It emerged that beads were worn to ward off colds; one mother pointing to a little hollow in her neck, said: 'You keep your bronchitis hole covered up and you're all right.'[12]

Nurse Pearce soon became the confidante of many mothers, and an important source of information to Margaret about the experiment. Some mothers told her their children were suffering from 'general nobility', 'comic asthma', 'yellow jarments', 'S.Viper's Dance', 'nervous ability', and 'apathetic fits'. Other mothers made earnest requests for guidance and reassurances such as 'Nurse, does it 'urt to 'ave your nostrils [tonsils] taken out?'

Some of the accepted habits of families must have hindered rather than promoted health. Speaking of toothbrushes, one child said that Uncle Ned had one 'and we all use it when we like'. Spectacles were shared too.

The parents' ignorance about health matters demanded tolerance on the part of doctors who needed a new kind of social communication for their task of educating parents as well as curing children. They, together with the dentists, had to learn to speak in simple language to parents. Miss Grant noticed how the professional men improved their communication skills; one dentist progressed from talking to mothers about 'deciduous' to 'temporary' and then to 'milk' teeth.[13]

Margaret was anxious neither to undermine whatever confidence the parents had in their own ability to deal with their children's minor ailments nor to encourage them to take less responsibility than hitherto. Margaret's constant concern was to educate mothers through the clinic so as to equip them to deal with minor ailments and to support them in their Herculean task. For, as her article 'Clouds and the Rain'[14] indicates, she knew only too well that many mothers, living with irresponsible husbands in grimy surroundings, carried heavy burdens yet bore them heroically.

The McMillan sisters watched the advance of the treatment centre with interest and it was a proud moment for them both when the report of the first six months, drawn up by Dr Eder and Dr Tribe, came to hand. Two factors emerged clearly from the factual picture of their work – the gravity and extent of suffering, and the preventable nature of most of the ailments. Here was clear evidence of the wastage of human resources.

Considering that it was only possible to open the clinic on two afternoons per week, and that the patients had suffered for years before attending the clinic, the figures showed a remarkable improvement in those who had been treated. Reporting in July Margaret said: '141 children have been treated since December last. Of these 77 have been cured, 48 are still under treatment, and are for the most part greatly improved.' Dr Tribe reported that 'Out of the 18 ear cases, 7 were cured and 10 are still under treatment . . . Of the 6 adenoid cases, 5 are cured – one without operation. Of the 39 eye cases, 24 are cured, 9 are still under treatment.' Similar figures were shown for children suffering from skin diseases, tuberculosis and anaemia. Reviewing the figures, Margaret made an impassioned plea for LEAs to provide treatment centres for children, saying:

> Surely this is a good result . . . The after-effects of rickets are being investigated at the Bow clinic, and it is hoped that in the near future Dr. Eder and Dr. Tribe will furnish some useful studies of individual cases from the experience they are now gaining . . . 'Is it nothing to you, all ye who pass by?' We have the power now. The will, surely, will not be lacking to save them.[15]

Margaret insisted that the doctors be paid at the standard rate. They did excellent work and testified publicly to the value of clinics. Dr Eder, reading a paper at the Third International Conference on School Hygiene in Paris, spoke of a child, aged 8 years, who suffered from Croupous Conjunctivitis, for which she had been attending the hospital for eight months. He said, 'The nurse, treating this child daily with a solution of silver nitrate, cured her in a week.' His colleague, Dr Tribe, said:

> When we started work in the school clinic at Devons Road we had nothing to guide us, but only the consciousness of an enormous amount of untended disease amongst school children and a passion to do something to cure it, as far as we could . . . I, being a general practitioner among the comfortable classes, was anxious to do the same sort of thing for poor children as I was doing for the well-to-do . . . I think we left a permanent effect of improved health upon a few children – but only a few . . . we were practically dealing with only one school, though a few from a neighbouring school came in later.[16]

In her fight for medical treatment to be offered to school children nationwide, Margaret tackled an area of need in Bow and simultaneously challenged the holders of the nation's purse strings. In her press articles she often addressed Members of the House of Commons, Whitehall officials and servants of the Board of Education, urging them to provide more medical treatment in clinics. Her article, 'Ten Hundred Thousand Philips',[17] is typical of many she wrote in which she gave case-histories of sick children who were unable to gain admission to hospital though they needed help urgently.

One of her articles had an unexpected spin-off. In the summer of 1909 a fund was started at Bedales School – a private fee-paying co-educational school in Hampshire – to provide a few weeks' holiday in the country for poor children in London. Having read Margaret's article on 'School Clinics', the secretary of the fund decided to invite children from the Bow Clinic as the school's guests. A report on the first batch of children includes:

> As a result of the good food, fresh air and loving care of the matron, the children 'grew fat and rosy'. When Charlie was leaving, half buried in a big bunch of flowers, he sighed, 'Oh, I shall miss my little bed.' At home 'he has to sleep across the foot of his parents' bed'.[18]

As LEAs were reluctant to provide treatment because of the expense, in 1909 Parliament introduced the Local Education Authorities (Medical Treatment) Bill which was designed to induce them to provide treatment by giving them the power to recover the cost involved from parents as a civil debt. If parents could pay for treatment they would be expected to do so, if they could not they would suffer no legal penalty. Before the Act was passed Margaret was busy trying to put her own views forward as she knew these proposals might reduce rather than increase parental responsibility. She wrote:

> There are areas where not 5 per cent of parents notified of serious diseases affecting their children take the smallest notice of the warning. How can these be reached? By summonses and threats . . . No! These summonses are not only costly, they are for the most part useless. It is not punishment but education and opportunity that are wanted . . . The Bill that makes treatment unpopular from the very outset is near its third reading.[19]

Margaret's friends, Doctors Eder and Tribe, used the press to publicise their professional views about the new provisions for treatment. They tried to explain that many cases needed prolonged treatment which could prove too expensive for parents:

> According to this Bill the parent is to be charged with the cost of any treatment provided by the local authority unless that body is satisfied that the parent cannot pay . . . The prolonged treatment and scientific application of remedies is beyond the reach of the wage-earning classes . . . As a result of this the parents will quite naturally refuse to saddle themselves with the expense of such prolonged treatment.[20]

In due course, the Bill became law and, as Margaret felt the provisions were unsatisfactory, she would sometimes plead the children's cause to her friends, with a view to encouraging them to use their influence to change things. Typical of this approach is a letter she wrote, while in Denmark, to the Countess of Warwick.

Copenhagen,
August 23, '09

Dearest Lady Warwick,

The spirit moves me to write to you. I think you will be at the Trade Union Congress, and certainly you will be able to influence the Parliamentary Committee as I could not even if I attended the Congress, which I can't do.

I want to say that in my opinion not much progress can be made in elementary education till we get school clinics.

Now at Portsmouth and elsewhere we asked for them riotously five times over. But that is not enough. What is wanted is really effective action in Parliament. Since January there had been no action so far as I know in Parliament in this matter, and I fear no voice was raised when that nasty little 'Medical

Treatment Bill' (well calculated to kill the infant clinics now in existence) was read and sanctioned.

Now I don't want to touch on this matter again with the Labour members. I have written to Mr. Thorne, as well (at every stage) to Mr. MacDonald. What I want you to do is to see that the Education Estimates shall not be brought up again without action being taken from the Labour benches. They *can* make a difference. It is easier for Labour to do these things than for advanced Radicals to attempt them.

With love,
Yours always,
Margaret McMillan.

P.S. There is not the smallest use in asking for clinics everywhere. What is wanted now is some more clinics at once.[21]

Margaret tried relentlessly to reach local and national centres of power, and to rouse the general public to demand treatment centres for school children. Yet despite dedicated work she and Rachel had many disappointments not only in regard to the inadequate regulations in the 1909 Act, but in their long, protracted fight for medical treatment.

Besides disappointments about the slow progress of her national campaign, Margaret had other troubles in Bow. Although at first the clinic seemed successful, the second report of its work showed that, economically, it was not a viable concern. As it served only one school, the doctors had too few patients; on some afternoons only six children attended the clinic. Consequently the running costs proved to be too high. Many parents decided to use the already busy hospitals rather than the clinics. As Lowndes reported they turned up 'in uncontrollable masses with their Alberts and Lizzies at the out-patients departments of the hospitals. "Damn the L.C.C." was the reaction of one famous hospital.'[22]

Writing about her centre at this time Margaret said:

It proved everything it should not have proved. The small attendance made the cost appear great . . . The clinic dwindled like a perishing child so we took the bull by the horns and in March 1910 announced that we must withdraw from Bow.[23]

Thinking of the draining experience Bow had been Margaret said: 'The clinic has nearly killed me; I'm going off now with Rachel for a few days. I'll do anything when I'm better.'[24] So she went away for a short break.

Although the Bow Clinic was not a financial success it made

visible the high incidence of preventable and curable diseases among school children in this area. Thus it contributed to the debate in medical circles about the gap in existing facilities for treatment. These comprised four major avenues of help. Children could be given medical care under the auspices of the Poor Law, but this was unacceptable to many parents; they could use the services of charitable or semi-charitable dispensaries, which would be similar to the ones which the Reverend ffarington Clayton gave to Ludlow; they could become out-patients at hospitals; or they could visit their family doctor. That diagnosis without treatment was next to useless, doctors conceded; but how treatment should be administered and paid for remained the subject of bitter controversy.

While many were embroiled in controversy about the fiscal and administrative aspects of treatment, Margaret was thinking about the question of prevention as distinct from treatment. None of the four existing agencies, she thought, concentrated enough on promoting health: they were engrossed in curing disease, yet made no attempt to educate parents about the causes and prevention of children's ailments. Pointing out that hospitals did not cater for these aspects of health care Margaret argued that the solution lay in the provision of more clinics. She said:

> The hospitals of London are not only crowded with patients, but their work is not, and cannot, become preventive . . . The great majority of ailing school children are not hospital cases at all: they are cases that need food, fresh air, warm and cold water, restoratives, play, and also the care of a nurse. A great many need also medical advice, but not hospital advice or treatment . . . Yet the school clinic must come. It is the next step towards getting humane conditions of life for the children of poverty.[25]

In the discussion about treatment in medical circles the idea of a number of clinics within schools gradually emerged. But while this idea commended itself to many doctors and parents, local authorities feared the financial burden clinics would impose on the taxpayer. However, Doctors Eder and Tribe continued to give their full support. Speaking to the Progressive League about the Bow Clinic, before it was closed, the former said:

> Working mothers cannot afford to spend hours at the hospitals attempting to obtain attention for their children. Even where it is secured, treatment cannot be given systematically and regularly. At the Devons Road School Clinic the nurse sees the child twice a day. Thus she can attend to the syringing of ears, bathing of eyes, and other little necessary operations.[26]

By degrees officialdom was won round, albeit reluctantly, to the provision of medical treatment and clinics in state schools, and Margaret played an integral part in this.

By now Margaret had affected state provision of meals, school medical inspection and treatment. In starting the Health Centre in Bow, she had also made the public aware of the tremendous amount of untended disease among school children and helped to change opinion about the need for school clinics. Paying tribute to her efforts to improve the physical condition of working-class children Gilbert, in his study of the development of national insurance in Britain, wrote: 'Her outstanding contribution to the health of children lies in her work in the establishment of school clinics.'[27]

Margaret's first-hand knowledge of the appalling conditions of many poor children in schools was later to lead her to initiate a series of interlocking experiments on behalf of needy children.

Chapter fourteen

Nothing Less than a New Crusade 1910

While admitting the financial failure of the Health Centre in Bow, Margaret believed in the idea and began to think of opening another similar establishment and capitalising on her mistakes. Knowing that the Deptford schools she visited regularly had long lists of children who had been medically examined but whose ailments remained untreated, she decided that a clinic was urgently needed in that district. So in 1910, she went to Deptford to pioneer a Health and Treatment Centre in its poorest part – the East Ward.

Deptford was steeped in history. There was, as Chase reported: 'The King's Head public house mentioned by Pepys . . . Up Deptford Creek came Francis Drake in the "Golden Hind", fresh from his voyage round the world; and from Deptford, Raleigh fitted out a successful expedition against Spain.'[1] But despite its glorious past, Deptford in 1910 was a decaying, depressed inner-city area. One of its social workers described it as 'a grey human unit lost in a background of depressing greyness'. She spoke of 'a greyness about everything – grey skies, grey streets, grey faces'.[2] Margaret painted the same gloomy picture:

> In some streets there is always an odour of death . . . On summer days you see scores of dirty, uncombed and ragged children playing on the hot pavements. Pretty baby hands seize refuse from the gutter . . . Lithe, half-naked boys play pitch-and-toss in the street.[3]

Deptford covered an area of 1,563 acres containing 53 miles of dingy streets and little open space apart from graveyards. In 1911, it had a population of 109,496, and a higher population density than many neighbouring boroughs. Whilst Deptford had 72 persons per acre, Greenwich had 26, Woolwich 17, Lewisham 24.8 and Camberwell 59.6. It had six wards, throughout which the people were unevenly spread; by 1921, census figures show that Deptford's population had increased and the East Ward with which Margaret became increasingly involved, had 131 persons per acre whereas the South Ward only had 45.

The same dismal picture emerges from the figures on over-crowding. In the East Ward there were 1.37 persons per room, in the South Ward there were 0.74. The parents often lived in one room with up to five children.

Table 14.1   Population density of the Metropolitan Borough of Deptford 1921

	Area in statute acres	Persons	Persons per acre	Structurally separate dwellings occupied	Rooms occupied	Persons per room
East Ward	163	21,327	131	3,184	15,347	1.37
North Ward	290	23,942	83	3,552	19,605	1.22
North West Ward	349	24,084	69	3,577	20,132	1.19
South Ward	288	13,063	45	2,403	17,542	0.74
South East Ward	175	13,094	75	2,126	12,902	1.01
South West Ward	299	17,024	57	3,033	19,911	0.85

The poor conditions in the East Ward are also reflected in the infant mortality figures. In Deptford in 1909 and 1910 there were 104 and 124 deaths per thousand. In 1910 the figure for the South West Ward was only 77, but in the East Ward it was 189 – a figure well above the national average. Roughly one-fifth of the children born in this ward died in their first year of life. In many London boroughs the infant mortality rate decreased but in Deptford's East Ward the figure increased. One journalist said: 'This appalling increase in the sacrifice in child life has occurred in a year that was healthy for children.'[4] Deptford was also the only borough in London where the 1910 general death rate was higher than that of the previous year.

The underlying causes of these unusually high mortality rates were low wages, intermittent employment, large families and insanitary dwellings. Poverty and poor household management often went together; poor housing led to ill-health, and sickness created ever more poverty. Low wages meant that few wage-earners could afford to live in a whole house – many of them could only rent rooms, and the resultant overcrowding made its own contribution to the high incidence of disease. Then, because of poverty, few could afford to send for a doctor.

In the East Ward some of the children lived in one-room tenements. The average number of children in a family was five, and their one-roomed home was living room, bedroom and, on occasion, mortuary too. There was rarely enough room for two beds, so the whole family usually slept in one bed at the end of the room.

In Deptford in 1910 there was a shortage of good housing stock at a price poor families could afford; the accommodation available for the lowest paid workers was usually in a deplorable condition. Making landlords improve and maintain their property adequately was difficult, if not impossible. When in 1911 there was an outcry about the high infant mortality rate in Deptford, it transpired that certain members of the council owned some of the worst property and were disinclined to improve it. *The Daily Chronicle* drew attention to the situation by disclosing the unpalatable facts to the general public in this way:

> In the past year the Mansion House Council has repeatedly urged on the Deptford Borough Council the need for increased vigilance in public health, but it had been met by the apathy of many of its members and the determined opposition of others. A great number of the members of the Deptford Council are owners of small property.[5]

There was a shortage not only of good houses, but also of reasonably well-paid jobs. In the East Ward many men were either unemployed for years or classed as casual and general labourers. Their chief sources of employment were a variety of light industries scattered throughout the dock area: engineering works, brick works, tin, sack and jam works, laundry and rag-sorting trades. Some men were warehousemen, railway workers and drivers of vehicles. To supplement their husbands' wages, some women undertook work in the cattle market where they did nauseating jobs on carcasses, others became seamstresses, domestic servants or factory workers. The average weekly earnings for 83 per cent of the population was twenty shillings; many earned less.

By B. S. Rowntree's[6] minimum needs scale, calculated for his 1901 survey in York, more than four-fifths of the families in Deptford's East Ward were living in dire poverty. From Table 14.2 it can be seen that as many of the families in Deptford East contained at least seven persons – the parents and five children – twenty eight shillings and ten pence was needed to meet their barest physical needs, not the twenty shillings 83 per cent of the population earned.

Where families had no more than two children, provided the wage-earner stayed in regular employment and the mother was a good housekeeper, they might have been able to live just above

Table 14.2 Minimum necessary expenditure per week for families of various sizes

Family	Food	Rent	Household sundries	Total
1 man	3s.	1s. 6d.	2s. 6d.	7s.
1 woman	3s.	1s. 6d.	2s. 6d.	7s.
1 man and 1 woman	6s.	2s. 6d.	3s. 2d.	11s. 8d.
1 man, 1 woman, 1 child	8s. 3d.	2s. 6d.	3s. 9d.	14s. 6d.
1 man, 1 woman, 2 children	10s. 6d.	4s.	4s. 4d.	18s.10d.
1 man, 1 woman, 3 children	12s. 9d.	4s.	4s. 11d.	21s. 8d.
1 man, 1 woman, 4 children	15s.	5s. 6d.	5s. 6d.	26s.
1 man, 1 woman, 5 children	17s. 3d.	5s. 6d.	6s. 1d.	28s.10d.
1 man, 1 woman, 6 children	19s. 6d.	5s. 6d.	6s. 8d.	31s. 8d.
1 man, 1 woman, 7 children	21s. 9d.	5s. 6d.	7s. 3d.	34s. 6d.
1 man, 1 woman, 8 children	24s.	5s. 6d.	7s. 10d.	37s. 4d.

the poverty line. But once the third child arrived it would be difficult to make ends meet. The inability of many parents to regulate family size to income was undoubtedly another major cause of poverty.

Rowntree,[7] drawing attention to the cyclical pattern of poverty that ran through the lives of working-class people, showed that most labourers' children were born into poverty and were underfed during their school years. Then they returned to poverty again in early middle life, when they married and started having children of their own; later they were in the same state again when they became too old to work. This pattern could be clearly seen in most of the families in Deptford and was probably reflected in the high general death rate and in children's poor physique.

Added to the problems of low wages, interrupted earnings and inability to relate income and family size, were the intemperate habits of many of the parents in the East Ward area. Beer often took the money that was needed for food and clothing. Drunkenness was common. The brewer's dray was one of the children's most familiar sights. At the turn of the century Deptford had 132 public houses – roughly one for every 760 persons – in addition to many off-licences. On Monday morning in Deptford bundles and jugs were the commonest sight. The former went to the pawnshop and the latter to the beer shop.

Gambling was another social evil that robbed many homes, not of real comfort since that was unknown to most of them, but of the barest necessities. A bookmaker in Deptford often took £70 in bets in less than two hours. Men, women and even children were known to have the gambling mania. While changes in living and working conditions were certainly needed, changes in the people's domestic habits and attitudes were needed too.

Most of the children in the East Ward were dependent on school meals and charities for their food. Many of them would have had no breakfast had it not been for philanthropists. One voluntary agency alone served between 1,200 and 1,800 breakfasts daily, but even so some children went to school on an empty stomach because they could not procure the free tickets which entitled them to a mug of tea, a roll and a piece of cheese. One agency reported:

> Many a touching sight was witnessed . . . Two children were seen to save about half their roll each morning. On being asked what they were going to do with it, they said: 'We are taking it home for mother and father and our little sister.' Their statement was found to be quite correct. Imagine five people existing on two rolls![8]

The inadequate food and clothing of the majority of the children often led to ill-health. Compulsory schooling meant that children had to go out in all weathers, but their shoes often had holes right through them. So they regularly sat in school with wet feet. These, then, were the kind of children and families that Margaret and Rachel sought to help. (For a fuller account of conditions in Deptford see Bradburn, 1976.[9])

After their experiences in Bow, the McMillans knew that to be viable any new health centre in Deptford would have to be well-used and serve several schools. Apart from routine medical inspection, they wanted to help children with eye diseases, decaying teeth and conditions requiring minor operations. For private individuals without means this seemed an ambitious scheme but, as on other occasions when the sisters took bold action in accordance with their deeply held convictions, financial help came.

First of all, on hearing of their proposed venture, Greenwich Borough Council offered them free use of the Old Vestry Hall, 3 Deptford Green, in the East Ward, for a Health and Treatment Centre. Then Joseph Fels promised them an income of £400–500 per annum; the Ogilvie Trustees gave £200 for two to three years; many private individuals also gave monetary help, and Margaret expected parents to pay something, however little, for treatment.

The balancing of her books was never Margaret's priority; if children needed treatment she gave it, whether parents could pay or not, but at the same time she encouraged them to shoulder their own responsibilities. Along with other members of the ILP

Margaret was spreading the idea that socialism was not state charity, and campaigning for workers to have better wages so that they could pay for their children's treatment and be independent of the state.

Once she had secured premises and some finance, the next task was to find people to share the responsibility for the running of the centre. Speaking of her early, abortive attempts to enlist local people and set up a committee, Margaret recalled:

> We wrote to the ecclesiastical guides of the people. Only one answered, and we made him chairman, but before the first bills were paid or cards issued, he said he must have a written and signed document from Mr. Fels, saying that Mr. Fels would be responsible. Mr. Fels, whose word was always as good as his bond, replied in language that I cannot possibly reproduce . . . Later we wrote to an influential lady and asked her to come on the committee, but she said she would go 'Only to people who were disinterested' . . . Worst of all, our secretary, who was very sensitive, resigned on the spot.[10]

Ultimately a small committee, which rarely met, was formed consisting of the McMillans, Mr and Mrs John Evelyn, Mr Joseph Fels and his private secretary, Walter Coates. The main responsibility for setting up the centre was undertaken by the sisters but as Rachel was in full-time employment the day-to-day administration fell on Margaret.

Prior to the opening of what Margaret referred to as 'The Health Centre' but which the locals persisted in calling 'the clinic', she read every available description of similar establishments. At this point England only had three recorded clinics, the voluntary one in Bow, now closed, and two others in Bradford and Cambridge.

Margaret envisaged that this new Centre in Deptford would be a working model. It would undertake medical, hygienic and educational tasks. It would be more like a home than a hospital – a place where parents might lose their fear of doctors and learn about the prevention and cure of disease.

In her article 'Faith and Fear' Margaret stressed that parents needed 'a familiar place close by', a friendly nurse and a teacher who could establish confidence and explain to them 'why Jane stoops and how Mary's neck can be made straight and supple again'.[11] Speaking of the teaching role of health centres, she said they would teach 'not only child, but parent', otherwise children would sink back into their old life of infection after treatment. Outlining what she envisaged she said: 'We should have to make the clinic not the appendage of a school, but the germ of the school.'[12]

An example of how Margaret hoped the clinic would influence the homes can be seen in the clinic card which she designed to help parents and children to understand about the care of teeth.

Help to Save Your Teeth by
Keeping Them Clean.

Brush them after supper, and after breakfast, also brush them after eating sweets.

Wet the brush, then scatter a little prepared chalk on it (you can get a penny-worth at the chemist's). Brush across then up and down the teeth, and brush the back teeth.

Wash out the mouth with a little water, and wash the brush.

Card from Children's Health Centre, Deptford

The Centre, which was furnished for under £30, comprised three clinics in one, a general clinic, a dental clinic and one for the treatment of malformations. When it opened, on 21 June 1910, it included a ground-floor waiting room, and a first-floor, sunny medical treatment room. It had a dental chair, a dark room 'where eyes were tested', 'tall narrow cupboards in which ointments and salves were stored' and over the mantelpiece a 'lovely picture of the "Guardian Angel" by Dvorak'.[13]

117

When the great day came to open the doors to the public, 'children arrived in torrents' from various schools and different social classes. The need for the Centre was obvious; in the Creek Road school alone, it was found that of 1,100 children, 500 required medical treatment immediately. Reporting on the first few months Margaret said: 'A new crowd is pouring in for hours and out again like water through a tube.' Ultimately about 6,000 children per annum attended the Centre. Speaking of the different kinds of parents who accompanied their children Margaret said some were 'ladies in soft shining clothes', others wore 'quiet hats and tailor-mades' and came from homes where hitting children and swearing were uncommon. A few mothers were drunk on arrival and staggered in with children in their arms. But Margaret commented: 'the staff does what it can, even for children carried away or led away by a reeling mother.'[14]

Rachel had seen the need to build bridges between divergent groups of people in her work in Kent. Now the Health Centre gave both the sisters the opportunity they sought of caring for children of all classes and the chance to meet their parents.

The staff at the Health Centre were all dedicated to their task, apart from the first dentist who, assuming there was plenty of money available, ran up a bill for £105 for three or four visits; he was sacked forthwith. The members of the staff were all part-time; there were two doctors who between them saw about 200 children per month; there was a visiting dentist, a nurse, who worked three hours every day, and a teacher of physical culture who taught five hours a week. Margaret's assessment of them was: 'Never was there such a wonderful staff . . . They turned every difficulty and limitation into a means of discovery, or triumph.' Describing the atmosphere they created, and how sorry children were to be discharged, Margaret explained:

> It was a happy, homely place, and when the children on a cold winter's afternoon trooped up the stairs . . . they sat round the fire with their much-loved nurse and told her all their family news . . . 'Please nurse I still have a pimple', said one little patient ruefully when she was gently told that she need not attend any more.[15]

Legally children could not visit the Centre in school hours; so some attended during the lunch hour, others between four and eight o'clock in the afternoon and some on Saturdays. When the children arrived many were in an appalling condition; they were dirty, diseased and inadequately clothed. They roused Margaret's pity and made her long to help them. Her vision of what these children could become, given a little assistance, never faded, though she never under-estimated the size of the task she was taking on. Looking at the children and the district she said: 'The work is as difficult as it can be, and if success can be won here, it can be won anywhere.'[16]

Although from the outset the Health Centre did useful work, the McMillans encountered fierce opposition. But after much patient endeavour, this initial hostility began to abate and occasionally turned into support. Mr C. – a rich Tory who openly opposed Margaret's work on the grounds that clinics would weaken parental responsibility – constantly argued with her. However, he modified his views after visiting the Centre and watching the staff at work. Margaret related: 'When he rose to take leave, he put gold in my hand . . . this gift, and one or two others offered by friends, is too precious to be declined.'[17]

The staff too had to get used to facing suspicion, resentment, ignorance, as well as blatant opposition. One parent said to one of the helpers, 'If the Lord Almighty wants my child's teeth to grow one way, why do you want 'em to grow in another?'[18] Typical of the many encounters the dentist had, which Margaret reported were:

> 'We've come here to see what ye're up to . . .' 'Why, if there was anythink wrong', said the father, getting angrier . . . 'I'd a gone to my sixpenny doctor at the top o' the street, who'd 'a pulled out 'is teeth a sight quicker 'n you.' But the dentist was as cheery as ever, and as kind. 'I don't want to pull his teeth out,' he said; 'that's just the one thing I don't want to do. I'm here, you see, to save teeth, not to pull 'em out.'[19]

Doctors met the same lack of understanding and initial opposition as the dentist. One parent complained that his child had 'been stripped', that fingers had 'bin pushed down her throttle', and again Margaret had to try to explain what medical inspection involved.

Nevertheless, despite recurring antagonism, the number of children using the Centre grew steadily. In 1910, 7,000 ailing children were treated. As the clinic was obviously meeting a need, in 1911 the LCC gave Margaret a grant towards the cost of the dental service and followed this, in 1912, with a medical grant.

Realising the effectiveness of Margaret's work and the way it was growing, the philanthropist John Chichester Evelyn offered her a gracious three-storied house with a large garden in Evelyn Street at a rent of one shilling a year. Margaret gladly accepted it, named it Evelyn House and had 'Evelyn Medical Home' painted on the door in letters of black and gold. From 1911 onwards, Evelyn House became the valued annexe of the Health Centre and was used at once for minor operations. This enabled Margaret to invite 20 children each Saturday to have their operations there. She and Rachel devoted their weekends to this and nursed the children until they were well enough to go home.

Deptford School Clinic and Medical Home.

FOR PARENTS AND GUARDIANS.

As every effort is being made to ensure that operations shall be carried out with perfect Success and Safety, the following rules are now being drawn up for the help of parents. It is certain that many fathers and mothers do not need the advice, but it is offered so as to make the Medical Home a safe place for every child.

1. Do not allow your child to have anything on the evening before the operation, except a cup of milk or liquid food.

2. Give a dose of castor oil or other safe medicine on the evening before the operation.

3. Let the child have a warm bath and change of clothing if possible on or just before the day of the operation. (All children having the operation for Adenoids are expected to go to the Clinic to receive breathing lessons).

4. Bring your child to 353, Evelyn Street, on Saturday morning at nine o'clock.

MARGARET McMILLAN,
DEPTFORD SCHOOL CLINIC.

This must be signed by Parent or Guardian before the operation is done.

I, the undersigned, being the parent or Guardian of

———————————————————, *hereby give my consent to the performance of the operation that is advised, and for which I understand an anæsthetic is necessary.*

Signed————————————.

Dated——————— School————————————

A fee of 1s. is charged. The money to be paid when the operation is agreed upon.

Deptford School Clinic.   Miss Margaret McMillan.

Notices sent to parents before operations at the Deptford School Clinic

The Health Centre increasingly did excellent remedial work. Margaret was able to cite case after case of improved health in children, sometimes resulting in better educational performance as in the following instance of a deaf boy who could not read but received treatment. 'Two months later he is full of eager desire to learn. He attacks the reading book, and begins to master the new art.'[20]

But despite good reports Margaret was dissatisfied with the overall results of the Centre. She realised that while many diseases were temporarily arrested, only a few were permanently cured. In one three-month period, the nurse treated 950 cases of skin ailments, such as impetigo, but 927 of these returned to be treated again for the same ailments. Hundreds of children went back to the clinic five and six times within twelve months, because they invariably returned to the same home conditions which caused the disease in the first place. Thinking over this problem, Margaret came to the conclusion that a fence at the top of the precipice would be better than an ambulance at the bottom, and that a preventive scheme was needed alongside good clinics.

Though Margaret was heavily involved in working for Deptford's children, she continued to plan and work for the children of Britain as a whole. She was not one who suffered from tunnel-vision. Having the whole country in her sights, she undertook to address many gatherings in different counties and wrote informative articles with the aim of stimulating members of the Labour Party and others to agitate for the needed reforms.

Despite all her efforts the spread of clinics was slower than she anticipated. Many authorities provided little help for their children. Even in 1914, seven years after the Act sanctioning medical inspection, only 241 of the 317 local education authorities were providing treatment. Another 53 were contributing to hospitals for the treatment of their school children; in addition 84 authorities had established dental clinics. It was not until 1918 that new legislation obliged all local authorities to provide medical treatment for children in state schools. So Margaret felt that she had to keep on bringing this matter to the notice of the general public through her lectures and writings.

Speaking in the Temperance Hall, Hanley, on 'The Doctor in the School', at a meeting arranged by the Stoke-on-Trent Association of Head Teachers, she gave details of what was happening in Deptford and tried to give her listeners a vision of what could result from medical treatment in schools. She explained that school clinics could help to keep children out of hospitals. Continuing, she said:

From our schools will appear a new generation, re-invigorated, strengthened, purified, trained in thought and habit; then the curse of disgraceful diseases, consumption, all kinds of loathsome skin maladies, diseases of the sense organs, complaints that are really the result of wrong living will be banished.[21]

Although Margaret took Deptford's sick, disadvantaged children as her starting point, she aimed in the long run to change the educational system so that it took responsibility for the physical and educational development of children, and for regenerating their neighbourhood communities. It can be claimed that she achieved considerable success in reaching both these objectives, which she saw as steps towards the new society of which ILP members dreamed.

Time and again in London Margaret challenged the settled order of things and succeeded in effecting a shift in the thinking of administrators and teachers, as she had done in Bradford. Opening the Deptford Health Centre, Sir John Gorst was reported as saying:

It was quite a new idea that education authorities were responsible for the health of children – only a few years ago it was the firm conviction of the Board of Education that it had nothing to do with the bodies of children, but only to stuff into their little brains reading, writing, and arithmetic.[22]

Speaking of the new acceptance in education of responsibility for the physical welfare of children, Margaret said: 'Everywhere is experiment and evidence. And if one fact emerges continually it is this: Primary education, at least, is mainly physical.'[23]

Frequently she helped to focus attention on the child himself, on the need to study him and put him at the centre of planning rather than, as was customary, try to force him into some existing theoretical framework. Discussing new approaches she said: 'Now they are leaving this wilderness – they are beginning to think of the child himself, of his aptitudes, his defects, his health and his growth.' To those who argued that medical treatment was not part of education, she retorted that, unless you put the child and his physical well-being into discussions about education, 'book-learning is of very little value'.[24]

Explaining the wider aspects of health and her ideas about building up the community and the nation she declared: 'The whole purpose or aim of Public Health is . . . not the health of individuals but the security and progress of the whole nation which is here involved in the elimination or tolerance of preventable disease.'[25]

All of Margaret's health experiments were part of her larger goal which Katharine Bruce Glasier described as: 'Nothing less than a new and nobler human race in a new and nobler social order.' Speaking of both Rachel and Margaret she said:

To the McMillan sisters, intent on 'whole' men and women . . . the plight of the workers whom they found, literally dehumanised . . . unable to save either themselves or their children, called for nothing less than a new Crusade – a Crusade to rescue the ideal of human life itself.[26]

Chapter fifteen

Night Camps and a Camp School 1911–13

Thinking of the prevention of disease rather than its temporary cure, Margaret, with Rachel's agreement, decided to start an open-air night camp for girls in the garden of Evelyn House. She wanted children to leave their overcrowded homes and be in the open-air for long stretches of time, so that they and their resistance to disease might be built up. She pictured them having simple but nourishing al fresco meals and sleeping outside. Another of her aims was to remove 'the disabilities that come to the children of poverty and make even the best teaching difficult if not impossible'.[1]

Margaret launched out on this new venture with enthusiasm and friends gave the financial help needed to get the scheme off the ground. Occasionally she was able to buy indispensable materials with small sums of money left over from the LCC grants for the Health Centre, but of necessity the Camp had to be furnished cheaply. With her usual ingenuity Margaret managed to procure or contrive the basic equipment needed. Simple beds were made of gas piping, trestles and canvas, all of which were lent, and primitive washing facilities were devised. Sir Robert Morant's wife gave the towels and his daughter hemmed them. Boys from the neighbourhood cleaned up the garden and helped with other practical jobs. Describing how the Camp was made operational Margaret said:

> Walls were tarred or white-washed, and a hot-water apparatus was rigged up in the garden fence communicating with a neighbour's boiler. It was a very clever arrangement . . . but we had to fall back on our own boiler house which we used as a bathroom. There was no bathroom in the house . . . but Miss Sewell fixed a pipe and hose over the yard drain, and enclosed it with canvas fastened down with stones in the hem. This cold shower cost 2s. 9d., and it was more amusing than a tiled and marbled indoor bathroom![2]

Despite many trials such as storms which blew down the improvised appliances and frequent skirmishes with local builders, surveyors and architects, the Camp opened in the spring of 1911 with 17 girls, ranging from six to fourteen years of age, who were put under the guidance of Miss Sewell, the Camp guardian. Describing the first girl to camp – Marigold, a nine-year-old who had never slept out before – Margaret wrote:

> She had seven bodices on and as many underskirts, and was never allowed to have a breath of (night) air. In spite of all she could eat nothing, and her parents were miserable. This tragedy was disposed of by Miss Sewell in two nights. She took a great many of the 'things' off, covered the little one warmly, but lightly, in a camp bed under the elder blooms. The result amazed and delighted the father of Marigold, who now arrives joyfully at dusk every night with his smiling daughter.[3]

The joy and excitement of the children after their first experience of sleeping out in the garden were immediately apparent. Margaret said that hardly any of them had ever seen a moonrise or a sunrise. They were staggered by the vastness of the sky. One child, with sparkling eyes, said, 'I've nivver seen it before, nivver!' Some saw flowers and butterflies for the first time in the Camp.

The children arrived in the late afternoon, played in the garden, then they were invited to participate as a group in all the domestic jobs connected with the running of the Camp such as arranging and setting the tables for a simple evening meal; this was followed by bathing where the older girls were encouraged to look after the younger ones. At seven o'clock the beds were put out and the children, most of whom had never had a bed to themselves before, slept outside under a flimsy awning. (Fortunately the spring came early that year, 1911.) The next morning the children breakfasted on porridge made with fresh milk, and the oatmeal which Margaret bought in Inverness; then, when replete, they set off for school.

From the beginning the Camp children ate well and slept soundly, with the result that their general health improved appreciably. Margaret, who gave her undivided attention to the experiment, kept a watchful eye on each child and was gladdened by the faintest sign of progress in their condition. After a while in her article 'The Child of the Future',[4] she was able to give case histories of children who, having slept out in the Camp and used the gymnasium she made in Evelyn House, had greatly improved physically. She claimed that every trace of dirt and disease vanished.

The following recollection of a visitor to the Camp, when it was well-established, gives a glimpse of the personal attention Margaret gave children; he recalled her not as a remote, august planner, but as one concerned with every detail of the children's lives and readily available to them.

> Perhaps the vision that will remain with me longest is that of Miss McMillan moving amongst the beds in the girls' Camp with the night wind blowing through the open sides of the simple wooden structure where they sleep, waiting to see them safely tucked in for the night . . . she bends over them to say some tender final word before they fall into the deep refreshing sleep that comes to them so swiftly. That is an unforgettable memory.[5]

Margaret longed for children in low-income families to be offered camp facilities. Speaking of this she wrote:

> If only there was land for, say, a thousand open-air bedrooms as humble as is this one . . . Since we cannot all claim good homes for all the year, at least can we not secure for all children camp-beds and canvas, and the kiss of the night wind for months in every year?[6]

As the girls' Camp proved to be such a success, she decided to provide similar facilities for boys. The need for these Camps was obvious. TB alone claimed many victims in Deptford; in 1900, 170 people died of it. So, having decided to open a Night Camp for boys, she looked round for a suitable site, and finding that the only free open space in the neighbourhood was the graveyard of St Nicholas' Church, she asked the vicar for the use of it. Margaret describes the incident.

> 'There you are,' he said, waving his hand, 'there is your garden.' It was not, perhaps, a cheerful scene . . . The upright stones, fallen long ago, for the most part are stacked up against the yard walls. The place has been a burying-ground for a thousand years. It has been closed for half a century.[7]

Having gained possession of the graveyard, Margaret engaged a gardener-teacher to look after the children. Initially eight boys camped there and the numbers steadily increased to forty. Again the equipment was of the simplest kind. Camp beds were made out of wooden trestles, French flour sacks and gas pipes. Blankets were made like bags so that children could button themselves into

126

them when the nights were chilly. There was an old boiler, which the boys stoked to obtain hot water; they bathed in their own tin bath and slept out under the elderberry trees with the tombstones standing about them like four-posters. Within a month, the fresh air, regular sleep and wholesome food made their mark on the campers. They put on weight and got visibly stronger and healthier. A newspaper article on the progress of some boys reported:

Take the case of Master George Lehean, who has visibly put on weight in a few weeks. 'I feel heaps better', he said yesterday to *The Daily Mirror*, 'I think sleeping out of doors is splendid . . . I can go to bed at eight and sleep on until eight again easily.' Master George Franklin was of an exactly similar opinion. 'Mother says that I don't look like the same boy' . . . 'The fact is', said Mr. Mickleburgh, the master who is looking after them, 'they have grown so tremendously fond of sleeping there that my present form of punishment is not to allow them to sleep out of doors.'[8]

As with other ventures that she initiated, Margaret ran into strong opposition. This time she became a target for abuse because her equipment was simple and the Camp was on consecrated ground. Some of the residents even implied that she and her sister must be making money out of it and called the whole thing 'disgraceful'.[9]

The *Daily Mirror* reported that initially some parents objected to the Camp's location. 'At first there was some opposition from some of the mothers who could only look upon graveyards as creepy places rather given to a ghostly population.'[10]

Speaking of the hostility she faced from outside, Margaret tells us that:

People came from all kinds of places and representing all manner of societies. 'Here is a disgraceful thing', they said. Some would-be trouble-makers questioned the boys to see if they could extract adverse comments from them, which they could then publicise, but were disappointed. 'Aren't you afraid, my boy, to be out here in the dark all night in a graveyard?' said a serious old gentleman. 'No, I aren't', said Jim . . . 'I'm asleep.'[11]

Margaret who, although realistic, had the gift of seeing beauty in the most unpromising situations, said of the site:

Early in the mornings the boys were awakened by the twitter and warble of birds round the church tower . . . They were

building already in chinks in the old walls, and in the Clinic
window, just opposite, and in the trees . . . I came once very
early. The sky was suffused with light . . . Gold and rose-
coloured clouds sailed overhead and a sweet breath blew fresh
from the river. Deptford is wonderfully pure and sweet at
midnight and in the morning.[12]

As time went on opposition mounted. Even *The Kentish
Mercury*, which usually reported Margaret's experiments favourably, said that this time her commendable zeal had outrun her
discretion. Then the vicar, who at first told Margaret: 'Don't
bother about the complaints,' changed his mind and said firmly,
'Move on.'

After this ultimatum, the sisters walked the streets of Deptford
for weeks looking for alternative accommodation for the Night
Camp but discovered nothing. In the end Margaret had to leave
Rachel to carry on the search alone as she was due to lecture in
Derby on 'School Clinics', at a meeting arranged by the local Co-
operative Guild. Rachel went to the station with her and insisted
that before she came back, a new site for the Camp would
certainly have been found. But Margaret was sceptical. 'It's all
right,' Rachel said, as the train moved off.

In Derby Margaret gave an impassioned speech on the need for
more clinics. After giving an outline of the many curable diseases
doctors were currently dealing with in her own in Deptford, she
said:

Mr Lloyd George had given £1½ millions to sanatoria, but if he
gave half-a-million for school clinics he would not require £1½
millions for older children . . . To put it at its highest, for a cost
of four shillings per head per annum dental and medical
treatment could be given to every child in the country or for
half-a-million they could have school clinics and camp schools
for all . . . With two not very large clinics they could deal with all
the children [in Derby] at a cost of £1,000.[13]

On returning home, Margaret found to her surprise that Rachel
had found a rough parcel of ground for a boys' Night Camp, close
to the Health Centre, which could be rented for five shillings a
week. This piece of waste land was a dump for nearby houses; it
contained refuse of every kind, and had an old stable on it. The
sisters quickly obtained the tenancy and with the help of children
and others the site was cleared at such speed that they vacated the
graveyard and moved there within a week.

Unfortunately, on arrival they found once again that many

residents strongly objected to the ground being used as a boys' Camp and took every opportunity of showing their disapproval. A typical reaction was that of a local woman who shrieked as she passed the Camp, 'Riff-raff I call 'em. Nasty riff-raff.'[14] One neighbour flung tins, boxes, broken plates and rubbish on to the site. Another threw out slices of bread and scraps of food with the result that soon several cats made a habit of gathering there in the evenings and serenading the campers until the small hours of the morning.

Undeterred, Margaret pressed on with her plans. First, she erected a tent to protect the boys from the weather. Later she saw she needed a more permanent structure with good toilet facilities and a sound roof. After designing this she soon became locked in heated, protracted battles with officials and builders. Recalling them, she said:

> I applied for the right to build, and sent in a rough sketch of the proposed shelter and bathhouse . . . The first plans were condemned, and I think very wisely. (A high official of the London County Council said we could not have a school bath worth anything for less than £2,500).[15]

In the end a German firm built her a bath at a cost of £30 and a shelter for £120 which had three open sides and enough space to allow 50 boys to sleep there. Then she set about creating a garden round it out of the rubbish dump. There she helped the boys to grow flowers and vegetables which they all sampled in due course.

On the white-washed fence of the Camp she put clothing-pegs for the children. After examining the clothes hanging there she wrote:

> I wish the members of the Cabinet and every well-off person could see a few of the clothes that are hung on these pegs every night. Mere dirty rags, alas! . . . I live in hopes of putting all the coats and many of the shirts, etc., under the boiler fire soon, and of bringing in the era of washable jerseys and new footgear . . . We confiscate tobacco (for actually some little boys take it to bed with them), and our manual training consists very largely of sewing on buttons and learning to hold spoons. It sounds very humble work, and yet it has to be done first apparently. University education, higher technical education will follow. They cannot very well precede it.[16]

Notwithstanding bad weather and the many difficulties which cropped up daily, Margaret was able to keep the Night Camp open winter and summer alike; the boys flourished; the experiment was a success.

Margaret's next project arose out of her contacts with the girls and boys in the Camps. She observed how deprived, socially and culturally, these children were. Speaking of them she said:

> One in thirty had a hair brush. Not one in thirty had a nail brush . . . Of religion in the deepest, highest sense, they knew little . . . the boys take in comic papers of a very vulgar order and would like to show the pictures to everyone . . . in many homes there is not even one book![17]

One day, after asking the girls to write an account of a night spent in the garden, she realised how poor their literary skills were and wondered about their general standard of education. These were children who had been taught by traditional methods, in large classes, in badly ventilated schools and whose low attainments were obvious.

Thinking about them she wrote: 'We begin to understand why employers complain bitterly of the letter-writing of boys and girls who have left school.' One irate master said: 'Why can't any of 'em be trusted to add a column of figures or write a decent hand and spell properly?' Her comment was: 'The proof of any kind of education is that it makes children able to do things well, and not that it makes them hopeless in spelling or arithmetic.'[18]

After reflecting on the children's standard of achievements and believing that schools should provide the information and skills home could not impart, Margaret decided to start a school – a Camp School – for boys and girls from six to fourteen years. Instead of children spending long hours in over-crowded classrooms, she believed she could give them a sound education in the open-air. She visualised children having their meals outside and being taught by teachers who could introduce them to the excitement of learning. At night she envisaged that the boys would sleep in their existing Camp while the girls would return to Evelyn House. During the daytime the boys' Camp would be used as the School.

As soon as Margaret thought of a new scheme she started to tell all her friends about it. Doctors in the Clinic at once began to recommend children, who had been certified as unfit to attend LCC schools because they had anaemia or other curable diseases, for this school. In quite a short time Margaret had the names of 57 pupils and she promptly engaged three skilled schoolmasters who wanted to experiment with a new kind of education. Speaking of the School and its teachers Margaret explained:

The teachers are all specialists. The headmaster, Mr Norman, for example, is an expert in normal subjects and drill; the second master, Mr Greenfield, has specialized in drawing and painting and our night master gives attention to hygiene. The children should not only attain a state of physical well-being . . . They should hunger to learn, and they do, even now, though the hunger must get keener.[19]

Describing the Camp's interesting curriculum to a visitor, Margaret said:

Geography becomes a much less formidable thing when one learns it by means of such actual models as the children make themselves on the floor of the open-air school with sand and chalk and pebbles; and history is felt to be much more than a matter of dead Kings and forgotten battles when events can be recreated in miniature, and each child takes its part and feels its relation to the whole scene. Then there are baths and exercises – not the stiff wooden drills of the playground and classroom, but the intelligent use of all the muscles, proper breathing, and the free, natural play of the limbs.[20]

Aiming to develop these children socially, Margaret invited many interesting personalities to the School.

Ladies from the West End, learned professors, medical men, and chairmen of education committees, come to tea . . . It is remarkable how everyone (however poor) began to brush his clothes, wash and scrub his finger-nails, take pains to wash and also comb his hair, and discovered the importance of his new handkerchief. And how carefully we study the table manners of the guests and try to model our own on them. It would appear that table manners can be easily taught when children are allowed to be hosts.[21]

Occasionally, to extend children's horizons, she arranged for them to visit places of interest locally and go to London theatres. Sometimes she organised social evenings in the School. Thinking of the different possibilities these afforded she wrote:

On warm June nights one can, given a good lantern and slides, take one's guests to Norway, to Italy, to Canada and the Isles of Dreams. You can have open-air plays on some evenings with the children as actors, and why should not the greatest singers come down and sing to us?[22]

Although Margaret was able to enrich the lives of the campers

Mention
what *they*
learned.

one of her deep regrets was that she could not keep the children longer, perhaps until they were 16 and over. Some of those who had to leave, asked if they could come back, just to sleep in the Camp. At first she agreed but decided later that it was not a good idea. She said: 'They are not the same boys. Yet they do not all forget that which they learned.'

Although busy with the multifarious activities of the Camps, Margaret often thought of the degrading, depressing circumstances of the people in the neighbourhood, and of the ultimate aim behind all her experiments – the building of a better future for all mankind. After ruminating on this objective she wrote:

> Outside (as well as in the homes of those in the Camp) stalks the Spectre of Famine . . . It is all very strange, very cruel. No camp-school is worth anything that has not as its goal the making impossible of such things to-morrow.[23]

She yearned to help young and old at the sharp end of things to shake off ill-health, escape from their cultural desert and find a higher quality of life. But she felt that this needed to be tackled in a systematic fashion – camps for children one to five, then others for secondary age-groups. In 1914, she said:

> Why should we not have higher-grade camps and keep them until they are eighteen? . . . We could teach older children as easily as the younger, and they could have the benefit of the open-air life and all the advantages that richer children enjoy.[24]

Due in no small measure to the staff, the Camp School was a great success; despite hard work and poor conditions many of the teachers stayed there for years. Margaret's own personality and commitment to helping children elicited from all her work force the co-operation without which the School could not have functioned. She never treated her staff as puppets; they shared the decision-making with her; they were more than colleagues; they were partners in a joint enterprise. Yet it is clear from what her old scholars said that Margaret was the moving spirit behind an enterprise which brought great benefits and happiness to the children. Dorothy Lob recalled:

> One cannot think of one's schooldays and its happy memories without thinking of Miss McMillan. To me she *was* the Camp School. Her strong character and personality was always felt in her presence and in everything she said and did. I remember so well the way she would recite a certain poem she wished us to learn. She made one *see* Wordsworth's Daffodils fluttering and

dancing in the breeze! Her hands were full of expression – I used to watch them a lot. She would finger her long gold chain as she spoke to us. One incident I remember well, was on the occasion when the then Prime Minister, Stanley Baldwin, came to visit our school . . . I think it was always a proud moment for her when she was 'showing us off' to her celebrated visitors.

Another thing I can remember clearly was the time she was summoned to Buckingham Palace for lunch or tea with the late Queen Mary. She came into our classroom while waiting for the taxi (our classroom was the little hut by the gate) and told us where she was going, and that the next day she would tell us all about it . . .

On another occasion I well remember I had been off school with 'flu. She had missed me. After my first day back I don't think I saw her, but when I got home a young student was waiting on our doorstep and told me to come straight back with her as Miss McMillan wanted to see me. I was rather puzzled and bewildered, but upon entering her tiny sitting room she greeted me with open arms and said I certainly needed building up after 'flu. On the table were all sorts of things, calves' foot jelly, codliver oil and malt etc., which she gave me. She was indeed a wonderful woman . . .

Her image is still very prominent in my mind. I shall never, never forget her. She was so proud, so full of love, for her children and her school. She did so want us to be something useful in life and do great things. Not until one has grown up does one realize what she was striving to do . . . Where was there ever a school where the children were showered with so much love? What fun we had at Christmas parties – magic man, presents etc . . . visits to the 'Old Vic', Tower of London, British Museum, Albert Hall, besides many others. She would bundle as many of us as possible into a taxi – we were packed like sardines, but it was always great fun.

Gladys Woodhams, another old pupil, wrote:

The things that the school children do to-day were unheard of when we were little, but Miss McMillan came and opened new and wonderful doors for us . . .

Yes, to us she was all powerful, we could face anybody or anything with her beside us. I can still hear her saying – you may be poor now but if you want to there is nothing to stop you sitting in the House of Parliament. I remember too the morning when I must have been extra stupid and trying, and eventually the tears came and continued after the lesson had finished. Then on looking up there was Miss McMillan, putting her arms round me, telling me to stop crying and asking *me* to be friends again. I can still hear the gentleness in her voice.

How she enthralled us with her beloved Scottish songs, and the stories of her early life in America . . .

I recall her untiring efforts in teaching us to portray the works of Shakespeare, and how we had to understand the beauty and meaning of the words we were speaking . . . She always insisted that we never miss lessons, and would even have us by her bedside when she was too ill to get up.

She was a truly great person, stern, yes! How her eyes would flash at silly stupidness and laziness, but how gentle, patient and understanding the rest of the time.[25]

Many evaluations of the School indicate that it was a school of excellence. Hugh Railton Dent, the publisher, and Albert Mansbridge both designated it 'the finest venture in adolescent education we had ever seen'.[26] One Director of Education asserted after visiting the school, that the level of education in the eleven-year-old pupils was two years in advance of that in the schools of his county.[27] Robert Blatchford suggested that if we were a wise people 'we should make Miss McMillan Minister of Education'.[28]

Some members of the London County Council who viewed Margaret sceptically and thought her experiments irregular and administratively untidy, began to feel uneasy about the children of school age who attended the Camp School. Looking for reasons to close it down, they sent two inspectors to examine it. Dr Ballard, the senior inspector, reported:

We inspected the school – inspected it thoroughly. We examined, tested and questioned the children on all points. We left no aspect of the school unscrutinized. We made independent observations and gave independent tests. And when we compared notes we found that we had arrived at exactly the same conclusion. We agreed that this was not only a highly efficient school, but that it had points of excellence not to be found in any other school that we had ever seen. These children of the slums had a charm of manner and a grace of diction of which the best school in the land might justly have been proud. They spoke the mother tongue beautifully. They even recited 'Lochinvar' with a glorious Scottish accent, which hugely delighted my colleague, who was himself a Scotchman. We had looked at the school, we had found that it was very good, and we reported accordingly. The Camp School was safe.[29]

Wanting to keep abreast of up-to-date thinking about child-rearing, Margaret and Rachel went to America in the autumn of 1912 to attend a Conference on Education and Medicine in Washington, and stayed in America until Christmas Eve. They were widely received and visited the White House and met Mr Taft – the then President of the USA.[30]

Once back in Deptford Margaret again threw herself into the work of the School. Although it was deemed to be successful, she was dissatisfied; she searched incessantly for more effective ways of preventing ill-health and other problems of the disadvantaged. Asked what the leaders of the Labour Movement could do in the meantime to help her to help children, she began to articulate her feelings about the needs of pre-school children and replied:

> There are two practical proposals they might make when the Government's education proposals come before the House which would have immediate value. They should urge that money granted for the treatment of children should be made available for little ones below school age. And they should urge that a certain proportion of the huge sum of money that will probably be voted, should be earmarked for the promotion and encouragement of experimental schools run solely for the benefit of children and proved to be efficient . . . Expenditure in these two directions would be immediately productive.[31]

Margaret's ideas about prevention were part of a new stream of thinking which was currently flowing through the nation. Some put their faith in housing schemes as a means of preventing disease, others stressed legislation. Philip Snowden, in speaking on the National Insurance Act of 1911, said that one likely development of it was that the 'function of the medical service' would become 'increasingly preventive rather than curative', and that the activities of the medical profession would be 'devoted more and more to preventing disease'.[32] George Lansbury, writing after the 1910 election, said he was elected because he averred that the Socialist Party would work for prevention.[33]

Margaret's own views on the part open-air schools played in the prevention of disease spread far beyond Deptford. Writing in 1913 she said:

> It is pleasant, for example, to hear that in Wales the managers of a certain school . . . have decided that walls may slip back like folding doors and allow the classes of young Welsh girls and

boys to feel Heaven's breath on their cheeks as they learn their tasks . . . Fresh air is not a dangerous thing, but a blessing.[34]

Some of her ideas on school baths were taken up outside Britain. Some of her leaflets on hygiene were circulated in Germany, Austria and the United States. Some authorities based experiments on her ideas, some started but unfortunately did not always continue with them. Writing once when dispirited she said:

Though Bradford built baths, it was only seven years after that she began to use them as classrooms . . . London has practically no school baths, and the school children suffering from dirt diseases can be numbered by tens of thousands. How weary one grows of writing of all this! When will these times pass?[35]

Alongside the supervision of her different experiments, Margaret now began to turn more and more attention to the needs of children below five years of age. Having observed that children starting their compulsory schooling at five were already dirty and diseased she realised that true prevention needed to begin in the pre-school children and in homes.

Chapter sixteen

A Camp for Pre-school Children 1911–14

The important part played by the first five years of a child's life in the educative process has been recognised for over 2,000 years. The long list of philosophers and writers who subscribed to that view includes Plato, Comenius, Oberlin, Rousseau, Pestalozzi and Froebel, just to mention a few. Margaret McMillan, through her study of the writings of earlier educators and her own observations of children in Bradford and Deptford, belonged to the same school of thought.

Through her various experiments on behalf of disadvantaged children she gave fresh emphasis to that idea, and applied in practice theories which men from different disciplines were currently propounding. Speaking of the awakening interest in early childhood which she encountered she said:

> The new thinkers, the psychologists . . . began to show why the first five years of life are the most important of all . . . They told us how the first five years was the time of swift events and that destiny was settled then.[1]

Considering the needs of pre-school children in Deptford, she realised how little attention health and education agencies were giving to the 2–5 age group in particular. Yet during a child's first five years infectious diseases were often rife and the time before formal schooling was a vital period, when children were capable of learning skills quickly and effectively. The 1837 Notification of Births Act ensured some supervision of children up to their first birthday. Welfare centres, where they existed, concerned themselves with the health of babies from birth to two years; school doctors began to examine children at five and elementary schools catered for those above five. But for the vast majority of the nation's children, the years from 2–5 were years of preventable suffering and boredom. While Margaret was considering the best way of approaching this problem, she was precipitated into action by the pleas of Maureen, one of her Night Camp girls, who said:

> 'I don't half wish our Rosie could come here and play. She's only a nipper, Miss, just two – and she doesn't go to school yet. My mum says she's always under her feet.' . . . 'Maureen,' said Margaret, 'run home and ask mother if you may bring Rosie here, to spend the day . . .'
>
> Soon she returned, leading Rosie by the hand . . .
>
> 'We must open our doors to the toddlers, Rachel,' Margaret said as she watched her thoughtfully. 'We must plan the right kind of environment for them and give them sunshine, fresh air and good food before they become rickety and diseased.'[2]

Shortly after this, Margaret invited pre-school children in the district to come to Evelyn House and play in the long, narrow garden which she had made attractive with colourful flower beds. As the Night Camp girls were only there from 6 pm onwards, it could be used in the daytime as a safe playground.

Margaret knew the kind of homes these children were likely to come from because their older brothers and sisters were already in her Camp School. She was aware of the condition these children were likely to be in and the problems they would present. Nevertheless, believing that most diseases were curable and most habits could be changed, Margaret viewed the project optimistically. When the Baby Camp first opened in 1911 only six youngsters turned up. As Margaret expected, most of them came from poverty-striken, unstable families. Many mothers were out all day working and some fathers had left home.

Although the McMillans were keen educators, they saw the importance of developing healthy bodies before trying to train the mind. One journalist wrote of Margaret: 'She early saw, through her own observation, the truth which Havelock Ellis proclaimed in 1908: "Education has been put at the beginning when it ought to have been put at the end." '[3]

Once the children arrived – at a time convenient to their parents – the McMillans devised a simple, flexible timetable for them. Large blocks of time were allotted to free play in the fresh air. In the bathrooms provided for the Night Camp girls, children were washed and trained in hygienic habits. Later they were given plain, nourishing food, followed by rest in wooden cots made from banana crates. After the rest period, they played outside again and had tea before returning home.

Margaret watched the children carefully and would often modify her plans to meet individual needs. She never viewed children in the mass. A journalist who spent a day at Deptford gives us a picture of her individual care of children.

> Very little can escape her eyes. The little boy who has remained mentally and physically stationary for a whole year, a cretinoid, is now under observation and treatment, assured of the fullest attention and care, because Miss McMillan detected him among the fifty other boys in the camp. The other boy wearing a thick muffler under his sweater, overheated and on the way to catch a cold because his throat and chest are unnaturally muffled, finds himself face-to-face with her and gets a little lesson in an elementary principle of camp life.[4]

As news of the pre-school experiment spread, so the number of children in attendance grew and the need for extra staff and a larger site became apparent. Fortunately, Margaret found a suitably trained teacher – a Miss MacLeod – who was willing to help her. After discovering that one of her old Camp School girls was willing to be a nursery assistant, she promptly engaged both of them and presumed that, as always, the finance for this new venture would be found and that mothers would contribute according to their means to the running expenses. Margaret usually received the children and greeted their mothers; Rachel, when free, often supervised the children in the bathrooms. As this was a new venture, both of the sisters had to feel their way and adopt a pragmatic approach to the daily programme.

Reviewing the way her work always seemed to be branching out in new directions, Margaret said:

> In some curious way, which I cannot explain, the work seemed, nevertheless, to be always opening out and finding a way for itself, almost, as it seemed, without our design or desire. Like a tiny streamlet, it found a way.[5]

Due in large measure to Joseph Fels, this humble beginning with the pre-school children at Evelyn House grew first into the Baby Camp, then into the large Open-air Nursery School, for which Margaret became nationally and internationally renowned.

In 1913, just a few months before Fels died, he wrote to the London County Council pointing out that the Stowage, an acre of vacant land in front of the Deptford Clinic, could be used to great advantage by the McMillan sisters. The Stowage, so named because at one time Thames smugglers hid 'the stuff' there, had been earmarked for a three-storey elementary school, but as the Council did not intend using it immediately, because of a decline in the local child population, they decided to let it to Margaret.

They offered the site at a rent of a shilling a year, with the free use of a house on it, but only on condition that the agreement could be terminated at a day's notice. However, from that time to this, the Stowage has been in continuous use for nursery school purposes.

Despite the absence of any security of tenure on the Stowage, the sisters with characteristic courage accepted the LCC's offer, levelled the ground, and made a play area and garden. Then they started to design buildings for the Baby Camp. Margaret recalls how the task of planning the first building fell on Rachel.

> Very early in 1914 I was stricken by illness and laid up in a nursing home for weeks . . . So Rachel was left alone to plan the first open-air nursery . . . she designed the first shelter and bathroom and saw the plan carried out by the builder-caretaker of Evelyn House.[6]

The Baby Camp building was simple, and witnessed to the sisters' belief in the value of fresh air and the need for cheap, functional buildings. It comprised a series of sheds, open at the sides, and equipped with good toilet facilities. Margaret said that they were not ideal but that they were a vast improvement on indoor schools; they offered space and moving air. The McMillans called the buildings shelters; they envisaged that children would play out in the garden whenever the weather allowed and only use the buildings as shelters from bad weather. When the first shelter was completed in March 1914, Margaret, with the help of a handcart, moved the equipment from Evelyn House to the Stowage and the group of twelve pre-school children took possession of the larger site.

Children attending this new camp were expected to stay there all night just as members of the Boys' and Girls' Camps did. Margaret tells the next part of the story.

> They were not to go 'home' at night, but to camp out in this strange new house. This was found to be, on the whole, very amusing . . . The school had thirty children in steady attendance ere April was far spent. And the way these children flourished astonished everyone . . . the doctors say that they could not have foreseen and had not expected this triumph of little children. It was new – this kind of school – like the aeroplanes and the wireless.[7]

Margaret was delighted to see how these children, many of whom lived in cellars, enjoyed the space in the Camp, the good food, the bathing, the rest periods and play facilities. Thinking of this she wrote:

On warm evenings, after the bath, they would run in couples, these little three and four-year-olds, down the length of the oblong shelter and back, rejoicing that there were no tables, no chairs, no rules to keep them any more from this new, strange life and movement. They ran and ran and would hardly stop running . . . Life fell in new rhythms – of sleep and waking, play and rest . . . Meals were a new kind of experience and carried new joys. Sleep. It was a pleasant and renewing world . . . The camp grew lovelier and the children more resistant.[8]

After the outbreak of World War I, when married women were needed in the munition factories, Margaret undertook to open her doors to their children, many of them babies, and in return received a government grant of seven pence per day for each munition worker's child. This supplemented her scanty finances.

When munition workers brought babies only a few months old, then nurses were required to look after them. But as the war went on good nurses became less easy to obtain. Many members of the nursing profession joined the armed forces. Because of staff shortages, the Camp became increasingly difficult to run and extra strain fell on the two sisters. Although they trained a number of young girls as nursery assistants they were constantly in need of additional help. One teacher who applied for a job there at this time tells of her experiences.

In November 1914 I went to Deptford to be interviewed by Miss Margaret McMillan who wanted a teacher to run her Babies' Camp. I found a tall rather ungainly woman with a large rather heavy face, sallow complexion, and big luminous eyes . . . I think she told me a little about the Camp . . . but what I do remember clearly is that she brought the interview to an end by saying, 'I don't know anything about you but I like your face'. And then she asked me to come for a month and see how I got on . . .

She left me very much by myself to run the school but occasionally she would wander round and see how things were getting on . . . Rachel cooked the mid-day meal for her sister, herself, and the tiny teaching staff (and what entertaining meals they often were, with Margaret to lead the conversation).[9]

However acute the staff shortages, and however difficult the running of the Camp became, the McMillans never shrank from the personal cost; their eyes were set on the advantages the Camp offered children. Writing of this time, Margaret exclaimed:

To let them live at last and have the sight of people planting and digging, to let them run and work and experiment, sleep, have regular meals, the sights and sounds of winter and spring, autumn and summer . . . to get these things we sacrificed everything else.[10]

When the children's gains in weight were monitored[11] the results gratified the sisters. But despite the children's appreciable progress, Margaret was not allowed to continue her experiment without opposition. Many neighbours were extremely vocal. Margaret tells us:

At first, and for a long time, the neighbours said, 'You will never dare to let them sleep out. What if a storm came on, and at night?' We had no answer, but the babies had a good answer ready. For when the rain descended and the flood came and the thunder roared they slept right through the storm and woke in the morning as unconscious and merry as birds.[12]

The children continued to eat and sleep outside and stay at the Camp from Monday to Saturday for the first years. But by the autumn of 1917 *The Crèche News* was reporting a change in procedure.

It is not at present found possible to keep the Camp guests for the whole week, as used to be done; now they go home to sleep. During the day, however, they receive three meals: lunch, dinner and supper. The rest of the day is spent in play, in sleep, and for the children over four years of age, in play-education.[13]

While Margaret was convinced that her first task was to build up children's bodily health, the question of how to educate the mind continually exercised her. Pondering this she felt that life in the fresh air would help children to grow and develop mentally, as well as physically, and wrote:

We have to find means to let the young live and move in close intimacy with the forces, and changes that develop not only the muscular brute force organs, but the higher and finer nerve processes and brain centres as well. To understand this is to understand education and the rest is mere padding.[14]

As a student of Séguin's work, Margaret had come to believe that the senses lie at the base of intellect, and that man first perceives through them. Consequently she tried to give her children such experiences as would assist sense development. Experiences, she said, filled the well-springs of the subconscious life 'long before any impression is tossed higher into the consciousness'.

Thinking of the garden, which she was still in the process of creating round the shelter, she realised that here was an instructive environment which could be used for sense training and other educational purposes – an environment which children would not have otherwise. So she planned to exploit the garden to the full for the youngest as well as the oldest children. When a child was awake his cot would be moved about the garden so that, she declared: 'His vague and wondering gaze is arrested, it may be by the bright foliage of a rosebush, or the tossing green of the privet hedge.'[15]

According to Margaret, many of the children had had their senses dulled, if not perverted, before arriving at the Camp. Some of the young babies already knew 'the taste of ale, or vinegar and even of pickles. But they are glad enough to start on a better system and have better experiences.'[16]

Explaining how she helped children to develop their sense of smell in the garden, where she had deliberately planted many herbs including mint, lavender, sage, thyme and rosemary, as well as many roses, she wrote:

> The toddlers go round the beds of herbs, pinching the leaves with their tiny fingers and then putting their fingers to their noses. Coming back with odorous hands, they perhaps want to tell us about the journey . . . But besides the herb garden, there are Roses . . . And they are so low-growing, just tall enough for toddlers . . . Gustav Grunerwald and W. R. Smith have a row of tiny worshippers smelling them and gazing at them hand in hand.[17]

Throughout her planning for the Camp she tried to devise a curriculum of relevance. Describing how, as well as planning for sense training, she worked on the muscular system and helped children whose muscles were weak through want of exercise, she said:

> We furnished the Baby Camp more or less as an open-air gymnasium . . . There are low steps to climb, there are hillocks and planed tree-stumps. Children frisk up these little hills and down again. One is reminded of lambs all the time.[18]

Because children were not taught to speak properly at home, she gave practice in pronunciation, but felt this, like other language learning, could be done informally whilst a nurse was washing or dressing a child. Handkerchief drill she felt was essential if children were to learn to speak well; they could not make distinct sounds with blocked nostrils. So she encouraged children to bring hankies, then taught them to enunciate nursery rhymes and jingles clearly.

Much time was spent too on helping children develop independence, self-esteem and confidence. They were taught to wash and dress themselves; ears, necks, eyes and teeth were regularly inspected. 'These things have to be learned and learned early', Margaret said.

> Elsa, a timid, helpless child of three, put on her coat frontwise. Then she held it wrong way up, but after a good many trials got it on alone. Then (as it had only one button, and that a big one), she finished this new task and was very proud.[19]

The older children were given more advanced tasks. As members of a community they learned to serve others in setting the dinner tables and Margaret saw the positioning of cutlery as a preparation for the teaching of reading. These children also learned to draw and write. In the garden she hoped they would learn to discriminate, to compare and classify plants and that this would help them when they came to do arithmetic later. Singing, dancing and listening to stories were a regular feature in the Camp and when children were thought to be mature enough they were taught the beginning of reading.

As Margaret observed children growing and developing so she devised schemes to meet their new stages. Not only did she care for their physical and intellectual development but also for their all-round growth. She believed that a beginning could be made in fostering emotional and spiritual development through the love shown in 'the smile of welcoming faces and the touch of gentle hands'. Social graces she hoped to encourage at mealtimes.

After children had been in the Camp for some time their parents began to notice a difference in them. Margaret too saw how much they had improved physically and benefited from the Camp life. When she compared new entrants with older campers she believed there were gains other than physical. Commenting on this she maintained:

> The newcomers . . . are not so much alive as the others, and in them the real effect of indoor and street life on the nervous system is seen only too plainly. It is they who tread down things, who break young stems and tear blossoms . . . It is not they who grow excited over the silk-weavers who eat the mulberry leaves, and who ask questions about the dark chrysalis and butterflies, the tadpoles, and the fish. Frozen and stiff are many of the newcomers.[20]

These results, especially the spirit of enquiry she saw in the older children, encouraged Margaret to believe that the Baby Camp was an experiment worth developing, that it was the beginning of something new in education and could be provided relatively cheaply – cheaper than a system of fostering. While a place for one child in her Camp cost the parents no more than two shillings a week, foster-mothers in the district charged between six and eight shillings. So she thought it likely that mothers would welcome a service of this nature, and that it could set the feet of many children on firm foundations.

During these pioneering years in Deptford, Margaret maintained her many wider interests and commitments. The Workers' Education Association, with Mansbridge at the helm, was one of the many societies which she supported, because she was eager for adults as well as children to share the benefits of education. Appointed to its Executive Committee in 1910, she served with enthusiasm for many years. As well as undertaking committee work for the Association, sometimes she spoke at WEA Summer Schools, and was photographed at the 1912 Oxford gathering of the Association with William Temple, the future Archbishop of Canterbury, on the lawn at Balliol.

The Feminist Movement was another of Margaret's commitments. From her Bradford days she had been concerned about the sweated labour and poor working conditions of women in industry. However, as progress towards reform on women's questions was so slow, she was drawn into the struggle for women's education and suffrage and frequently spoke and wrote about the need for women to become involved in politics. Believing that they should have a share in shaping laws, she urged them to take part in decision-making locally through membership of such committees as were open to them.

In working for women's emancipation she did not seek to embroil her sex in fierce competition with men; she aimed to enlist them in a fight for equality for all people and a struggle against injustice and discrimination. Once closed doors were open to women, she believed, they would be able to make their own contribution to society and bring their wisdom and feminine qualities to public life.

Addressing a gathering of the Women's Freedom League at Joseph Fels's home in 1908, she said:

> This world – this wretched world! – has need of women. The whole population is debased by the existence of an immense

number of persons who never have enough to eat, and this will never be put right unless women come into the arena with new power, new impulses, and new love.[21]

She longed for women to be able to influence public opinion, but felt they were hampered in this because they had no vote. Writing on 'The Case for the Industrial Women' in *The Men's League Handbook*, she maintained:

Women have no Parliamentary vote . . . how can millions of voteless working women influence the destinies of their country in a beneficent and effective way? . . . There is now no turning back. Every path has been closed except the road to votes and higher education for all women.[22]

So for several years, inside and outside the ILP, she fought for women to be granted the franchise. Because she believed in non-violent methods, Margaret was a suffragist rather than a suffragette. Suffragists held meetings, distributed leaflets, arranged peaceful demonstrations, used non-disruptive methods and kept within the law. But suffragettes damaged public property, engaged in violent acts and broke the law.

The Labour Party was divided on the issue of women's suffrage. There was agreement in principle, but strong disagreement on the voting rights to be given. It was argued that giving women identical voting rights with men might increase the political power of many upper- and middle-class propertied women, and thus be a gift to the Tory Party. Some Labour politicians feared that the granting of votes to some women might damage the prospect of universal suffrage for all men, and that they should support complete adult suffrage both for men and women.

The Independent Labour Party was inclined to be sympathetic towards women's suffrage and put it in the forefront of its programme. Mrs Pankhurst, the leader of the militant suffragettes, was one of Margaret's colleagues on the National Administrative Council of the ILP for many years. Although agreed on the need for suffrage, they disputed the means to it.

Both Keir Hardie and Margaret spoke openly in favour of women's suffrage, when to do so in Labour circles was to court unpopularity. At the 1907 Annual ILP Conference, where many members of the party showed they were not in agreement with votes for women, Hardie said publicly he would be ashamed to belong to a party that turned its back on women. He wanted adult suffrage and wanted 'to let the women feel that, whoever deserted them, the Socialists of Great Britain would stand by them until they were political equals'.[23]

At the same meeting, Margaret stated that women were political outcasts, and stood in an entirely different relation to the political issues of the day than men, but that this injustice needed to be fought wisely. She declared 'She was in favour of taking one step at a time to reach the goal, rather than trying to put undue pressure on the Government as the suffragettes were doing.'[24]

Between 1907 and 1912, a succession of Private Members' Bills before Parliament, proposing to extend the franchise to women, came to nothing. This exasperated suffragists and suffragettes alike and led suffragettes to become increasingly militant. Those in the Women's Social and Political Union, founded by Mrs Pankhurst in 1903, felt that as rational argument had failed, force was now the only way open to them.

Once Mrs Pankhurst publicly stated that the time had come to attack property, suffragettes smashed windows and set fire to empty houses, churches and railway stations and engaged in activities which brought them into confrontations with the police; some of them were imprisoned. Then, seeking to secure public attention as well as their early release, they went on hunger strikes. The government's response to this was to order forcible feeding. Nurses and wardresses were directed to hold women down while prison doctors pushed tubes into their mouths thus forcing them to take nourishment. This regulation outraged the McMillans; moderate men and women who were not particularly in sympathy with suffragettes were revolted by it too.

Eventually, public opinion compelled the authorities to find an alternative to forcible feeding and a way of avoiding hunger strikes. When Parliament passed The Prisoners (Temporary Discharge for Ill Health) Act in April 1913, women were allowed to be set free on licence for recuperation purposes, but were made subject to re-arrest. This Act, which soon became known as 'The Cat and Mouse Act', was hardly more acceptable than forcible feeding. Consequently, feminists decided to work for its repeal and the McMillans too became involved.

During the summer of 1913, they took part in a demonstration outside the Houses of Parliament, which was meant to be peaceful but became violent. Margaret describes the incident:

When the Cat and Mouse Bill came into operation . . . we joined
a committee . . . and went with many other women to the House
of Commons, with a protest signed by a great number of people
. . . we reached the House and mounted the steps leading to the
foyer in front of the ante-room, whose swinging doors were
closed to us. There we stood a long time . . . suddenly a force of

policemen swung down on us like a Highland regiment. We were tossed like dust down the steps . . . A moment later, I was on the floor, the crowd behind flung over me in their wild descent. Then I saw a policeman and Rachel standing over me, he dragging me up, she holding her arm behind me.[25]

Rachel maintained that Margaret would have been killed if she had not been there to pick her up. Reporting the débâcle, *The Christian Commonwealth* said:

Miss Margaret McMillan, whose very appearance in the group should have been a protection to her . . . was frightfully ill-treated. She was thrown violently and deliberately down the steps, and lay prostrate while the mob of policemen surged and stumbled over her. Happily, some of the police picked her up and pushed her before them, or she would unquestionably have been trampled to death . . . Miss McMillan was to have spoken at the evening meeting in Kingsway Hall but was too bruised and shaken to appear. One felt the surge of hot anger which thrilled the meeting when the fact was announced.[26]

Future novelist Rebecca West, then a political writer for *The Clarion*, wrote indignantly about what she saw.

I do not know whether you have ever seen an elderly and heavily built lady thrown down a flight of stairs by half a dozen policemen. It gives one a peculiar buzzing sensation in the head. And when you look again and see that two more elderly ladies behind her are being thrown from side to side as dockers pass sacks of grain into the hold, the sensation increases . . . The first elderly lady is pitched forward on the dusty pavement, and is seen to be Miss Margaret McMillan.

Miss West went on to speak of Margaret as 'one of the few constructive statesmen of this country'.[27]

Thinking back over this incident, Margaret recalled:

This was the only time when I ever saw Rachel stirred to real and deep resentment . . . the iron had entered her soul. She appealed to various members of the House to make impossible the recurrence of such violence to persons engaged in a peaceful mission. Quite in vain. She was not flouted – but ignored.[28]

Margaret was so seriously hurt that she was forced to cancel all her speaking engagements for several weeks. While she was recovering from the effects of this encounter with the police, in August 1913, Rachel decided to relinquish her employment in

Kent, in order to work with Margaret full-time. From this time onwards both of them could be seen regularly in Deptford's streets. They were known leaders in a locality short of initiators. By now neither sister had an assured income of any kind. They had a little family money, were content to live economically and trust to providence. A friend who called on them told of their frugality, saying she saw them sit down to 'a meal of a cup of tea and a bloater'. They had to struggle to make ends meet. Lowndes reported:

> In reality money had but one meaning to them. It helped their work. All they could get out of their own small personal store, from their friends, or from public resources went willy-nilly into the common stock . . . Margaret never understood 'money' any more than a child understands a 'key'. It worked. If she thought that the organisation for which she lectured needed the money more than she did, it went back.[29]

After recovering from her injuries at the Cat and Mouse demonstration, Margaret took a renewed interest in the welfare of her socialist friends. Not infrequently she used her pen to help those facing hardship – those laid low by sickness and unable to work. Her article 'A Pioneer',[30] in *The Labour Leader*, is typical of the many she wrote pleading for money for staunch ILP members who had fallen on bad times.

Sometimes she was busy with groups of students and teachers who, from as early as 1914, visited Deptford to talk to her about her work for pre-school children. At other times she left Rachel in charge while she went away to lecture on school clinics or open new ones. Lord Sanderson of Ascott reports:

> In 1913, my wife, who had met Margaret McMillan and had become much interested in her work, started a school clinic at Ascott – one of the earliest experiments of the kind in a rural area – and Margaret McMillan came down to open it.[31]

It is hardly surprising that amidst all these activities Margaret was sometimes so fatigued that her friends became anxious about her. Mansbridge stated that in March 1914 the Mayor of Deptford wrote to her:

> A large body of friends, many of them working folk, are very anxious you should have a complete rest. They have asked me to become the intermediary for sending you the enclosed cheque for £25, and a similar amount for the next six months. It is, of course, their desire that you should devote this sum entirely to your personal benefit.

Margaret McMillan

Apparently not satisfied that she intended to use the money as the contributors intended, in April he wrote again:

'As Trustee of the Fund I do feel that I owe it to your friends to guarantee that the money shall be used in the manner that they wish and not simply for your work . . .' Her answer to this has not been preserved.[32]

Margaret became increasingly involved in developing her plans for pre-school children, but unfortunately a more systematic working out of her ideas for a pioneer Open-air Nursery School had to be delayed. First war and then personal tragedy were to interrupt her progress.

Chapter seventeen

With Rachel in the War Years 1914–17

At the end of the first term at the Stowage, in July 1914, Margaret and Rachel went to Norway for a holiday. Unfortunately after a short stay the Norwegians urged them to depart. Margaret tells us:

'You must go,' they said to all the visitors, 'War is declared. England is going into it . . . Take the train to Bergen at once, and you will get home' . . . At Bergen, crowds were waiting with trunks on the quay, and only by special favour and pleading were we allowed to go on the crowded ship bound for Newcastle.[1]

Margaret was not only surprised by the outbreak of war on 4 August, she was deeply distressed by it. Believing firmly in a brotherhood of nations, war was abhorrent to her. With her comrades in the ILP, she had struggled to establish an international order in which humanity gave of its best to each nation, and each nation gave of its best to humanity. That was her dream but now it was shattered.

She arrived in Deptford with a heavy heart, only to find that events there depressed her further. Recalling this time she explained:

When we got back to Deptford in August 1914, we found that Deptford and all its people were changed . . . Hitherto our staff had been a stable one. We had all worked in a spirit of mutual trust and fellowship. Now all this was changed. War had breathed upon them all like poison fumes rising from the pit . . . Our good caretaker threw off the mask of years and stole all the clinic sugar and camp groceries. Everything in the way of stores vanished. The cook left suddenly, carrying off with her the Sunday joint. This was only the beginning . . . But above all, the Nursery School was in danger.[2]

Soon Margaret had difficulty in obtaining and retaining teachers and nurses. Conditions in her school were poor, the equipment was primitive and jobs elsewhere were plentiful. Because men were called up for national service, women teachers were at a premium. Nurses, attracted by the uniform, new comradeship and the possibility of foreign travel, were keen to join the forces. Margaret's staff became birds-of-passage; some didn't even bother to give notice, they just disappeared.

Then there were air raids. Zeppelins dropped bombs which created havoc throughout the district. Some parents and children were killed in their own homes. Some disturbed people vented their spleen on the McMillans and their Baby Camp. ' "They're Germans," said one. "Their nurses doan stop wif 'em," cried another . . . "How can you expect girls to stay in a danger zone?" asked parents . . . But they were clear that we were to blame in some way.'[3]

Often the sisters were left to look after the babies by themselves. In addition, they were asked to take full responsibility for two boys – Peter and Totty – aged seven and five. Their mother had died and their father, a miner, had enlisted. The sisters accepted the children, took them to live with them at Evelyn House and kept them until the father was released from the Army. One of Margaret's trainees recalled: 'The elder, Peter, was deaf but Margaret got a surgeon to deal with this and he recovered his hearing . . . Totty suffered from rickets on arrival but was given the means of getting over it.'[4] After a week Totty fell desperately ill. Margaret reported:

> Rachel nursed him . . . Sometimes she sat up with him at night, holding him long in her arms. 'He will die,' said three doctors. A week later, he sat up in bed and looked out at the deep, dormer window and asked for 'all me toys'. Rachel had bought him a great many. She had also brought him back from the grave.[5]

Margaret took a lifelong interest in these boys. Unfortunately Totty contracted tuberculosis and died aged eighteen. After that the father went to America with his remaining son and settled there. Margaret often thought of Peter and left him £100 in her will.

As the war continued the staffing problems worsened. Many people moved away from London to safer places. Some of the people Margaret managed to employ turned out to be liabilities rather than helpers. Some were highly critical of her work and scornful of her equipment.

'We engaged two Belgian refugee teachers,' Margaret reported

. . . 'One of them was a good teacher and gave good lessons . . . She had a great contempt for our "meeserable furniture", for our shelters, our tables – everything; and she assured our now wildly oscillating staff that we could not go on long. "Thees place will be taken away from them", she said. Even our faithful clinic staff were inclined to believe her. I had fears, too.'[6]

When Margaret was away either lecturing or on committee work, Rachel was in sole charge. It was Rachel who stood in for absent staff after night raids. Speaking of such an occasion, Margaret reported: 'Rachel might have looked sad as she worked alone, she looked strangely happy . . . A kind of exultant look came to her at times. It was not the look of one who succeeds, but of one who obeys.'[7]

In June 1915, Margaret was re-elected to the National Administrative Council of the ILP. While Hardie topped the poll with 264 votes, she was third from the bottom with only 60. This low poll may have been due to her increasing involvement with her Deptford experiments.

Hardie died in September 1915 a broken man. One of his friends wrote:

In the outbreak of war he saw the madness of mankind in the furious struggling which he believed would never occur, and to a body overworked, the shock of the European conflict and the spectacle of Socialists fighting and divided, added the signs of a broken heart.[8]

While his death robbed thousands of a much loved comrade and fellow fighter for justice, it also made many, like Margaret, all the more determined to carry on his struggle.

Despite wartime conditions, which made her work in Deptford even more onerous, Margaret wrote forward-looking articles for different newspapers which aimed to instil hope and inspire courage. In *The Teacher's World* in 1916, she gave her vision of what teachers might contribute to the nation after the war.

There is little doubt that England's future will depend largely on her schooling, for, though the schools cannot create a great race, yet they must in future determine whether any race can keep abreast of the demands of the new and transformed world. We cannot draw (as we must) on a large supply of skilled labour and original thinkers if the schools do not help to equip these.[9]

As well as writing she continued to speak at public meetings, in spite of the difficulty of travelling. For instance, she spoke on

'Votes for Women' at the National Union of Women Teachers'
Conference at Buxton in 1916, and wherever she went she tried to
raise morale.

In addition to writing and speaking Margaret received many
visitors in her Baby Camp. Some appreciated her experiments,
some went away critical. Speaking of the latter she reported:

> Some noted that we had not the things that were needed to give
> us full success. They went away and shrugged their shoulders.
> They would do things better than this. They have done nothing
> better than this. If we had grants for the Camp School, then we
> could do better. 'After all,' I said once, 'it is the germ of a great
> tree.' 'Not of a tree – a forest,' said Rachel. So we went on,
> though at times we were ashamed.[10]

Sometimes even Margaret herself doubted whether the general
public would ever understand what they were trying to do as her
remark to Rachel shows: ' "Oh Rachel!" I said to her again and
again. "No one wants it. No one cares. What you see, nobody else
will see." '[11]

As the war continued, conditions grew worse. Eventually, after
one of the biggest raids on Deptford, Rachel and Margaret left
their home at Evelyn House and went to live at the Stowage; later
they had to close the Night Camp and send the children home
every night. This meant children went back to the poor living
conditions from which they had been rescued and some of them
died soon afterwards.

When mothers, doctors and nurses said those early deaths
could not be helped, the sisters felt they were trying to excuse the
inexcusable. 'It *could* be helped,' Rachel said. 'There would be no
great difficulty in saving them all if we will it. For it is a question of
building up these little bodies, of giving them new life in the
sunshine.'[12]

Rachel gladly spent herself for the children and they responded
to her love for them. Speaking of her Miss Stevinson said:

> She bathed and tended her babies herself when skilled help
> could not be obtained, and it was her loving hands which lent
> refinement to the poor equipment. All the ailing babies, we are
> told, held out their little arms to 'Miss Rachel' – and she
> instinctively knew which of her little ones needed her most.[13]

Though her spirit remained willing and buoyant, wartime
conditions were taking their toll on Rachel's strength. After weeks
of exceptionally heavy work, one of the cleaners noticed that she
looked ill. When Margaret was told this she hurried home, only to

find Rachel entertaining some of their many visitors. After they left, Margaret took a closer look at Rachel. She was so disturbed that she suggested they went away for a holiday, but at first Rachel refused to leave Deptford.

'Strange!' she said, 'how I feel – we must not let go here.' A little later she said: 'Yes! Let us go away for a little while and take the boys.' The boys flung into the room at this moment. They were well now, thanks to my sister. 'Miss Rachel,' said the younger, 'if I was in town and if I had a penny, I would buy you some medicine.'[14]

They all went to Hastings but had only been there two days when news reached them of a relative's death. So, taking Peter and Totty back to Deptford, they set off for Edinburgh.

After their return to Deptford, they were harassed by repeated air raids. Thinking of one perilous evening Margaret recalled:

The Zeppelin hung over the 'Plume of Feathers.' . . . 'I ain't bin as good a woman as I'd orter be,' said the fat little cook, wiping her eyes. 'I orter 'a' thought more o' me 'usbing in 'orspital.' In that moment the Zeppelin rose with a lovely gliding movement and sailed gently away.[15]

A week later the raids began again. Margaret relates how one night Rachel woke her and advised her to get up and rouse the boys.

A terrific blast struck the house as we went downstairs. I looked up and saw that Rachel had not followed us . . . She had just time to join us when a third crash sent all our windows in, and the ironwork along the outer wall . . . A policeman's torch appeared at the great open place where glass had once been. He looked at us in amazement. 'Is there anyone here?' he said. 'Yes,' we said, 'we are here.' 'You're in a hot corner,' he observed, and disappeared as suddenly as he came. There were deaths around the corner.[16]

After one of the raids, Margaret became ill with septicaemia. Rachel, as well as nursing her, looked after the Camp and was determined to keep it open. Margaret tells us:

Once, when, owing to some little mischance, the Head closed for the day, Rachel was vexed. 'It is just because it is all so hard,' she said . . . she was busy from morning to night observing and looking after the weak children and sometimes even teaching (for we never closed the school for older children) . . . she did not believe in the primrose path, but in the joyful goal.[17]

Still the raids continued, until in the end, utterly worn out, Margaret and Rachel went to Chelsfield near Orpington to rest for five weeks, taking with them Peter and Totty. After so many disturbed nights in the city, they were glad to be away and took delight in seeing the fields and the hedgerows 'wreathed in tangles and bunches of "traveller's joy" '. At Christmas they made a party for the children. Then on Boxing Day, the boys danced with glee because their father came home on leave and took them to Manchester for the New Year.

Soon after the boys' departure, the McMillans found new rooms in Farnborough – four miles away from Bromley. In their exhausted state they half hoped that Peter and Totty wouldn't return for a while, but they did. The father brought them on his way back to Flanders saying that they wouldn't stay away; they just longed to return to Deptford. So the sisters found a nearby school for them and Margaret began to travel to Deptford two or three times a week. Sometimes the bus services were disrupted, and on occasion, after a long day at the Camp, Margaret had to walk the last four miles in the dark. But whatever hour she arrived, Rachel was always there to greet her.

In March 1917 they decided to take up residence again at Evelyn House and only to return to Farnborough for the weekends. But ere long Rachel became utterly exhausted. A doctor was called; medicines were prescribed, but her condition steadily deteriorated. She went downhill so rapidly that death seemed imminent. Though she spoke infrequently, her thoughts always centred on others. She managed to say to Margaret:

'I don't want to leave you' . . . 'Try to be very brave, Margaret,' . . . Her thoughts wandered then to the desolate children she had rescued. 'Poor little Peter . . Totty . . .' They were her last words. Earlier in the week she had asked Margaret to send for an Edinburgh cousin . . . 'She will be tired.' said Rachel in a characteristic way. 'Tell her to rest at Carlisle.'[18]

Rachel died on her birthday, 25 March 1917, aged 58. While hundreds of Deptford's parents and children lost a true friend, for Margaret it was more; she not only lost her last remaining close relative, but a partner who shared her life's purpose. Margaret was stunned by her bereavement – she could not grasp what had happened, this was the greatest blow of her life. For a time her grief knew no bounds. She blamed herself for not noticing Rachel's fatigue sooner. She felt she had failed the one who was closest to her. Of the funeral Margaret wrote:

On 28th March we laid her to rest in Brockley Cemetery. Mr and Mrs Mansbridge were with me. It was a very small funeral. But the children were there – all our older camp children. They stood round her grave, wistful, astonished, and laid their offerings of spring flowers at her feet.[19]

Chapter eighteen

State Provision of Nursery Schools 1917–19

After admitting pre-school children to her garden at Evelyn House in 1911, and her Baby Camp at the Stowage in 1914, Margaret was totally convinced of the need for more nursery schools and that the state should face up to its responsibility for providing them. But governments seemed to be reluctant to become involved with provision for children below school age. However, kindergarten and nursery school teachers who had long been convinced of the beneficial results of pre-school education were shortly to feel that at last their dreams of nursery expansion would come true.

Soon after H. A. L. Fisher – an outstanding President of the Board of Education – was appointed in 1916 by Lloyd George to plan the reconstruction of education in the post-war era, he began work on an Education Bill which became a milestone in the history of education in England and Wales. Once it was known that he was thinking about new legislation, representatives of different sections of education sought the opportunity of putting their views before him.

Unfortunately, when much of this was taking place, Margaret, who normally would have been in the heart of agitation for nursery schools, was still benumbed by Rachel's death. Her grief was so excessive that she was unable to take an interest in her own Baby Camp, let alone in the possibility of a new Education Bill. From this time to the end of her life, she gave Rachel the credit for everything that had been accomplished in Deptford and believed that her influence lived on: 'My sister's life-work being done, grows every year in significance . . . It seems as if it could not perish and fade away,'[1] she wrote. Mansbridge declared that after her loss, Margaret was always ready to explore ideas about the after-life but 'never went to a séance or consulted a medium'.[2] However, she was not allowed to remain in the slough of despondency for long. One of her friends recollected: 'One day she distinctly heard Rachel's voice saying to her "Margaret, I am tired of your grief, when will you get on with our work?" '³ This acted as a spur in her flank. Interests which had been held in check by personal sorrow began to stir in her again. Mansbridge believed that she felt that she owed it to Rachel to be interested in the experiments at the Stowage: 'She had to discharge her debt to Rachel . . . but she was obviously hungering for the old human touch.'⁴

Margaret only regained her interest in practical issues slowly, but a new incentive came from an unexpected quarter. A friend left Rachel a legacy of £1,200 the very day after her funeral, and straightway Margaret decided to spend it on rebuilding and extending the four-year-olds' shelter, and make that a memorial to her sister.

Planning began at once, although by the terms of the site agreement the LCC could have evicted her from the Stowage at a day's notice. Being firmly convinced that her work with pre-school children was destined to continue, she spent the whole of the legacy on the extension, plus £500 provided by the Board of Education. Thinking about her tenuous hold of the site and her faith in the work being carried on there, she wrote:

> We are here by the kindness of the L.C.C., who allow us to have the ground rent free so long as they are not using it. 'And if they should want it, where would your work be?', it may be asked. The answer is: Nothing will destroy the work done here.⁵

Within a few months the new building providing extra accommodation for 30 children, together with a memorial room to Rachel, neared completion. At this point, Margaret, who knew many of the nation's leaders personally and often asked influential men and women to visit Deptford, invited H. A. L. Fisher to open her new premises and he accepted.

Although Margaret's short-term aim was a better start in life for the children in Deptford, her vision was better chances for young children everywhere. Speaking of the two million children who had little or no nursery education, she wrote:

> The street is still the only playground of poor little toddlers and of older children too, where, nearly every week, some find violent death or life-long deformity and weakness. It was not the sudden end that shocked my sister most. It was the deliberate neglect that issued in spoiled lives and characters.⁶

For all children to have nursery education, Margaret knew that more than voluntary effort was required; the state needed to provide schools. So this was a particularly propitious moment for her to have an encounter with the President of the Board of Education. By the time of their meeting, Fisher had already decided to include clauses about nursery schools in his 1917 Education Bill, which he was due to present to Parliament for its first reading in ten days' time. At the opening of the newly-christened Rachel McMillan Baby Camp, on 3 August 1917, he and Sir Robert Morant spoke of Margaret's pioneer work in education. Fisher was reported as saying that the McMillans had

> seen some of the fundamental truths of education: that the education process begins at a very early stage, the close connection between education and health . . . the value of the open-air and the importance of unremitting attention to the minor ailments of the child.[7]

Admitting that at the time his department did not give grants for nursery education, he believed that those who showed initiative and originality should at least 'receive ample encouragement and a large measure of freedom from the Department of Education'.

In her reply, Margaret emphasised that 'she did not wish to open a place for minding babies': it was a school she had opened and hoped children would be able to stay there not just until they were five, but up to seven. Real reform in education she stressed was to be found in the kind of preventive work that nurseries attempted.[8]

Sir Robert Morant, who as former Permanent Secretary to the Board of Education had first-hand knowledge of the difficulties Margaret had faced in setting up her experimental establishment, commended her vision and determination saying that at the beginning people called Margaret's pre-school establishment 'a wild-cat scheme . . . But there was tremendous faith and energy behind it. It needed that to get it a chance of germinating and to fight for it against all the barbed wire entanglements of officialdom.'[9]

Sir Robert added that when the nursery school idea was taken up on a wider scale they must all try to ensure that it was not spoiled. Replying, Fisher said: ' "this venture should not be allowed to fail . . . it would serve as a working model of a nursery school," and he hoped that it would have "imitators all over the country".'[10]

The Kentish Mercury, Margaret's local paper, commenting on the fact that Fisher's new Bill aimed to encourage the establishment of nursery schools for children under five years, hinted that Margaret had influenced his thinking.

> One is inclined to speculate as to how far Mr. Fisher was led to this belief and guided in his plans on it, by his acquaintance with

the experimental work carried on in Deptford by the Misses
McMillan. To those ladies, we are inclined to think, credit may
fairly be given for initiative in the matter of this desirable
reform.[11]

Two weeks later, the same paper announced that Margaret had
been appointed a Commander of the Civil Division of the Most
Excellent Order of the British Empire 'for services in connection
with the War'. It proudly stated: 'South-East London will
unanimously approve the honour bestowed on Miss Margaret
McMillan, whose splendid social work Deptford has learned
to value, even though it may not yet appreciate to the full
its possibilities.'[12] This was an honour which Margaret gladly
accepted but rarely mentioned.

For the next few months while busy with her diverse establishments, she continued the clearing of Rachel's personal effects and
left final instructions about her own. The following extract from a
letter she wrote to their Edinburgh cousin, months after Rachel's
death, shows how she still felt in close contact with her sister: 'I do
not believe now that death ends all . . . I am not only in touch with
my darling, I do nothing, and will never do anything without her
guidance.'[13]

When Fisher's Bill was going through Parliament, Margaret
disseminated information about the many issues it raised. For one
thing, the term nursery school was ambiguous and needed
clarification. Sometimes it was used to mean a fee-paying
kindergarten in charge of teachers. On occasion it was applied to
day nurseries where nurses or parents looked after the children of
working mothers. At other times it was intended to describe baby
classes in infant schools. Many members of the general public were
unaware that trained teachers were in charge of nursery schools
and that they provided the foundation of the whole system.

A major public relations exercise was called for before the Act
reached the statute book. At once Margaret committed herself to
speak about nursery education to influential individuals and
groups. Addressing members of the Association of University
Women Teachers in January 1918, she said:

It must be understood that there cannot be any serious system of
education unless it is pursued unrelentingly from the beginning
of life up to the end of adolescence. It must be carried on as a
consecutive task, and inspired by a great aim – the freeing of the
higher powers of man and woman for the pursuit of what is best
in human work, endeavour and influence . . . My address this

afternoon is designed to interest you in nursery schools and nurseries where the first great drama of education will be played out.[14]

To focus the attention of workers on the nursery schools issue, Margaret wrote at the editor's request in *The Labour Leader*:

Mr. Fisher's new Education Bill . . . asks that children of 2 to 6 years old shall have out-door nurseries . . . it makes provision that the elementary school shall not in future receive damaged material, but shall on the contrary, start work with children who are not merely healthy, but also intelligent and cultured.[15]

To allay the fears of infant teachers about losing their jobs, she explained that the Bill did not 'propose to scrap infant mistresses as such. It foreshadows for them a brighter future.'

She believed that nursery schools would bring benefits to the whole education system, because they would give each child 'a sub-structure of health and intelligence' that would 'alter its outlook and revolutionise its work'.[16]

Nevertheless, misconceptions about the aims of nursery schools continued to abound. Some members of the public thought that these schools sought to become substitutes for homes and argued that young children should be kept in their own homes, irrespective of their quality. Others showed that they thought nursery schools were welfare centres rather than educational establishments. This belief can be clearly seen in the debates in Parliament when Fisher's Bill reached Committee stage.[17]

Clause 19 of the Bill, which received the Royal Assent on 8 August 1918, authorised Local Education Authorities to make arrangements for:

1 the supplying or aiding the supply of Nursery Schools (which expression shall include Nursery Classes) for children over two and under five years of age (or such later age as may be approved by the Board of Education) whose attendance at such a school is necessary or desirable for their healthy physical and mental development.
2 attending to the health, nourishment and physical welfare of children attending Nursery Schools.

Furthermore, the Act confirmed that 'The Board of Education . . . may pay grants in aid of Nursery Schools, provided that such grants shall not be paid in respect of any such school unless it is open to inspection by the local education authority.' Later, it was stipulated that the first expenditure eligible for grant would be that incurred during the year ending 31 March 1919.

Unfortunately, Fisher's Act was advisory rather than mandatory and so state provision of nursery schools was slow. Consequently Margaret once more considered how she could inspire different groups to exert pressure on LEAs to implement the new Education Act. Among these were women who, because of the fight for suffrage, were for the first time admitted to the Electoral Register in October 1918. Addressing them, Margaret exclaimed:

The entrance of women into Parliament should, and will, we believe, be the death knell of misery, slow torture, early death and neglect of children. The nation will be disgraced whose women, having power, do not take care of its little ones.[18]

The Act opened the way for state provision of nursery schools. But such schools were still, even within education circles, not a widely understood idea. Needed urgently were schools which, to use Fisher's words about Margaret's, would 'serve as a working model' for others and have 'imitators all over the country'.

Once the Act was safely on the statute book, Margaret took up the task of developing the Rachel McMillan Baby Camp into the Rachel McMillan Open-air Nursery School and Training Centre. But, before examining that stage of her pioneering work, let us pause to take a closer look at the initiator at her maturity. More remarkable than any of her notable experiments was Margaret herself.

Chapter nineteen

Our Maggie

> She was a big woman, stately, well proportioned, quick in her
> movements and walk . . . Her skin was fair and fresh, her
> features regular and attractive, but it was her eyes that revealed
> her power and personality. They were large and arresting and
> could become piercing, scornful, thoughtful, compassionate and
> at times mystical and far-seeing.[1]

Such was the recollection of one who knew her well.

Margaret was a person who stood out in a crowd. 'Meeting her
by chance say in a railway train', remarked the poet Walter de la
Mare, 'I would have said she was one of those invaluable
phenomena England used to be so rich in, "a character".'[2]

She was an unforgettable person who riveted even casual
acquaintances by her personality. A pupil in a school she once
visited recalled: 'After fifty years, I can still see her flashing brown
eyes and hear her voice and even yet feel the vivacious strength of
her inspiring personality.'[3] Mansbridge spoke of 'the dignity and
power of her presence throughout her mature life'.[4]

Margaret was not interested in herself, or in her appearance.
During her brief spell with Lady Meux, she wore the fashionable
clothes chosen for her, but afterwards spent little time or money
on dress. 'Clothes became for Margaret a regrettable necessity, to
be forgotten as soon as possible', observed the Labour MP,
Margaret Bondfield, adding: 'The duty of seeing that all her strings
and buttons were fastened was distributed among her fellow
workers. Even so, her personal appearance was arresting.'[5]
Mansbridge tells a similar story: 'When she wanted a new hat she
sent the charwoman out to buy it, and the charwoman, with a
wisdom which is common among south London ladies, chose one
to suit herself, and secured the reversion of it – very rapidly.'[6]

She was an extrovert, so engrossed in her care for children of the
slums as to be unaware of her own feelings. Lowndes reported:

She would limp through the whole day half conscious of some vague discomfort and find a terribly blistered heel at night caused by a tight shoe . . . Without thought of her own comfort, she spent her life in trying to bring comfort to 'these little ones'.[7]

However, it was not her oddities so much as the spirit within her which lingered in the memories of those who encountered her. P. S. Ballard, the LCC Inspector of Schools, who often visited her at the Stowage, perceived something of the deeper side of her life. He wrote: 'What a rich personality was hers, and how strange a destiny . . . To converse with Miss McMillan was always a delight; she was so frank, so fresh, so whimsical.' Then he added:

She brought with her a sense of largeness. One had a feeling that she breathed a larger atmosphere, and lived and moved among larger things than ordinary men and women. It was not merely that her life was dedicated to great causes, but that she was ever conscious of the deeper purposes and the wider destinies of the human race itself. There were no barriers in her mind, just as there were no solid walls in her school. Her sympathies were as wide as the world.[8]

What others thought of her or her enterprises concerned her little. Like many pioneers she often had to stand alone and learn to steer her way through years of loneliness and ostracism, until her schemes became socially acceptable. Dr Mallon, a one-time Warden of Toynbee Hall, wrote:

For years we called her a 'crank'. We loved to think of her as protectress of the children. But we called her a crank, and said she had one idea. Now many of us think she had the one idea that matters . . . Had Miss McMillan lived 500 years ago, she had lived as the Saint of Poor Children for ever.[9]

Commenting on Mallon's remarks, some twenty years later, a writer to *The Times* observed: 'To the unthinking, saintliness perhaps connotes detachment, but Margaret McMillan was as competent in worldly affairs as was Catherine of Siena. She fought her battles on soap-boxes in the parks and in town councils and education committees.'[10]

In an article headlined 'The Nuisance Who Worked Miracles' J. B. Priestley described her as 'One of those beastly Agitators who are always bringing up awkward subjects and making decent people feel uncomfortable.' Then he confessed:

I believe such people single-minded, pure in heart, and blazing with selfless love, to be the salt of the earth. There is more essential Christianity in them than in a multitude of bishops. If it were not for them and a few glorious artists, this world would be one huge ashpit.[11]

Another contemporary describing her as 'disquietening', said:

All her life Margaret McMillan was that disturbing element in human society – the practical visionary. She left you feeling that something ought to be done, but that you ought to do it. And you knew she was doing it. You had seen the wonders of Deptford, and with her you said: 'If there, why not here?'[12]

Many well-known writers tried to convey their impressions of Margaret. Mansbridge likened her to Florence Nightingale. Another writer, claiming that both 'were mystics' conscious of and in communion with 'an unseen world', added:

Both were by nature artists; Florence Nightingale's early dreams were of music as much as of medicine; Margaret McMillan trained first as a teacher of music, then as an actress. Both sought to release the spirit of man by care for his body . . . Both were natural feminists, yet both subordinated direct work for the emancipation of women to their own particular missions.[13]

Sometimes, because she said she was directed by her voices, she was compared with Joan of Arc. Robert Blatchford saw her as 'A blend of Joan of Arc and Florence Nightingale, tempered by the humour of Jane Austen.' He said: 'I stood in awe of that strange woman. She was a good deal of a poet and still more of an angel . . . a strange, beautiful, gifted woman, great; but odd.'[14]

The actress, Dame Sybil Thorndike, who knew both G. B. Shaw and Margaret McMillan, said that the former frequently referred to Margaret in her presence, saying, 'There's a Saint Joan for you.'

Shaw declared that Margaret was 'Not only one of the best women of her time and in her orbit, but also one of the most cantankerous', and added, 'she owed a good deal of her effectiveness to the latter useful quality'.[15] Once, when a fellow Fabian said, 'She has bees in her bonnet', he at once retorted, 'Yes, but she manages to produce very large rabbits from very small hats – the hats of county councillors.'[16]

In public Margaret could be both wooing and waspish. She could win people to help poor children by her perseverance and oratory. Mansbridge recollected her persistence:

Presidents of the Board of Education have told me that if she wanted to see them she saw them. No private secretary was skilful enough to stay her, and she was quite capable of waiting on the steps of the Board all day if any one she wanted to see was out, and there was a chance of his coming back.[17]

In committees Margaret could be pertinacious and impatient with those who tried to obstruct her plans for poor children. Lady Norman, who worked with her on the LCC's Education Committee, recalled:

> She didn't suffer fools gladly. Those who knew what they were talking about, she listened to . . . But to those who thought they knew all the answers to the difficulties of educating the young, she was very intimidating and often quite rude.[18]

However contentious Margaret may have been on public bodies, in private she was a friendly, agreeable person, on good terms with her neighbours. One who used to live next door to her and Rachel wrote:

> When I was a child in Albury Street, my father used to do their garden and built them a potting shed . . . when I was just over three years old I had been in hospital for four months and they brought me a doll and they had knitted a complete outfit for it in royal blue . . . My mother used to mind their big black cat for them when they went away for a holiday and at Christmas time; they were two wonderful ladies.[19]

To the ordinary folk who worked for her, Margaret was an understanding, forgiving employer. Alderman Dr Kathleen Chambers of Bradford relates how once when Margaret was due to speak there:

> A first-class ticket was sent to her. She arrived with no ticket, having travelled third-class. She had no luggage, no warm coat. She had come 'just as she was'. It transpired that her housekeeper at Deptford, who was of a convivial nature, had gone off to celebrate with the key in her pocket. Despite all advice, Margaret refused to dispense with the erring and not very capable helper. Margaret McMillan was the most selfless person I have ever known.[20]

She was not by nature a home-maker, though she greatly appreciated the different homes Rachel created around her. She loved entertaining in her own home and particularly enjoyed planning simple, but special, dishes for guests. One visitor recalled:

> I was privileged to be invited to lunch with her . . . in the early nineteen twenties. She had a special mulberry pie made in my

honour and said that the mulberries had been gathered from a tree in the grounds, planted by the Duke of Wellington.[21]

She frequently received people of different ages and classes but greeted all of them with the same old-fashioned courtesy. She could, to use Kipling's words, 'Walk with Kings – nor lose the common touch'.

Well-travelled and well-read, Margaret was a stimulating person to meet. Her warmth of heart, keen sense of humour and great capacity for friendship earned her many friends. She was good company and at the same time one whom others could rely on for a sympathetic ear, though she could be blunt and abrasive if need arose. She was extremely shrewd; Walter de la Mare once said she had an 'inexhaustible knowledge of human nature'; at times she seemed to have the gift of second sight.

She was sensitive to the deepest needs of people and on occasion spoke to them of the faith that meant so much to her. In a letter to Mrs Robert Blatchford, sorely grieved by the death of her baby, she wrote:

> Yes, I do think he lives yet, and that you will see him again. We are still so gross I think it no wonder we can believe very little. Faith is not credulity to me, but a kind of gift or vision: and the pure in heart *see*. I believe that everything is very well. I don't like writing any more because it seems weak and poor. When I see you, I will try to tell you better what I think.[22]

To a young lady who told her that she found the current teachings about religion unconvincing, but was enthusiastic about the writings of Emerson, Margaret replied:

> Yes, his essay about the Over-soul is very fine. But you are young and may still come to have personal experiences that will convince you of the great realities . . . If only you could *see* the Mighty Powers . . . Without Those behind us neither Rachel nor I could have achieved anything.[23]

Her teaching staff knew her as one who had a keen sense of humour and as a mimic *par excellence*. She was an engaging raconteuse who enjoyed telling funny stories against herself. One of her teachers recounted:

> One day she came into lunch convulsed with laughter. As she came over from the Camp School she passed two old men from the Doss House. One said, 'There's Lady McMillan!' But his companion replied, 'That's no Lidy – she's a H'orator.'[24]

Margaret was passionately fond of children; they were drawn to her and felt secure in her presence. After visiting the Stowage, a School Medical Officer from New Zealand wrote:

> The first thing I noticed was the attraction that Miss McMillan had for the young children, many children leaving their own teachers and going to her directly they saw her. On the whole of our tour of inspection we were accompanied by a little girl of about three years of age, a new-comer to the school . . .
>
> The child was in new surroundings, and the first thing for Miss McMillan to do was to gain her confidence and affection . . . I took farewell of Miss McMillan at the gate of the school. A small person of three or four was holding on to her skirt. (When a statue is made to Miss McMillan, one or more children holding on to her skirt and looking up into her face should be included.) . . .
>
> The piety of Miss McMillan was so much part of her being that one could not fail to observe it. Undoubtedly herein lies the mainspring of her life's work – 'Inasmuch as ye have done it unto one of these little ones . . .'[25]

Margaret loved nature. When in search of rest and refreshment, she would make short visits to the countryside. Being specially fond of Scotland, with its lofty peaks and remote islands, she went there whenever possible. On her return she would write about her vacation, and try to convey something of the loveliness she had seen with an artist's eye to others – especially to city dwellers. After one holiday, when she had obviously revelled in a brief spell in the Highlands, she wrote:

> Between the rocks the slopes were golden with primroses, and in the clefts of the rocks the hollows thrilled with the cooing of wild pigeons. Near the spouting cave – where the water tosses up in a great column, visible for miles – the dark, sharp pinnacles were spanned with rainbows where the sun caught the drifting mists of silver spray. All this you may see in any spring-tide in Iona.[26]

Margaret loved beauty in all its forms. The arts, especially poetry, music and the theatre, gave her great joy and she longed to introduce others to their delights. One of her old pupils wrote recently:

> I am now telling my grandchildren about the times she took us to London, the Old Vic, the Albert Hall, the British Museum and other places. The funny thing was she used to bundle us all into one taxi . . . How we enjoyed those outings![27]

The actress in Margaret never quite died. She frequently undertook to produce plays in the Camp School and was known to give the performers a rigorous training. Writing some 30 years after her death an old pupil who took part in her productions of Shakespeare's plays, said:

> I can remember playing in several . . . She seemed to lose all sense of time when she was directing the class in one of them. As a kid I was always ready for my lunch but if Miss McMillan was taking the class it had to wait until she was satisfied we had our parts somewhere near the mark. On several occasions I saw the dinner go by the classroom but for the next ten minutes or so had to shape my mouth like a pipe so that people at the back could hear every word I had to say, only then could I chase after my lunch.[28]

Colour meant a great deal to her and she had definite views about its use. Although negligent of her own clothes, she observed what others wore and the colours they chose. After meeting Walter Crane (the artist) she noted that he 'wore a horrible magenta handkerchief'. On another occasion, she reported that Rachel was 'dressed in a soft dove-grey'. Her ideas about the use of green were unusual as the following incident, recalled by one of her old students, shows: 'I went on duty one day wearing a spring green overall. She came up to me and said, "It's very pretty dear, but don't wear green. It's the fairies' colour, they won't like it." A Highland superstition perhaps?'[29]

In the garden, Lowndes said: 'she liked large splashes of colour, particularly delphiniums, larkspurs, roses, nasturtiums and zinnias. Once in her absence the old gardener planted the geraniums intended to create such a splash of colour singly, here, there and everywhere.' Feeling disappointed about this she remarked on her return, 'It looks as though the garden has measles.'[30]

Margaret was a loyal subject of the Crown who had a great respect for the monarchy. During a period of political unrest, when many Labour supporters protested against singing the National Anthem, Mansbridge consulted her about singing it at a WEA meeting she was to address in Sheffield: 'Of course we'll sing it,' she flashed. 'The King needs our prayers.'[31]

Although usually in good spirits, Margaret could become a prey to moods and depression. Feelings related to personal attacks she could shrug off fairly easily, but she found vexation caused by opposition to her schemes more difficult to dismiss. At such times she would unburden herself to Rachel, or to close members of staff.

Her awareness of the darker side of her own nature and her appreciation of the finest qualities of others can be seen in the comment she made about Rudolf Steiner of the Waldorf School Movement: 'He seems to see one. He knows already when you come near and yet he never condemns or criticizes, or has bitter thoughts like me.'[32]

Perhaps Mansbridge gives us the key to a true understanding of 'Our Maggie' in saying: 'Her real life was, in a word, otherwhere . . . To understand her it is necessary to regard her as one who was so deeply rooted in things spiritual as to be indifferent to all else.' She was not 'one who valued material things at all . . . Throughout her life she was conscious of the communion of saints. "I always obey my voices, because they come from God", so might she have spoken any day of her life.'[33]

If, as Mansbridge maintained, the inspiration and driving force of her life was spiritual, perhaps it can be seen in retrospect to have been the product of costly moral decisions made over many years. There seems to have been a thread running through her life which linked the different periods into a discernible unity.

When, after her spiritual experience at Ludlow, she turned her back on the settled, secure life of a governess to follow an unknown road, she was led to take up voluntary work for the Labour Movement. Moral indignation at the low wages of the workers impelled her to help the dockers fight for a rise in wages. While involved in that struggle she learned to write for the press and address public meetings. Both of these activities took her out of obscurity into the public eye, then into the Independent Labour Party and later to representing it on the Bradford School Board.

It was during her time in Bradford that she groped her way towards a personal destiny; she said she felt herself called to fight the battle of the slum child and to follow in Shaftesbury's footsteps. As she pursued that path, she came to believe that nursery conditions approximating to those in middle-class homes, were the birthright of every child. From that time onwards she waged a long, political struggle on behalf of a better start in health and education for all children. This fight, which demanded sacrifice and self-discipline, was the natural outcome of her firm belief in a more just society which she had held since her youth.

The ILP was an instrument which helped Margaret to reach her ideals. In her battles on behalf of little children she needed the support of politicians to get her ameliorative measures legalised. Children had no votes and therefore someone needed to present their case. So Margaret became the leader of a pressure group within the ILP, which succeeded in disturbing the settled procedures of many civil servants and initiating reform. Later, she sought to help the nation's children by pioneering a series of establishments, such as clinics and schools, outside the state system, many of which ultimately became valued prototypes.

The ILP gave her a vision of a new world from which grinding poverty and gross injustices had been eliminated. This not only inspired her but sustained her in a fight to which she was totally committed for over 40 years, and which claimed her to the end.

It was probably the combination of that vision and her new-found Christianity which enabled her to become one of the most moving and creative forces of her age. The East Ham Labour Party and Trades Council, in viewing her as a pioneer of social progress, said that 'in her work for very young children she was the most successful revolutionary of her day'.[34] But her success never came easily. Looking back over the slow, steady advance she made towards her goals, she wrote:

> To live through such years is to win new faith and trust in a beneficence that outsoars the little dim circle of our sense perceptions. To live through them is to win faith in humanity too. Progress is not a triumphant riding on; it is a painful stumbling on.[35]

Chapter twenty

The Rachel McMillan Open-air Nursery School 1918–19

'Miss McMillan is a social reformer first, an educationist second. Living in the midst of submerged humanity, her ideal has been to bring the submerged portion of humanity up to the existing standards of living.'[1] Thus said *The Times Educational Supplement* when reviewing her book, *The Nursery School*, published in 1919. While that view is a matter for controversy, what is beyond question is that from then to the end of her life she was involved in nursery education.

Even prior to this involvement she was a firm believer in education's intrinsic worth and felt it was everyone's birthright. Combined with sound health, she believed that education could 'lay the foundation of a happier social life and a new era of human progress'.[2]

Convinced that the poor provision of education was a national scandal, she urged the electorate to ask their MPs to work for its expansion. She herself pursued that policy through her own political party. But she was not only interested in spreading the benefits of traditional education more evenly, she was concerned about curriculum content and educational reform. When 29 Independent Labour candidates were elected to Parliament in 1906 and the Labour Party declared its belief in 'free and ample opportunities for all', she immediately pressed it to be more precise in its views, saying:

> We realise that the time is now come, when mere phrases will not suffice, that we must have clear notions as to what constitutes good education, clear views as to how the present obstacles towards the attainment of it can be removed, and above all, definite ideas as to the nature of the constructive reforms to be advocated.[3]

Margaret was concerned about workers who were only given a few years of elementary education before being flung into industries. Some fathers, she complained, threw their children into jobs 'as kittens might be thrown into water'. Consequently, she urged the Labour Party to agitate for Day Continuation and Further Education courses. She yearned for labourers to have a qualitatively new life, a life containing something more than material improvement. Believing that the desire for education and enlightenment lay buried in the hearts of many workers who had been denied access to them, she wrote:

> Indeed, the whole desire of the workers to-day is touched with Idealism, however material their demand for more wages, better houses etc, may appear to be . . . The materialism itself is largely a result of this baulked desire for something else. Even the vice that degrades our cities is a kind of revolt against this monstrous denial. Nevertheless, the new hope is alight . . . To fan it and feed it, is one of the highest duties of a Labour or Socialist Party.[4]

Once more systematic instruction was given, she believed that education would create its own demand for further education. 'The History of Education is really the History of Democracy', she said, 'as people advanced slowly in social hope and faith, the level of their demands in education and nurture rose with the tide.'[5]

However, when she thought about laying the foundations of a nobler social order and a more educated democracy, she always came back to the idea that the best place to begin was with the health and education of young children; that was where reforms needed to start: 'Sanatoria, housing, pensions, scholarships, even better wages – what are these without early culture or education? . . . The first years decide all.' Thinking of Rachel and others she wrote:

> It was not for . . . reforms divorced from early education, that our dear ones lived and died. They refused to build on sand. Inspired by their long, obscure and glorious record of faith and hope, we will work as they worked in the presence of the Unseen.[6]

Looking at Deptford's poverty-stricken pre-school population, she was aware that their deprivation was caused first by a cluster of social, economic and political factors, and then in many cases exacerbated by the ignorance and moral degradation of their parents. Through her Party, Margaret fought unremittingly to remove the causes of poverty; through her clinics and camps she had sought to alleviate its consequences. Now through the establishment of the Rachel McMillan Open-air Nursery School, she aimed to offset her children's background of deprivation. The scheme she envisaged would be preventive as well as curative. It would help young children and their families; it would be an extension of the home, though not a substitute for it.

When Margaret began to plan a curriculum for this school, there was little objective research on the education of young children she could consult. Research in this field only appeared after doctors learned how to preserve children and research workers improved their measuring instruments.

She herself was not a trained nursery/infant teacher, but she had been a frequent visitor to schools since her time on the Bradford School Board. As already mentioned, she was exceptionally well-read on education, whose literature at this time was largely influenced first by philosophy and experimental psychology, and later by biology and physiology. She had a knowledge of writings in all these disciplines and was familiar with the ideas of Plato, Locke, Rousseau, Pestalozzi, Froebel and many others.

As well as being acquainted with various theories of education, her writings show that she had taken note of practical experiments in the field, and was aware of the ideas of prominent teachers and thinkers outside England. She knew of Robert Owen's Nursery/Infant School in Scotland, Séguin's work with retarded children in France, Grundtvig's Folk High Schools in Denmark and Dr Montessori's work with poor children in Italy.

She herself was an eclectic, a pragmatist who was aware that she needed to consult authorities and at the same time create something new.

Are we to turn to Spencer or Herbert, Froebel or Séguin? Who is to be the supreme guide and teacher? . . . None of these in the sense that we should follow any of them blindly. Our task is new. It has never been attempted. All the teachings of the greatest men and women halt long before they come abreast of our needs. Therefore we have to do our own research work.[7]

As a former Manager of a group of schools in Deptford, she regularly visited a number of London primary schools, and was well-acquainted with their conditions and educational practices. But she questioned much of the established thinking of her day about school buildings and the education of young children. In her own nursery school, she intended to cut loose from current practices and produce a positive alternative to the existing order.

Most elementary schools were surrounded by asphalt yards; she believed in schools set in gardens. State school buildings were prison-like, badly ventilated, had poor toilet facilities and were

175

crammed with dirty, hungry, sick children. She favoured open-air buildings with good sanitary arrangements set in large gardens. Elementary school teachers, burdened with classes of 60 or more, were often forced to maintain strict authoritarian discipline, and deal harshly with children they could not keep in order. Margaret shunned that kind of an ethos. She liked smaller classes with a friendly, stimulating, informal atmosphere. Outside schools she saw prominently displayed notices forbidding parents from entering. She wanted visitors to feel welcome in her school – especially parents. So many things about state schools jarred and saddened her. She felt that most teachers were competent, but they were saddled with an impossible task – to give mass instruction in the 3 Rs to hordes of unhealthy children in poor buildings.

She firmly believed that the physical well-being of children was a priority in any scheme of education, and that only when the health of children was attended to, and accepted as a community responsibility, was there any prospect of success in achieving the aims of education. Yet she did not see how the nurture children needed could ever be given within the existing public elementary schools. Contrasting such schools with the nurseries she had in mind she wrote:

> The great services to humanity to which we now aspire cannot be achieved within these short school days that take account of nothing but life in the classroom. The elementary school opens at nine. The nursery school work is far advanced at that hour. The school has recess from 12 to 2; but these are vital hours in the nursery school – the hours, in short, when the great assault is made on the arch-enemies. Dinner and sleep are vital in a war of prevention. At four the school closes. But the nursery school is busy then with preparation of the evening meal. Holidays are welcomed by the school. Holidays are only a kind of desertion for the nursery school child.[8]

Margaret preferred a child-centred, rather than subject-centred system of education. Believing that the child and its physical well-being should be the first priority of all educational planning, she was critical of educators who tried to conjure up an ideal syllabus for children in a vacuum, irrespective of their ailments. Questioned by a journalist about programmes for children, she said: 'It is not possible to think that treatment is a thing altogether apart from "education". One might as well say that a violinist should not think of his violin – but only of his score.'[9]

While many thought of the body as separate from the mind, Margaret believed that the one impinged on the other, and that a good nursery school would provide for the development of both. Given a spacious, carefully planned open-air environment, which children could explore, she believed that children would grow both in body and mind.

As a result of the Fisher Act, she anticipated that nursery schools, surrounded by gardens, would spring up in different parts of the country and that they would lay the foundations of a better society. Dreaming of this expansion, she wrote:

> All neglected, suffering, dirty little children now playing in the gutter, and near roaring traffic and hooting cars, will be gathered into gardens at last . . . As they grow up, they will long more and more to make gardens everywhere, to mow down and root out the things that destroy, to rear and find a place for all that is beautiful and innocent.[10]

The philosophy of education underlying the nursery school Margaret eventually founded, was an integral part of her Christianity and socialism. She believed that each human being was a child of God – a unique person to be loved and reverenced. True education for all children in all classes, she thought, should be concerned with the whole child, with his dignity, his physical, social, emotional, intellectual and spiritual development.

Based on her experience as a governess in wealthy families, on her knowledge of state schools and her careful observation of deprived children, she devised a scheme to match the needs of Deptford's pre-school children. She had numerous ideas about learning. She believed that knowledge was senses-dependent, that children learned first 'not by thinking but experiencing through the sympathetic system'. Therefore she planned the school environment so that children would have sensory experiences, mostly in the garden, occasionally in the shelters. Trying to answer the question often put to her about the kind of sense-training she thought teachers could offer pre-school children out-of-doors, she replied:

> Suppose you want to develop the touch sense! Lo! here are a score of leaves, hairy sunflower, crinkled primrose, glossy fuchsia, and the rose. Do you want to compare colours, to note tints and shades? Well, here is wealth a-plenty. The herb garden will offer more scents than anyone can put into a box, and a very little thought will make of every pathway a riot of opportunities.[11]

Margaret always saw children as individuals with their own particular intellects and interests. Consequently she favoured individual methods rather than class methods of teaching:

Our blunder in the past was forcing all children to reach the same level in learning the 3 Rs, whatever their natural powers or aptitudes. If one child at the age of two can read (there are such children) this is no reason for asking all children to vex themselves with letters before they can speak.[12]

She thought teachers should study the individual interests of children, use their spontaneous attention, and provide learning experiences which appealed to individual tastes. In the account that follows she gives examples of the different interests of two boys who are playing alongside each other:

He (Victor) is our oldest toddler – nearly three and very musical . . . he lives for and answers to one thing – music . . . Harold gathers up his train and walks up to look at him, with the mute wonder that one little dog gives another. Harold hears no magic in the noise that comes out of the box. He will not understand, never will understand that; but after a while finding no further interest in watching Victor, he goes back to his toy. It is a tiny train, and he has fastened a string to the engine.[13]

Margaret thought that if teachers would observe children and wait until they were at the right stage of maturation before trying to instruct them, they and their pupils would achieve more in the end, and in addition children would enjoy their learning more. Maintaining that teaching when the children were not mature enough was damaging, she wrote:

It is . . . by premature use of the nervous tissue and by starvation of the nervous system with all its routes and centres that mischief is done . . . The 'entraînement' *follows* the slow work of silent growth . . . The child is injured by premature forms of learning.[14]

She believed that perception ripened slowly and that teachers should not try to make children do work that was too advanced for them. Driving home the point that 'perception takes time', she reported the following story of a conversation between Sam, a three-year-old, and Betty who was four:

'Betty' he says, 'have you washed your hands?'
'Of course, Sam.' . . .
'Are your hands kwite c'ean?' he says . . .
There is a long, long pause.
'Cook says her hands are c'ean,' says Sam, struggling with dim thoughts.
'She hasn't time on them . . .'

'I haven't time on my hands, she said to me.'
'Betty,' asks Sam, suddenly, 'what is time?' . . .
'Time is dirt,' said Sam very earnestly, 'that's what it is.'
(Sam does not take in the meaning of Time or other
abstractions. You don't gather grapes in February, even off a
good vine.)[15]

In her view children learned best in purposeful play in an
environment prepared by understanding adults and in human
interaction. Play to her was not the opposite of work; it was the
child's work. 'Most of the best opportunities for achievement', she
wrote, 'lie in the domain of free play, with access to varied
material.'[16] During play she expected teachers to teach, to interact
with children, explain things to them and, through speaking with
them, extend their thinking and language. She believed in children
being intellectually stretched, but not over-stretched: she wanted
them to be busy in school and purposeful.

As a former actress she considered training in speech and
language important, and felt that music, movement, drama,
poetry and art were just a few of the many activities which should
be provided for young children.

The three main practical objectives of the curriculum were: first,
to give children the much-needed physical care she referred to as
'Nurture'; second, to offer them an appropriate education; and
third, to strive to improve the child-rearing practices of parents.
Clarifying the first of these objectives, she said:

> The real object of our work is 'Nurture' – the organic and
> natural education which should precede all primary teaching
> and without which the work of the schools is largely lost. Many
> children from crowded homes today receive no nurture at all . . .
> They arrive at the elementary schools at the age of five suffering
> from the results of rickets, bronchial catarrh and other ailments,
> and their brain-growth is hindered by the evil of their first
> years.[17]

Of her second objective, she wrote: 'We are trying to create an
environment where education will be almost inevitable.' She tried
to create a home-like, happy, informal, stimulating atmosphere in
her School. Classrooms for children of all classes she said should
have: 'low chairs for the nurse, who is mother and sister for the
time; pictures and prettily coloured walls and light, musical
instruments, flowers and an atmosphere of joy and love.'[18]

Of her third aim, reaching the parents, and treating the child
and his home as a unit, she wrote:

It [the Nursery School] is going to take the child before disease
has got a strong hold on it when it is only two years of age, and
everything is promising. And it will get hold of the young
mother when she too is plastic. These two members of society
are going to be dealt with face to face, heart to heart, and hand
to hand.[19]

On the one hand, Margaret saw nurseries as schools where
mothers could learn more about child-rearing and home-making.
She aimed to give parents a new conception of home life which
included 'talks around the fire, stories, games, music'. On the
other hand, through parents' meetings, she hoped teachers would
learn more from the mothers about the children they taught. She
saw nurseries too as centres where mothers could further their own
education and become part of a more informed electorate;
nurseries were to be a focus for the community and influence the
whole district.

When the Rachel McMillan Open-air Nursery School started it
took over the site and buildings formerly used by the Baby Camp.
The centre of the acre of land at the Stowage site which, from all
accounts, formed 'a pleasant oasis in the drab neighbourhood',
was laid out in gardens. On one side there were shelters and a
small administration block; on the opposite side was another
shelter. At the beginning these housed 60–70 children between
two and five years of age, and about 13 children under two.

After the war ended no more babies were admitted, unless there
were exceptional circumstances. Those who were already there
were allowed to stay on during the transitional period and at two
became part of the School. The conditions of entry to the School
were simple. Providing children were normal, free from infectious
diseases and between two and five years old, Margaret enrolled
them. If she kept a child after his fifth birthday, because she
thought his health would benefit, he was transferred at five to the
Camp School.

Describing the School's lay-out, she said:

The form of the open-air Nursery School is not one large
building, but many small shelters . . . each one self contained.
Each has its own bathrooms and offices and is an open-air place
which can be turned into a nursery or dormitory at will. Each is
presided over by a trained nursery school teacher who is helped
by partly trained girls who are there to observe as well as to
assist.[20]

The routine was simple so that children easily got used to it and soon felt successful in it. Describing a typical day in the School, she wrote:

> The nursery-school day begins not at nine, but at eight o'clock in the morning, and the first hour of the day is the busiest of all. The little ones . . . are quickly overhauled, washed, dressed warmly, but with few garments, and made entirely comfortable, as every child should be, and is, in any good private nursery. At nine, all sit down to breakfast . . . On the tables and along the walls there is apparatus of varied kinds . . . Outside there are sliding boards, steps and rib stalls. All the best apparatus is in the garden . . . At twelve there is a two-course dinner, with two year old monitors serving, and at 12.30 [the] little ones are fast asleep . . . All the afternoon, and on fine mornings, they are playing, working, sleeping where He (the sun) can find them.[21]

Between 5.30 and 6 p.m. the children were collected by older children and taken home.

When the Nursery School opened, Margaret's financial position was weak. Once the munition factories closed, the Ministry of Munitions grants, given for children of munition workers, ceased. In addition, when mothers were made redundant, they could not afford to pay two shillings per week for children's meals. Yet she did not want to stipulate a fixed price for food, lest this would exclude the poorest children. 'Our experience', she wrote, 'shows that an appeal to the public spirit and sympathy of parents is far more effective than the most rigid and carefully thought out system of money payment.'[22]

However, under the Fisher Act grants in aid were promised to nursery schools which complied with Grant Regulations. To qualify, schools had to be inspected, run successfully for a year and deemed to be satisfactory. To become grant-aided was now Margaret's aim, but in the meantime, undeterred as ever by financial stringency, she continued to implement her plans.

Once she was determined to run a school rather than a baby-minding institution, she realised that more teachers than nurses would be required. She believed that 80 per cent of a school's success depended on teachers, but the kind she wanted were difficult to find. After several attempts she discovered that even trained and certificated teachers had little experience in teaching. In addition she declared, 'Those who came first were shocked. They had never been in a slum home. They were nervous about sleeping and living always in a slum area.'[23]

She required good experienced teachers who loved children, were willing to work and live in a depressed area and give friendship and practical help to the residents. But she did not easily find the teachers she required. Few of those she first interviewed had had any training for work in the slums or felt that the improvement of children's health was part of their professional duties and, understandably, still fewer wanted to live in Deptford's dockland. Thinking of her unfortunate experiences with teachers whose conception of education differed from her own Margaret wrote:

> The teachers stand a little aghast. This nurture is very well but it is not their business. Not their business! . . . The teacher of little children is not merely giving lessons. She is helping to make a brain and nervous system, and this work which is going to determine all that comes after requires a finer perception and a wider training and outlook than is needed by any other kind of teacher. So we had first of all to work out a new art, by taking on new tasks and doing them with a new motive.[24]

Margaret believed in accepting children as they were and dealing first with their obvious physical needs. 'The little ones were delicate. Many were dirty,' she wrote. Trying to move some teachers from their preoccupation with instructing the mind, to meeting children's immediate needs, she appealed to them passionately saying: 'Forget that you were teachers, forget even that you are students and try to help these children.'[25]

By degrees Margaret found teachers of sterling quality – teachers who, despite their low salaries, helped to lay the foundations of what became an outstanding school. Margaret herself gave her services. Even after the LCC helped to fund the School, she refused to take a salary from them, because, she said, 'then I would be their servant and have to do as they told me', whereas she felt 'it was her business to tell them and show them!'[26]

Her aim was to have a trained competent teacher as head of each shelter and to make her responsible for the practical training of the young students who helped her. Staff and students alike were expected to cleanse children's heads, and where necessary to treat minor ailments, so that children did not have to be excluded from school and so miss the benefits of the open-air life.

Margaret lived on the spot in a tiny bungalow. She was like the Managing Director of a large enterprise plus the Press Officer, the Public Relations Officer and much else besides, but, at the same time, she was servant of all. She was fully engaged with administration, meeting parents, working with children in the garden, discussing procedures with teachers in charge of shelters, and entertaining official visitors, such as the school doctor who visited once a week, and the dentist who called once a month. She did not undertake any formal teaching of children between two and five years old, though she did much informal teaching and often took classes of older children in the Camp School for music and drama. Although her various responsibilities might take 16–18 hours a day, she spent them gladly. She had an infinite enthusiasm for her experiments. But just as she felt children needed unhurried time to reflect on their experience, so she took time to dream dreams, dreams which later she turned into reality.

Margaret's experience with the teachers she encountered made her realise the urgent need for specific training for those who intended to work with disadvantaged pre-school children. Consequently she decided to initiate courses for teachers and to use the Nursery School as an integral part of their training. An outline of the course she designed follows on page 184.

As she thought about the practical side of teachers' training, she realised that the Nursery School could become a training ground for all who wanted to give service to society through their profession – for young girls who might not want to become teachers, but would welcome a practical training in the care of young children. Expressing this idea she said:

> In the nursery school there is no part of the work, however humble, that does not offer great opportunities for observation as well as service . . . The nursery school will become the practising school of to-morrow! Here our young teachers will learn by service . . . Here the future health worker can take part of her training. Here the nurse, the future mother, the social worker can learn by doing.[27]

A copy of the application form for the Probationers appears below.

When she advertised her course, at what she now called the Training Centre, 15 to 20 students applied for places. Those she accepted were expected to live in hostels in the neighbourhood. The Centre had no specific building of its own; its base was the Nursery School. In Margaret's mind these two new institutions – the Training Centre and the Nursery School – would complement each other.

Accounts of the residential accommodation provided for the students indicate that it was frugal. The records suggest that the early recruits were women of calibre – women with lofty ideals. The work was hard, the hours long, the equipment primitive and the food poor. Margaret had little to offer her trainees materially, but she could give them the chance to participate in a worthwhile task, and the by-products of this were a rare comradeship and

The Rachel McMillan Baby Camp
and
Training School for Nurse Teachers.

1. A complete course of training is offered to girls and women who will later enter Nursery Schools and Nurseries as Nurse Teachers.

   The training is for two years.

   Candidates must have a good general education. Small salary given, with board, lodging, uniform and laundry.

2. The course of training includes lectures from experts in physiology, psychology, hygiene, and child observation of children from one year and under up to seven years old. Great attention is paid to the nurture, help, and observation of young children under four. School methods are based on the free development and training of the senses in earliest years, making possible at last the effective teaching of the three R's. Dancing and singing, dramatic plays, and folk-songs and tales are features of the work. Also artistic needlework, with drawing and designing. Voice-production lessons are given to students by an expert.

3. Students are granted a Certificate sanctioned by the Board of Education at the end of their training, conditioned by their having passed the inter-examinations of the course.

4. Students have three hours off daily, two of which must be spent in study. The trial period is one month, and if the student is satisfactory her training dates from the beginning of the first month.

   MARGARET McMILLAN.

FORM——

for the use of Candidates wishing to enter as Probationers the Rachel McMillan Camp-School.

Candidates are received from the age of 16 to 30. They must be in good health, free from specific disease, and have received a good elementary, and, preferably, a secondary education.

Probationers must come on one month for trial.

Probationers, if accepted and desirous of taking the training, must sign, as below, an agreement to remain under training for two years following the date of entrance.

Every care will be taken of the health of candidates, and every effort made to ensure their future success. But no responsibility will be taken for unavoidable illness or failure.

Candidates must pay a premium of £40 for each year of training.

MARGARET McMILLAN.

All candidates or probationers are to be called " RACHEL McMILLAN NURSE-TEACHERS."

deep job-satisfaction. Students were amazed at the immensity of the task she had undertaken and challenged by the totality of her commitment to it. One of them wrote:

> There was a strong spirit of dedication among students constantly re-inforced by the example of Margaret McMillan. The daily living conditions were hard and somewhat bleak. The four Hostels in four different Deptford streets were set in the local community in Albury Street, Evelyn Street, King Street and Wellington Street, and we were often kept awake at night by drunken brawls in and around the local pubs.
>
> All meals we ate in the dining room shelter in the Nursery School . . . The food was simple, plain and not always adequate for those with large appetites. The open-air living was healthy and a joy in warm weather, but could be very spartan in cold winters. Most of us went home at weekends and returned with food parcels to be shared with others not able to get home. This entirely new life presented a great challenge to students, opening our eyes for the first time to the effects of dire poverty and ignorance in the lives of young children. These experiences which we shared with each other strengthened our personal relationships and common resolve to make some contribution towards the improvement of the lives of underprivileged children.[28]

The following account is from another early student:

> In August 1918 there was a group of 15 or so students who had accepted Miss McMillan's offer that they should join her at the Centre in Deptford, to train for Nursery School Teaching . . . In the group three at least were qualified and experienced teachers, and two others had experience of work with young children.
>
> During these early days students spent most of the day working in the 'shelters' as the first open-air nursery classrooms were called, with some time off duty, and had lectures in the evenings and later on Saturday mornings. On Friday evenings Miss McMillan herself took a French class – mainly spoken French, and on Saturday mornings the classes were on drama, movement and speech. Other classes were given in child health and development and dental care. Practical work included gardening, a period in the kitchen and another in the minor ailments clinic . . .
>
> The shelter known best to the writer in those early days was that of the 'toddlers'. Each student had a small group of children in her special care, and under the guidance of the member of staff in charge of this shelter, she took each of her special

children from his or her mother when they arrived – bathed each
one (every day) and after the necessary tooth combing of hair
re-clothed him or her in more suitable clothing, carefully storing
the child's own clothes for the late afternoon return home.
During the day the children played freely in the garden – or
shelter when wet . . . As mothers arrived after tea, each child
was redressed and taken to his mother by his 'nurse', as early
students were called . . .

Miss McMillan was often with the children in the early days at
Deptford. She joined them in the garden, and talked to them
when watching their play. She liked them to be free to use all the
opportunities of a garden – to play with stones, smell the flowers
and plants – a herb garden at the back of the shelters was a
special pride – and help care for the guinea-pigs and rabbits. The
development of all their senses was important to her, especially
through their surroundings. As the mothers passed her
Bungalow room window on their way home she would talk to
them, and listen to them, encourage them to let their children to
be as free in clothing as possible – persuading them particularly
to be bare-headed.

The garden meant much to Miss McMillan and indeed to all of
us at Deptford – To open the gate in the wooden palings along
Church Street and to enter there was to pass from one world to
another . . . Whenever the gate was opened it became a
common sight to see older men and women looking at their
children in a world of space and flowers, grass and trees.

Giving us a picture of Margaret's attempts to extend nursery
education, she wrote:

Sometimes a group of students would accompany Miss
McMillan when she went to lecture to different societies. The
titles of these lectures might vary but the subject was the same in
each case whether the members of the audience were those of
the Theosophical Society, or of the Labour Party – the early
nurture of children and the need for Nursery Schools. She was
single minded in pursuit of support for her work with children.[29]

The Nursery School and Training Centre were now launched,
but before Margaret could develop them further she faced a
financial crisis.

Chapter twenty-one

Developing the Nursery School and Training Centre 1919–25

Early in 1919, Margaret's financial situation, which had been deteriorating for several months, became critical. She was in low spirits. Tradition has it that she didn't know how she could pay the cook's wages. She wondered whether the School would have to be closed down. However, before she took any steps in that direction, money and cheering news came from a number of quarters.

The most unexpected cheque came in April 1919. Queen Mary, who was reported to 'miss nothing that was good on the social landscape', honoured and greatly encouraged Margaret by visiting the School. On hearing of the impending visit, Margaret took fresh heart saying to a member of her staff: 'If the First Lady in the land will come from Buckingham Palace to see my poor School, it means she has faith in us and the work must go on.'[1] The story of what happened after the Queen had made a tour of the shelters is told by one of Margaret's teachers:

> After tea the Head of the School went with Her Majesty to the gate. As they walked along, the Queen asked, 'Why is Miss McMillan so depressed – is there something worrying her?' Miss Chignell replied, 'It is possible we will have to close down in September for lack of funds.' At that time we had no Government Grant and you had to run successfully for a year to get one. The Queen asked what it cost to run the School for a month. 'About £100', was the reply. The Queen departed, but two days later a cheque for £300 came from the Palace. This just saved the experiment.[2]

Many years later, when Queen Mary learned, by accident, how her cheque had kept the School open, she said, 'I am very proud I was able to save such a fine piece of work.'

Another supporter was J. M. Dent – one of Margaret's publishers. Through many years he gave Margaret financial help and much useful advice. When, in February 1919, she mentioned to him her need to raise £1,000, he replied encouragingly: 'I don't think it should be too difficult to raise your £1,000, and if you could come and talk it over with me I will try to help you.'[3] In addition to giving money himself, he repeatedly enlisted his friends in the fight to keep Margaret's experiments solvent.

Writing to her in 1923, Dent said: 'Rely upon me for any money that you may need from time to time. I do not care what the cost may be, I am going to stick to the movement.'[4] Shortly before his death in 1926, he asked his son, Hugh, to give her a sum of money on his behalf which enabled her to build a much-needed new shelter.[5]

To raise money herself and spread information about nursery education, Margaret opened the School to visitors each Wednesday and sold photographs of it together with some of her own pamphlets. Hundreds of visitors came to these occasions and regular sums of money were made this way.

The Nursery School children also participated in the fund-raising efforts. They wrote letters in longhand inviting guests to their functions. Below is an example of one of these.

The Rachel McMillan Nursery School
232 Church Street Deptford

Dear Mr Dent

On June 5 from 2.30–6.0 we are having an open-day. We want some money for our new school and so we are going to ask all visitors on that day to give us half a crown towards expenses. We will give them an entertainment – The biggest of us are acting scenes from 'The Midsummer Nights Dream' and the next eldest are giving an Operetta 'A Fishy Case'. Of course the little ones cannot do much but they will do their best we are sure.

Please do come and bring others with you. We want so many things for our new school. Answer quickly because we want to know how many cakes to make for tea.

With love from

The Children of
The Rachel McMillan Nursery School

Sometimes small amounts of money came from anonymous donors as the following extract from one of Margaret's letters to Dent shows:

My unknown friend, the factory-worker, sent me her roll of notes yesterday – £6. The sum varies from £6 to £10 every 25th March and 25th September. My darling's death-day – and her 'little sister's'. It is not easy to trace it. It always comes from a new post-mark. Such a woman will surely be a Queen in Heaven, though she is nobody at all here. I'm going to put some of the money into a little library for the students: 'To the Unknown Friend Library'.[6]

Margaret's reach always exceeded her grasp and as fast as the money came in she had a purpose for it, and still additional projects in mind. She never quite found the level of funding which took her beyond the possibility of crisis, but this never stopped her planning further expansion.

However, a visit of three LCC Inspectors, in May 1919, in response to her application for the grant, led to greater financial security. The officials inspected the School thoroughly and the following extract from their report shows how highly they rated it.

This is the biggest and most thorough-going attempt made in London to provide a suitable training for very young children . . . Its most characteristic features are:-

1 The long hours. The children come at 8.20 and leave at 6 p.m.
2 The supplying of breakfast and tea as well as dinner.
3 The facilities provided for instruction and recreation in the open air. It is in fact an open-air school.
4 The attention that is paid to health and cleanliness . . . In most of the nursery schools visited more stress had been laid upon the school side than upon the nursery side: this cannot be said of this nursery school.
5 The number of activities with which the school is closely related. There was till recently a crèche on the premises, but most of the children under two have recently been excluded. Use is made when necessary of a medical and dental treatment centre and a cleansing station which stands in close proximity to the school. All these institutions serve with the school for the training in nursery school methods of 24 students for whom hostels are provided in the neighbourhood. Some of these students are already certificated teachers who desire special nursery-school experience . . .

We were very favourably impressed by the effect of the training upon the children. They are cleaner, better nourished, better mannered and better spoken than the ordinary children in the Deptford district. We regard the school and its adjuncts as a very valuable experiment in social regeneration.[7]

After such a favourable report the School was recognised for grant purposes and the first payment was made in September 1920. Although the grant by itself did not cover the School's total costs, it was a regular income. The Training Centre was also recognised in 1919 and qualified for grant purposes. Teachers taking a one year's course there, after they had trained for two years in other colleges, also became eligible for grants. But still Margaret was not satisfied with the courses provided for nursery school teachers. Thinking more of the nation's need for trained teachers than her own financial resources, she decided to admit students to a three-year course leading to her own certificate, although no grants were available for such a course.

Now that she had some grants, Margaret was freer to devote more of her attention to how she could make the School more of a therapeutic community and advance the education being given in it. The main teaching area – the garden – needed upgrading first and she took special pains over this. She believed that in the open-air she could provide children with integrated experiences.

Having little money to spend on equipment, she made the trees at the Stowage serve many purposes. 'Even though our little ones cannot scramble up the trunks,' she said, 'we need only help them to a seat between two strong branches to see their deep and vivid joy in this kind of "apparatus". Under them our toddlers and three-year-olds sleep safely in July afternoons.'[8]

Along with the trees and the shrubs, a wide variety of plants flourished. She planted them so that children could see some flowers in bloom every month. Believing that the garden was the best place for sense-training, Margaret wrote: 'When he has been in the garden, and only after he has been there, should a child try to recognize the colours in his boxes and tablets and match them. The first impression is the original, without it any colour work is artificial and vague.'[9]

In spring the garden was full of bulbs; in summer, Margaret said, it has 'fields of marigolds and rivers of blue veronica and larkspur'. She grew lilies, especially scented ones. Young children, like the one described below, loved to examine and smell them. Margaret reported: 'A delicate three-year-old little boy, often ill, whom I carried one day to see a dark-spotted lily, appeared to enjoy the scent very much. "It is like me", he said, noting the spots, "when I had measles".'[10]

She extended the herb and the kitchen gardens so that these city children could see vegetables actually growing. She planted fruit trees and found that children stripped them long before the fruit was ripe. When the mulberry tree had berries, she said older boys had 'purple streaks leaking from their pockets'.

The greenhouse, which the Camp School boys built, was full of plants too and Margaret attached a pipe from the boiler room to one of its walls to heat it in winter. The garden had wide terraces where children could push and pull their trains and enjoy all kinds of muscular activities. It had narrow paths 'that were straight and smooth'. On the walls were 'rib stalls for climbing', and a 'tall jungle-gym' and a slide. She longed for a fountain and running water, but could not afford to provide them. 'The only little brooks we have are the rain streams in the shallow concrete', she commented 'and we love them.' To supplement these she arranged for children to go down to 'the stream of the wide-curving Thames',[11] where they spent many happy moments. She kept animals for the children; there was a kid, a hedgehog, an aquarium and a bird-table. Describing the School she wrote: 'In the aviary, canaries twitter . . . Guinea-pigs squeak from the hutches, rabbits look out from their burrowing place and pink and brown mice draw the wondering eyes of many observers.'[12]

Through being responsible for animals, Margaret believed, children would learn to love and care for them, and this might encourage respect for all living creatures.

Early emotional development, an important factor in mental health, was assisted first by the satisfaction of children's biological needs, such as food, and then by the love which surrounded them. Children were encouraged to believe that life was good.

Margaret aimed to establish social ideals in the young and expected the adults around them to be trustworthy models for them. During meal times, she expected teachers to train children to have good manners and self-control. In play periods she hoped children would be taught to take turns, encouraged to show initiative and self-reliance, and helped to develop self-confidence.

In the School it was Margaret's custom to initiate ideas but to include others in their execution. She trusted teachers to teach well and give students a thorough training. Most members of her staff were well-schooled in the principles and practices of Froebel – the apostle of play. They were experienced teachers who were allowed to work out their own preferred teaching styles, providing they kept her main goals in mind. Those who knew her said she was 'a genius at getting others to work for her'.

Margaret wanted all instruction to be pleasurable, she wanted 'reading without tears'. Considering the intellectual training of three-year-olds she declared that they worked hard in school:

not under compulsion, but obeying an impulse that brings its own happiness . . . The teacher shares the gaiety of this work that is not only play but also adventure – an adventure that opens the door to every order of new pleasure.[13]

Recalling his school days in the 1920s, one old pupil explained:

Things that are now commonplace were introduced in the McMillan school, climbing frames, slides, and play as-you-learn gadgets. I suppose there was some drudgery. If so, I don't recall any until I left and went to the elementary school.[14]

Margaret believed that given the carefully prepared environment in the garden, as well as wise teacher-intervention, children would see and handle natural objects, form concepts and gain insights appropriate to their age and development. They were introduced to their literary heritage through stories, poems, nursery rhymes and jingles. There was dancing, singing, miming and acting, different forms of creative handwork and free play with natural materials such as sand, wood and clay.

Teachers and students were to do more than merely supervise play; they were to help children develop the skills of learning – attention, persistence, experimentation, discrimination and problem-solving. Margaret expected her helpers to make sure that there was continuity and progression in the children's activities, and not to leave the responsibility for that to the children.

The successive steps by which children are led on to make new efforts and new achievements have to be planned by adults. For young children as for intelligent animals, this very planning is too advanced a process to be voluntarily undertaken.[15]

Speaking of how children in elementary schools did not improve in drawing when lessons were first introduced, she wrote:

Children carried on the kind of 'free' work for years, gained nothing, and at last flung the whole thing aside . . . Because they were learning nothing, only marking time . . . the new power that should have been won in drills (into which a child will throw himself heartily) was lacking.[16]

Her own conception of nursery schools can be seen in an extract from a broadcast she gave later in 1927. 'Everything is planned for life . . . This world is full of colour and movement . . . The afternoon is filled with music and dancing, with tales and play and throughout all, the great function of speech is never forgotten.'[17]

Margaret, like other pioneers, had many heartaches in running her school. Sometimes she was frustrated by vandals. Recording this she wrote:

> Some boys of our neighbourhood are always making raids on the garden . . . and carry handfuls of fresh vegetables away, leaving some on the paths. They also smear our new-painted door and frontage, and shiver the new glass . . . 'The brazeness of them. The owdaciousness!' cries the dustman. 'They're walking down the roofs, like cats, at daylight.'[18]

Sometimes she was hurt by parents who took their children away from the School as soon as they recovered physically, saying they were sending them 'to a proper school' now. On other occasions she felt stabbed by the derogatory remarks of prospective students about her meagre amenities. Reporting one such incident she wrote:

> 'I feel disillusioned,' said an athletic young lady visitor. 'In fact, it is hardly fair. Here am I – been to a really good school, fond of games too; but you don't play hockey here. And I thought from your lecture, it was Paradise . . . I call it too bad.'[19]

Despite all setbacks, the intake of children steadily increased. Reporting in 1921 the School's Superintendent said the Nursery was overflowing.

> There was an average attendance of one hundred and thirty-five children, and almost daily we were obliged to turn away mothers who were seeking admittance for their children . . . and we were also training private students for Nursery School work.[20]

The number of students in the Training Centre, now referred to as the College, increased to 30. Margaret believed in large schools for nursery children, where the pupils were separated into small groups, but thought colleges for teachers should be small. She wanted the practical work of students to be linked to theory, and individually supervised by heads of shelters. In large colleges, she felt it would be difficult, if not impossible, to do this.

To gain acceptance for her ideas, Margaret had to battle continuously on two fronts; within the teaching profession over the size of colleges and the training given in them, and with the general public to accept nursery schools as desirable and the training of teachers for them as necessary. It was commonly believed that any nice motherly girl could do that job, by the light of nature, so Margaret felt impelled to write about the specific training needed for nursery school teachers and how it differed from that of infant teachers.[21]

Her vision for teacher-training was that the syllabus would always include aspects of community work. She said she was preparing students 'to deal not merely with childhood, but with environment'. One journalist, writing in *The Times Educational Supplement* in 1919, reported that, 'All Miss McMillan's teachers learn to be social workers.'[22]

She asserted that parents were often blamed for neglecting their children but few helped them to become better parents, or develop themselves as persons. She was determined that her students would learn something about both of these things in the Centre, and that home-visiting would be a recognised part of their practical work. Opening schools to parents for odd days, she thought, was no substitute for a carefully thought out scheme of working alongside parents.

Margaret struggled to know individual families as well as she knew individual children, and her expectation was that students would do the same. She knew that without the intelligent co-operation of 'the place called school and the school called home', money would be wasted and, even more important, parents and children would rarely fulfil their potential.

She believed that, although schools had a part to play in giving children a more equal start in life, they could never by themselves give equality of opportunity. Homes, children's informal schools, gave them unequal chances of developing their unequal genetic inheritance and sent them to schools with different attitudes towards learning. This made her think deeply about ways and means of rousing parental interest in children's education and of helping parents themselves become more effective educators. She found that their interest in education often developed when they were helped to understand their children's intellectual needs and shown how to meet them. Margaret proved in her own school, what later research surveys substantiated, namely, that more parents are more interested in their children's schooling than has sometimes been supposed.

Margaret's views about home and school relationships and her encouraging attitudes to parents can be seen in her own description of her Mothers' Club.

> They join the club so as to be a part of the new movement, a movement that has already changed in some degree their own lives and the future of their children. They express a desire to come abreast of the school, to understand its aims and to

forward them as they only can forward them. So from the outset there is a community of interest, and this is the basis of the new association.

At the club's weekly meetings, the mothers hear talks on topics related to the hygiene and education of children, or on public affairs.[23]

The following extracts from letters of old students show that Margaret deliberately trained others to know children individually, and visit their homes to offer help and friendship. One wrote:

Margaret McMillan loved children in a way I shall never forget . . . Her motto was 'Educate every child as if he were your own.' She knew all their names – when I was new this always amazed me. The first night at supper she asked me how Charlie was – I blushed and felt terrible. It taught me that children as individuals mattered to her. The next day I memorised the names of the 25 in the shelter, that, if nothing more, prevented homesickness for the Welsh hills.[24]

Another reported:

We knew the parents very well as visiting homes was a very important part of our duties. We as students and staff lived among them. There was no college building and we occupied houses in various streets around the school.[25]

Recalling her experiences one of Margaret's teachers said:

All the staff visited the homes of our children . . . One home I recall visiting, because the little boy hadn't been at school that day . . . While I was there Father came in. He had been out all day looking for work. He was exhausted and sat down on the edge of the bed. After a little I noticed a pool of blood on the floor by his foot. He had walked through the sole of his shoe – through his stocking and his skin.[26]

What then were the observable results in children of all this fresh air, nutritious food, sleep and contact with teachers? Did the School make any impact on the homes and neighbourhood?

When the Nursery first opened, 80 per cent of the children had rickets, but after one year's attendance it could be confidently stated that 'no trace of rickets existed in the school'. In addition, many of those who were pale and anaemic on entry became robust and built up a good resistance to disease; some needed no more medical attention after they had attended the Clinic for four weeks' treatment.

Reporting on the school children's resistance to disease, when the influenza epidemic raged in south-east London in December 1921, Miss Stevinson – one of Margaret's teachers – wrote:

> It is a fact worthy of record that there were no deaths and no cases of serious illness among the children of the older-established school. The children's power of resistance had been built up by the good plain food and fresh air they had enjoyed for months, in some cases for years . . . Outside the Nursery School the children died in great numbers.[27]

Reporting on the difference in health between children who had spent three years in the Nursery School and those who went straight from home to an elementary school at five, Margaret reported: 'The average of "delicate" children who remain delicate after three years in the Nursery School is about 7 per cent. This contrasts favourably with the average of 25 to 35 "damaged" entrants into the elementary school.'[28]

Improvements in physical health are easier to measure than those in intellectual, emotional and spiritual development. But, after becoming sturdier, many of the Nursery School children responded appreciably to the School's instructive environment which also fostered creativity. These children were educated within a framework of high expectation and Margaret was able to show that ultimately most of them, despite the multiple handicaps they began with, were in advance of the Binet intelligence tests devised for their age group.[29]

Thinking of the children's progress in language, Miss Stevinson reported:

> The children want to talk and they have a great deal to say to each other . . . They are anxious to remedy their own speech defects and good-naturedly ready to criticise and help one another.
>
> 'You'll never be able to take a good part in the play you know,' said one maiden scornfully to another. 'You still drop your aitches!' . . . But she made valiant efforts forthwith to conquer the troublesome aspirate.[30]

Thinking of children's use of speech, Margaret wrote: 'The good models provided in the nursery shelters do ensure, not only fair speech but the ability to use it for expression.' Speaking of the long-term effects of this early training in language, she said:

> The older children are often invited to give entertainments – plays, etc., – by the religious and other organizations of the

neighbourhood. What is even more satisfactory, the complaint that school language is overpowered by home language cannot be said to hold good for them.[31]

As a result of the enrichment programmes in oral work, music, drawing and dramatisation, Margaret felt that children who went on from the Nursery to schools for older children would find they could more easily cope with the advanced work there.

The increase in effective co-operation between parents, teachers, doctors and nurses as a result of the Mothers' Club was not quantified. However, Margaret and her staff maintained that the Club had helped to change attitudes in parents and teachers; it had encouraged some mothers to provide their children with better food, more rest, better clothing and raise the hygienic standards of their homes. Sometimes the Camp School children themselves set new standards in the home. One mother said to Margaret: 'Our house won't do for her, Miss, now. She's always a cleaning of her room and a keeping of the windows open, as it's a mercy we don't catch our death o'cold.'[32]

Margaret believed education would help parents to express themselves better, to increase their community participation and create a more knowledgeable society.

Miss Stevinson enables us to catch a glimpse of how the School tried to help parents to feed their children better: 'We talk to the mothers in the mornings, in the evenings, and at the club and the school doctor talks to them when she examines the children.' Speaking of clothing she wrote:

Many of our mothers put too many clothes on their children . . . One little boy came to us who suffered from a weak chest. We found that he was wrapped round and round in layers of newspaper soaked in camphorated oil . . . Some of the children are dressed much more warmly on Monday than on Thursday. The shadow of the pawnshop looms darkly and heavily over the Nursery School.[33]

While many mothers were undoubtedly helped by the School, some resisted change. Recalling how she sent a teacher home with a Lily Jacobs who was suffering from conjunctivitis, and the mother's response to it, Miss Stevinson explained:

'Bless you, Miss,' cried Mrs Jacobs, arms akimbo, 'that ain't conjunctivitis! That's the draughts in the house . . . Conjunctivitis? Not it, Miss! Why, look at our Georgie, he's got sore eyes. Look at me, ain't I got 'em? Look at our Bill! We're all the same, Miss, every one of us, and don't that prove it's the winders?' Alas! Mrs Jacobs must be registered as one of our failures. We could not prevail. There are still Mrs Jacobses amongst the ranks of our mothers – but not so many as there were last year.[34]

One of the many benefits springing from the Mothers' Club was that parents got to know each other better; they got a sense of belonging to a neighbourhood group. They not only met each other in the sewing classes, they joined in social occasions specifically arranged for them. Comparing the mothers who assembled for their annual outing in 1930 with those of 1910, Margaret saw a great difference – particularly in their heightened self-respect:

It seems strange to look at them in the lovely gardens, and remember that they live in the area where my dear sister and I worked, under such different circumstances, twenty years ago. What have these kind and charming women in their neat attire and with young smiling faces, restrained in all their joy – what have they to do with the people of yesterday? Doubtless many healing influences are playing now on many neighbourhoods. And among the healing agencies we venture to class our own open-air Nursery School.[35]

Members of staff noticed that, through the School, parents would sometimes get a new view of their children, then start to take a greater pride in them. Miss Campbell, one of Margaret's teachers, remembered such a case:

I recall a little gipsy-looking girl, Liz – one girl among several brothers. Liz never had any new clothes – hers came off a barrow. One day we had dressed her in a bright orange overall and hair ribbon. In the evening, coming down the steps, mother stopped and looked at her lovely daughter. 'Is that my Liz?' she said. 'I never knew she was pretty. Let's take her home to show her Dad, he don't know neither.' The result, dad gave mum a shilling every week for clothes for Liz.[36]

While engrossed in all this work for children, students, parents and the neighbourhood, Margaret gave little serious thought to her precarious legal tenure of the Stowage site. But, in 1919, the LCC made a new agreement with Margaret which allowed her to stay on at the Stowage, providing she relinquished all claim to the property, including the buildings, by 1924. What would happen after that date no-one knew, but Margaret held on to the vision she had of a large nursery school there.

Despite the many calls on her attention at the Stowage, in 1919, Margaret allowed herself to be nominated as Labour candidate for the LCC for Deptford. She was duly elected and appointed to serve on the Education Committee. This gave her the opportunity she had been seeking – to raise questions about the expansion of nursery work throughout the Authority. Typical of the many questions she asked in Committee in 1920 were:-

> Whether any provision is made, or about to be made, in the current year for the opening of nursery schools?
> Whether in view of the fact that hundreds of untrained teachers are now in the Council's employment, any provision is to be made in this year's estimates for the training of such teachers?[37]

It was obvious to her that if plans for nursery school expansion, as envisaged in the Fisher Act, were to be realised, provision needed to be made at once for initial and in-service courses for teachers. But she found it difficult to rouse much enthusiasm in the Education Committee, for these or for nursery education generally.

Ballard explains:

> The Moderates were then in power, Miss McMillan was a Labour member, and one of those awkward people who wanted things done . . . She tried to persuade the Education committee that a nursery school was as cheap to maintain as an ordinary council school – and immeasurably cheaper to build . . . But the statisticians challenged her figures, and poured scorn on the form in which her balance-sheet had been drawn up. Still she stood her ground and went on pressing her claims. And although she made many warm friends, she also made many enemies. Certain members of the Moderate party regarded her as a nuisance.[38]

Margaret's Nursery was by now over-full. She wanted accommodation for an extra 100 children and felt that at least two new shelters were required. In this proposed expansion Margaret was not only thinking of the needs of Deptford but of how she could promote the idea that large nursery schools, rather than small ones, were needed nationwide. The Board of Education was advocating small schools or units for about 50 children, but these were costly to build as well as to maintain. The initial and recurring expense of them acted as a deterrent to Local Education Authorities who, under the Act, were not compelled to provide them. Margaret thought that if she demonstrated that large schools could be proportionately cheaper than small ones, cautious LEAs might be encouraged to make some nursery provision.

Acting on the idea of enlarging her own premises, she wrote to the LCC asking for help and giving the *raison d'être* for this extra accommodation as:-

1 The testing at last by experiment what the size of these schools should be.
2 The actual knowledge of what they should cost.
3 The testing by experiment of how the staff should be trained.
4 The effect of the Nursery School on general health and intelligence.[39]

This seems to have been an inspired move, as it turned out that members of the Education Committee were currently debating whether to open some experimental nursery schools of their own, when they received Margaret's letter proposing an extension to her School. Out of the confluence of these two ideas came the suggestion that the LCC might erect an experimental nursery school on the land it owned at the Stowage, as an extension to Margaret's School.

Once this notion reached the Board of Education it was firmly resisted. Civil servants maintained that Margaret's financial methods were impossible and her grant claims so chaotic that they did not wish to cope with any extension of them. On one occasion an exasperated civil servant expressed the view that she could no more work in the public system than Livingstone could in the missionary system. In addition to negative aspersions about Margaret's fiscal abilities, doubts were expressed within the Board of Education about the wisdom of putting such a large number of young children together, at an age when they were most likely to catch infectious diseases.

However, after much haggling a new school was built as an extension to Margaret's, and was officially opened by Queen Mary on 22 November 1921. The two parts of the school, with accommodation for approximately 200 children of three to five years of age, were conducted for all practical purposes as one school, though they were differently financed. The original part, provided by Margaret, was merely aided by grant from the council; the other part was fully maintained.

Margaret was extremely fortunate in getting this building erected. It was perhaps more providential than coincidental, as by 1921 the economic state of the country forced the government to appoint a Committee on National Expenditure under the chairmanship of Sir Eric Geddes to seek ways of reducing expenditure.

Thinking of her oft-inspired moves, one of her friends said 'Margaret marched on in time with some music which most of us have not yet ears to hear.'[40]

The Geddes Committee immediately recommended that all educational development should stop at once. Subsequently, the Board of Education issued a circular to LEAs stating that it could not 'for the present entertain proposals for the establishment of Nursery Schools', except in special circumstances and where buildings already existed. Unfortunately this restriction remained in force until 1924. The 'Geddes Axe', as it came to be known, together with the Board's Circulars of retrenchment, dealt crushing blows to all nursery school enthusiasts, especially to Margaret. In 1922 Margaret failed to be re-elected to the LCC so was freer now to continue her fight for nursery schools.

One old student recorded an incident which shows how Margaret applied her faith to practical affairs:

> One day I was walking with Miss McMillan down the High
> Street – we met a Nun who stopped to speak to her. It was the
> time of the Geddes Act when there was little hope for Nursery
> Schools. Miss McMillan was very distressed. When she joined
> me after her talk with the Nun – she said with a radiance –
> 'Gwennie, they are going to pray for my work in the Convent –
> and I believe Tennyson was right. "More things are wrought by
> prayer than this world dreams of." '[41]

Margaret was unsure what to do next for pre-school children throughout the country. Her own school was thriving but this was never enough for her. She wanted to be a voice for all the voiceless; she knew public opinion would have to be roused on the nursery school issue. In 1922, while wondering how to do this, she received an invitation from Arthur Greenwood, MP for Nelson and Colne, who was on the Advisory Committee of the Trades Union Congress and Labour Party, to prepare a memorandum on nursery schools for the Party. This gave her the chance to put the case for nursery education, and the full implications of it, to a powerful body which could exert pressure on the government to withdraw the limiting Circulars and allow nursery school expansion to continue.

Her next opportunity came when she was approached about the founding of the Nursery School Association, a body which aimed to advance nursery school education and the training of nursery school teachers. One of her staff reports:

> On a cold and cheerless day in the spring of 1923 two visitors

came to the Rachel McMillan Nursery School to see Margaret McMillan. They were Mrs. Evelegh the wise and sympathetic Chairman of the Jellicoe Nursery School and Miss Owen, well known to the educational world as the Principal of the Mather Training College.

The three women who met in Miss McMillan's little sitting room had long been interested in the education of the pre-school child. They had worked many years for the nursery school and now they had come together to discuss the future of this movement and to consider whether the time was ripe for the founding of a Nursery School Association.[42]

Margaret, never one to underestimate the potential of a group with a common aim, gave the idea her wholehearted support. The outcome was the formation, after a conference in Manchester in 1923, of the Nursery School Association. Its three main objectives were: first, to secure the effective working of Clause 19 of the Education Act of 1918, which enabled LEAs to provide nursery education; second, to furnish opportunity for discussion; and third, to help form and focus public opinion on all matters relating to the nursery school movement. This was a milestone in the history of nursery education; the pattern of early childhood education in Britain, which later became the envy of the world, was largely shaped by this Association.

Between the formation of the Nursery School Association in 1923, and the decision to rename it the British Association for Early Childhood Education, in 1973, lies a half century of unremitting struggle for the establishment of nursery education, in which Margaret played a key role till her death.

When it came to choosing the new Association's first President, Margaret was an obvious choice. Once elected, she held the office with distinction for the next six years; she chaired meetings, gave lectures and led delegations to the Board of Education, to further the idea of 'Nursery Schools for all, beginning with those in greatest need'.

Despite the tremendous efforts made, politicians seemed apathetic about nursery education. In a Labour Party pamphlet written in 1924, and reprinted six years later, Margaret affirmed:

No great party has as yet taken the Cause of the Children much to heart. Busy as any party always is, it has no time to spare for it . . . A thousand objects claim the very close attention of the best people in the realm, so that – no! not the cry – rather the silent lapse of the children into lifelong misery and weakness does not touch them.[43]

At the same time as working for the Nursery School Association, Margaret helped other organisations. At a conference in London in 1923 called by Eglantyne Jebb, the initiator of the Save the Children Fund, she spoke about 'the principles of free play and open air education which the Fund was later to promote'.[44] In addition she entertained many important guests at her own School. Rudolf Steiner, whom she first met at a conference in Ilkley in 1923, was one of the many notables who visited her at the Stowage. As well as receiving visitors, she had to keep a close watch on the way her School was forever expanding. At her own expense she opened a new shelter, costing £600, in Wellington Street in June 1923. By 1924 there were 250 children on the register with an average daily attendance of 212, but still there was a long waiting list. More children in the School meant more staff and students were required. Although she already had five student hostels, the demand for places continually exceeded the supply.

By now Margaret's work was so widely known and respected locally that, in 1924, she was invited to write her name on Deptford's Roll of Honour. One newspaper comment on this read:

> If Miss McMillan accepts, her name will only be the fourth to be inscribed on the roll, but then any borough would be only too proud to be identified with the work of this eminent educationist ... Bradford has already perpetuated her name in the Margaret McMillan School for mentally weak children and the City's three nursery schools which have resulted from her efforts.[45]

In an official address, the Mayor, aldermen and citizens placed on record their 'deep appreciation' of Margaret's 'important and distinctive services to the Child Life of the Nation' and 'gratefully recognized' the 'honour which had redounded to the Borough by reason of the attention which has been directed to the Deptford Open-air Nursery Schools'.[46]

Although Margaret was nationally venerated, and her company eagerly sought in many different circles, perhaps she spent her happiest hours amongst the children in Deptford. One of her old students wrote:

> It is in the Nursery School garden that I like to remember Miss McMillan. Here in brief moments she would approach a small child and the two of them would wander off hand in hand to discover the beauty of a rose or the colour in a pigeon's wing.[47]

Chapter twenty-two

A Dream College 1925–30

Despite all the efforts made by the Nursery School Association and other nursery enthusiasts to encourage Local Education Authorities to establish nursery schools, development was slow throughout the country. In 1925 there were only 26 recognised nursery schools in England and 28 in 1929. Largely because of the expense involved, many LEAs improved the conditions in reception classes in infant schools for children between the ages of three and five, rather than build new nursery schools. Even so, in 1931 less than one per cent of the pre-school population of England and Wales was able to attend either a nursery school or class and the economic crisis of that year imposed restrictions on any further development.

Fortunately, however, there was an increasing acknowledgement among doctors, teachers and parents that nursery schools were desirable institutions. Once it became apparent that they provided nurture and education, a system of medical supervision before children began their compulsory schooling at five, and helped to improve child-rearing practices, positive attitudes to them developed. Though encouraged by the increasing recognition of the value of nursery education, Margaret agonised over the large proportion of the nation's children who still could not gain access to any nursery school or class, due, she felt, to public apathy about the implementation of the Fisher Act.

Her article, 'Those that are Sent Away', shows how much she cared about the mothers who had to be turned away from her own school daily and the children who had to endure preventable suffering:

Passing out of our gate everyday is a remnant of the army that must be sent away, . . . They are going back into the darkness of their squalid, hurrying lives. We have no room for them here . . . At the bottom of our hearts we know that the despair of these poor souls marks the water line of our own spiritual energy.[1]

D. E. M. Gardner, a former Head of the Child Development Department at the University of London's Institute of Education, who worked for a short time in Margaret's Nursery School in 1924, recalled Margaret's indignation at needless pain and distress: 'I remember the real agony in her voice when she pointed out a little girl suffering from neglected adenoids, "Look at that child – how horrible".'[2]

From now on to the end of her days Margaret concentrated on addressing the two interrelated issues of increased provision of nursery schools and specific training for nursery school teachers. Trying to spur the public into taking action about nursery education, in 1926 she wrote several articles in *The Clarion*.

> Please remember this, the open-air nursery school is on the Statute Book . . . The Education Bill of 1918 opened the door for this kind of school to every locality in the country [but] the people are not fighting for it.[3]

On another occasion she asked:

> What about the training of teachers? How are they going to learn their job – teaching? Can they master it by going to college for two years and giving lessons in a school for a few weeks? . . . I have no hesitation in saying such training is quite inadequate.[4]

Margaret's vision of the need for pre-school education often impelled her to speak about it far and wide. Eventually this began to take its toll on her. To a correspondent who expressed concern about her travelling so much (Margaret was now in her mid-60s), she admitted 'Sometimes I lecture and find all the travelling tiring – still.'[5] Before long her health seemed adversely affected. An entry in Katharine Bruce Glasier's diary for 13 February 1926 read: 'Went to M. McMillan's W.E.A. "Education in Danger" protest meeting at Westminster Hall – half full only. She is in great pain – arthritis in feet. God bless her.' (The meeting had been arranged to ensure that the needs of children below five years would not be sacrificed in the new administrative arrangements suggested in the Hadow Report, 'Education of the Adolescent' 1926).

By April, her health had seriously declined. Writing to a friend she said: 'Long ago I would have written you, but I have been and still am in a Nursing Home . . . I have an arthritic hip joint and am under an osteopath – the doctors being no use at all.'[6]

Forced now by ill-health to do less, Margaret was unable to attend meetings and conferences or accept lecturing appointments for several months. One of the many invitations she had to decline at this time came from Bradford. She was asked to be guest speaker at the 25th Anniversary Celebration of the Bradford Froebel Society. Though unable to be present in person she wrote an address which was printed and circulated to all members.[7]

Writing articles and letters in bed now had to be Margaret's main means of continuing her campaign. Often she wrote articles which related the children's cause to topical issues. During the 1926 Miners' Strike, she wrote in *The Clarion* comparing the cost of the strike with that of good educational provision for young children.[8] When it was mooted that a system of child allowances should be inaugurated to offset malnutrition in children, Margaret took the opportunity of saying that these would be no guarantee that children would be better fed or healthier. The money would be better spent on more nursery schools and she urged people to fight for 'the real salvation of the poor' by providing open-air schools.[9]

Challenged to put down 'in plain English' what her campaign was all about, Margaret outlined her ideas on nursery schools and colleges.

> To begin with, I want the infant schools of the country to become open-air nursery schools . . . and attached to these, small colleges with forty to eighty students . . . The girls should do practical work in the school from the start. They should have three years' sound practice in teaching before they are allowed to be responsible for the education of children.[10]

Thinking of the need for relevant teacher-training Margaret enquired of Sir George Newman, the Chief Medical Officer at the Ministry of Health, about the availability of grants for the building of a small college where women could train for work in open-air nursery schools. After receiving a discouraging reply, she once again turned her mind towards initiating a private venture.

Her Training Centre at the Stowage, loosely called the College, had no specific building. Students had to take their lectures in any available room in the Nursery School. Their residential accommodation consisted of four dilapidated houses in and around Albury Street, which Margaret had turned into student hostels. Originally many of these houses had decorated porticos, panelled interiors, Adam fire-places, carved ceilings and powder closets, but by now they had lost their pristine glory. These hostels had many disadvantages and few amenities. The following accounts by two students give an indication of the spartan accommodation together with the stalwart spirit of the students. One teacher, who trained in 1925, recalled going over the road from the Stowage 'to the Wellington Street Hostel each night, and using the outdoor bathroom in fear and trembling because of the explosive geysers'. But she remarked that she had 'no regrets', as she found it 'a very useful preparation for coping with Nursery School problems'.[11]

Another student recollecting her first introduction to the hostel at 24 Albury Street said:

My mother and I walked up several flights of stairs up to the top and went into a very small room with a sloping roof and off it was another small room (which people said was a powder closet when Queen Elizabeth's Ladies in Waiting were in Greenwich) . . . There was only a patch of garden to this house and then Carter Patterson's stables. On my first night I thought 'What on earth is happening?' There was thump, thump, thump practically all through the night and not altogether pleasant smells coming up, it was apparently these great big horses kicking against the partitions of the stables . . . My mother when she left me up there was very unhappy. It wasn't what I had been used to and I think she wanted to take me home, but I wouldn't go, and I loved every minute of the whole place.[12]

While recuperating in the Nursing Home, Margaret spent a lot of time dreaming of a purpose-built college. Although she had no idea how she could realise this dream, she never relinquished it. Fortunately, in 1926, she met Lady Astor, Conservative MP for Plymouth, who helped her achieve her objective.

Recounting how they first became acquainted, Lady Astor said:

One day Margaret McMillan telephoned and said that she had had a dream and something told her to get in touch with me. I went to Deptford with Margaret Wintringham [a former Liberal MP for Louth]; we saw the Rachel McMillan Nursery School, and realized then that here was a way of getting children out of the slums. I came home and told my husband.[13]

Christopher Sykes, Nancy Astor's recent biographer, commenting on the remarkable friendship which developed between her and Margaret, wrote:

Nancy and Margaret were both deeply religious, but in very different ways . . . Margaret McMillan's beliefs in the mystical significance of dreams, were normally somewhat repellent to Nancy, and for that reason the intensity of their friendship is surprising. Nevertheless it was formed instantly, and any doubts that Nancy had felt vanished on meeting this mild and formidable woman.[14]

Writing to Nancy Astor in November 1926 when she was back at the Stowage, Margaret said: 'I am urged by some influence to build a College, and I know it will go up presently.'[15] Ten days later she wrote her again saying: 'For some reason I'm called back and quite well – I'm going to build a College – perhaps that's why I've come back.'[16]

Margaret promptly set up a building fund and planned how to raise money for it. Subsequently, Nancy Astor used her influence and money to promote both nursery education and the proposed college – the provision of both would have been much slower had it not been for her assistance. Commenting on Nancy's doughty support, Sykes wrote:

> She brought that cause to the notice of the House of Commons. She saw that nursery schools could only expand if there were abundant training facilities for teachers and nurses . . . She interested Waldorf [her husband] in the enterprise and took him down to the nursery school and training centre at Deptford. He immediately shared Nancy's enthusiasm.[17]

One of the Astors said to Mansbridge on leaving Margaret's school, 'It is like a visit to heaven.'[18]

Waldorf gave money to buy land on which a college could be built and in 1927 Nancy gave £10,000 to the project. Paying tribute to his part in the venture Nancy disclosed that he 'had been very good in helping her to raise funds for the building, by allowing her to buy things like pieces of tapestry for £800 which later she sold for £2,000, the profit going to the building fund'.[19] Both of the Astors sacrificed and spoke to their friends about the fund. Few who visited them socially left without hearing something about it. Recalling the struggle for the college, Nancy said, 'I dropped everything and fought with her and for her – and I am grateful for the privilege. We had to close our house for two years, but to help her was worth it.'[20]

Margaret too spoke about the college wherever she went and mentioned it in her letters. Many thought that she would build her dream college in a more salubrious spot than Deptford, perhaps in Blackheath, but she was adamant that it must be erected among the homes of the children, so that future teachers could gain a better understanding of children's home backgrounds. Consequently, a site was chosen near to the Stowage in Creek Road.

In 1927, Margaret was granted a Civil List Pension of £75 per annum 'in recognition of her public, social and educational services'; this was a welcome lift to her own finances and enabled her to travel about to arouse more interest in the provision of nursery schools and colleges. When feeling impatient about the slow advance towards her ideals, she wrote pleadingly to her friend Katharine Bruce Glasier: 'There is no use trusting in Governments *of any kind* . . . O Katharine let's rouse *the people*. The politicians will follow.'[21]

Although so recently recovered from a serious illness, Margaret undertook a heavy programme of public speaking including a lecture tour in Scotland followed by visits to many large cities throughout Britain.

Addressing the Governors of the Yorkshire Loan Training Fund at Meanwood, Leeds, in 1929 – a fund established to help girls to have advanced education – she described 'the activity, aims and achievements' of her Training Centre and 'considered that girls who received grants from the Yorkshire Fund would do well to enter the Centre for courses of training'.[22] Trying to interest health workers in the training of nursery school teachers, in her article 'Nursery Schools: the Base of Education', published in *The Royal Sanitary Institute Journal*, she expressed the view that unless that training was attempted there could be 'no real progress or happiness for our race'.[23]

Inside and outside of the teaching profession she was recognised as an authority in her field. For years she was in great demand as an opener of new schools. Denby Street Nursery School, Sheffield, the Open-air School at Woodhouse near Huddersfield, the School for Educationally Sub-normal Children in Bradford, and the Kay Street Nursery School, Bolton, are just a few of the many schools she opened between 1928 and 1930, and wherever she went she mentioned her dream college.

Margaret's many public appearances and writings naturally attracted attention to her work. As a result, much of her time in the late 1920s was taken up with visitors to the Stowage. Mrs Bruce Glasier maintained:

Thousands of pilgrims, lovers of little children, earnest students of education from all over the world, have been making their way there in the past few years. Our Margaret McMillan's books have been more widely read in America alas than in Britain.

Outlining some of the School's achievements with children from one-roomed homes she felt she saw: 'The emergence not only of a new social order, but of the new and nobler type of humanity which is the object of all our striving.'[24]

The following appreciative letter from a Chinese official is typical of the many Margaret received from overseas visitors: 'On behalf of my Government I wish to express my appreciation of the assistance you have rendered me . . . Your work is simply the beginning of a realisation of an educational ideal which will probably take centuries to be fulfilled.'[25]

P. B. Ballard, the LCC Inspector of Schools, was one of many prominent British educators who paid tribute to Margaret's work. He wrote:

> I went first because I had to; I went afterwards because I wanted to . . . Later on when I extended my knowledge of nursery schools by visiting those in other parts of the country, I realized that Miss McMillan's school was the largest and most important, not only in London, but in the whole of England. And incomparably the best. So to see this school, and particularly to see its presiding genius, I often went for my personal pleasure and for the refreshment of my spirit.[26]

In between receiving visitors and fulfilling many speaking engagements, she completed her book, *The Life of Rachel McMillan*, in 1927, and dedicated it 'To Lady Astor', adding, 'Party is not enough!' Margaret deeply regretted that, while many were embroiled in party political strife, the sufferings of thousands of young children were going unheeded. She yearned for members of different political parties to work together for the benefit of all children and find a unity above political alignment as she did with Lady Astor and Mrs Wintringham. However, on occasion Margaret's fraternising got her into trouble with her own party.

When Lady Astor was seeking re-election as a Conservative candidate in the 1929 General Election, Margaret, though a well-known socialist, went down to Plymouth to speak on her behalf. Subsequently the General Secretary of the Labour Party wrote to Margaret pointing out that 'she had offended against the rule that members of the Party were under promise not to support the candidates of any other Party – especially so in a constituency where a Labour Candidate was standing'. In her reply, Margaret 'urged that she had gone to Plymouth because of all the help Lady Astor had given to nursery school projects and pleaded in extenuation that she had gone straight from Plymouth to Rochdale, to speak there for the Labour Candidate, W. T. Kelly'.[27]

One of the many devices Margaret used to draw attention to nursery education and the need for a college, was to ask influential men to come to Deptford. Stanley Baldwin, the Prime Minister, was one of these. Four months after visiting the Stowage, Baldwin mentioned this in a speech at Drury Lane where he said: 'I was very much impressed . . . when I went down to Deptford to see that wonderful child's school of Miss McMillan. I am quite sure that the next advance to be made by the State is the care of the children from the ages of 1 to 5.'[28] The Prime Minister's comment made a newspaper reporter rush down to Deptford immediately to interview Margaret. In answering his many questions, she said of Baldwin: 'He made no promises after I had shown him round, but it is clear that what he saw lingered in his mind.'[29]

As well as civil servants and politicians, Margaret would sometimes ask well-known literary men to come to meet her children and students. John Masefield, the Poet Laureate, Walter de la Mare and G. B. Shaw were among the many writers who visited Deptford. Her persistence, in pursuing the people she particularly wanted to come, can be glimpsed in a student's account of what happened when Margaret decided to invite G. B. Shaw. G. B. S.'s secretary sent a card, headed 'Mr. Shaw does not visit', followed by a list of places with nursery schools ticked. But Margaret wrote again and again. One of his replies included, 'I wish you and your D . . . kids were at the bottom of the sea.' Undeterred Margaret wrote again. Eventually G. B. S. visited Deptford, and the children Margaret had taught performed a play about St Francis of Assisi for him. He was thrilled and said he would write one for them.[30] The next morning he gave a talk on Russia. Later, according to an eyewitness:

> Peggy Mac [as Margaret was affectionately known] showed G. B. S. round the garden and picked up a toddler, Billy Stapely, and introduced him to the 'nice gentleman'. Billy responded by pulling hard at Shaw's beard, which caused great laughter from Miss McMillan. The only time the Lion was bearded![31]

Nancy Astor also persuaded Shaw to visit nursery schools. Collis, her biographer, relates: 'At one of them he is recorded to have asked a group of children: "Have you read any of my plays?" "No", they replied (They were all under five). "I am glad to hear it", said he.'[32]

At Margaret's Nursery School children were often registered before they were born and later proved to be good propagandists for nursery education, as were their mothers. One grateful parent wrote to *The Daily News*:

My children are in a Heaven on Earth. We live in one room – six of us – but they go into this Heaven every day. And I go with them, and forget, for a few moments, all that is sad and dark in my life. And I want other children to have a Paradise opened for them too. Then, even if their lives are hard later, they will have had some joy.[33]

While the money was being raised for the College, Margaret often dreamed about the teachers who would study there and how they could be fully equipped for the responsible nature of their work – the uplifting of humanity. Speaking some years earlier she had declared: 'To be a teacher in the schools of to-morrow is to be drawn into the very heart of a movement whose goal is the perfecting of the race.'[34] She believed teachers should realise that they were dealing with 'a brain and a soul', even when they 'seemed to be dealing with a nose and a lip'.

Writing to her students, when she was away lecturing in Glamorganshire in 1929, she tried to point them to a power that could sustain them in their work. Part of this letter ran:

Judge then how momentous is this hour, and how great the responsibility to which you in the days of youth, are called. I long, of course, to see you equipped with all the power that liberal education gives . . . But the new claim of the new hour is for new moral enthusiasm – yes, for Spiritual gifts before all. These alone can carry you through the period of transition through which we are about to pass. I do not know of any strength that can be found in even the higher forms of self-interest. They are all empty and futile. But there is another source, and in it is the needed power. 'Seek ye first the Kingdom of God' – here and now for little children.[35]

Margaret saw teachers as 'discoverers', 'inventors' and 'improvers of methods'. She expected those she trained to step out beyond traditional practices to pioneer something new. She was not only interested in distributing the benefits of existing pre-school education to more children, she hoped her students would continuously improve the quality of education.

Her ideas about teachers' training and their task in society largely sprang from her Christian Socialism, and were expressed in language similar to that Keir Hardie used. In *From Serfdom to Socialism* he wrote:

If anything is to be really done in this world, it must be done by Visionaries, by men who see the future, and make the future because they see it. The inventor and discoverer must see with the eye of faith the thing he wants to accomplish before it takes form and shape to the eye of flesh.[36]

Margaret's socialist principles and writings sometimes gave rise to suspicion about possible political indoctrination in her work. The letter below, written to *The Patriot*, but reprinted in full in *The Clarion*, illustrates this:

Sir, I notice that a public appeal is being made in the Press by Miss Margaret McMillan for funds in aid of the McMillan Training Centre at Deptford, and it would be most desirable to know if Socialist teaching is given, formally or otherwise, in the Centre . . . My reason for asking if any of your readers can furnish information in this case is that Miss McMillan appears to have been an active propagandist of Socialism, judging from parts of her biography of her sister Rachel, and from a passage in Mr. Lansbury's recent book, 'My Life'. Yours etc., PRUDENTIA.[37]

An extract from Robert Blatchford's answer to Prudentia follows.

It is not Miss McMillan's object to instil political theories into the minds of two-year-old babies; but to save them from rickets and scrofula and blindness and sores; to feed them and to love them and give them light and air; to teach them to use their limbs and eyes and voices and keep their souls alive and their bodies clean . . . Miss McMillan is asking for a college where the right kind of helpers and teachers may be trained . . . This college is the need of the hour . . . What she now needs is reinforcements. And she will get them.[38]

Margaret marvelled at the way the building fund for the College continued to grow. In 1929 she wrote to Robert Blatchford:

I'm getting the College to train people . . . The L.C.C. are helping me, but not enough to go on with without other help . . . Lord Astor bought the site for £4,000, Lady Astor gives £3,000. Mr. Wall gave me £1,000, and a lady left me £1,000 and Lloyds are getting £1,000.[39]

Later in the year she announced that the Foundation Stone of the Rachel McMillan College would be laid by Lady Astor on 6 November. When that great day came, Margaret reminded the assembled guests that the College was designed to realise Rachel's great aim 'to educate children as if they were our own'. Then she added:

We desire to turn out teachers who will be true gardeners in real child gardens, and, if these gardens are planted in poor areas so much the better. Education should make even the poorest district beautiful and create Edens in the heart of mean streets . . . This is a day for gratitude to all the friends of the College and School . . . They have aided the efforts of those teachers who desire to be social missionaries and whose training will be a dedication as well as a career.[40]

At the ceremony, Lady Astor described the work of nursery schools as 'the most important movement in the country at the moment', and told students that 'they would get from Margaret McMillan an inner light they would not get from anyone else'.[41] After the formal proceedings she made a tour of the School. But when she interrupted one three-year-old who was 'eagerly waiting to begin his steaming plate of vegetable stew', she was curtly told to 'Shut up and go 'ome.'[42]

On Christmas morning 1929 Margaret, half laughing at herself, wrote: 'I'm taking on the raising of £10,000 just now for a College . . . I, who had no sense about money, no training, and great caution. Why! All business ability, as well as great poetry comes from beyond.'[43]

Once the foundations of the College were completed, Margaret, though immersed in various activities, watched the walls rise with eager anticipation. At this time she was busy organising in-service courses in Deptford for certificated teachers. Among the many participants in these were groups of teachers from Yorkshire and Wales. H. G. Bannan of Bradford gives an account of Margaret's involvement.

In the April of 1930, ten Bradford teachers went to London to take advantage of the offer of a 3 months course in Nursery Education at the Rachel McMillan Nursery School offered to them by Margaret McMillan. She was at that time an old lady, but her passion for the well-being of the child was as white hot as her hairs were silver. She lived on the campus and spent her whole day amongst the children. You would find her in the garden, or near the aviary, talking to the little ones, correcting a wrong posture in child (or adult!), asking searching questions if she saw a child looking unhappy or distressed. She was always concerned with the child as a whole – his social, intellectual, spiritual and emotional development as well as his physical well being. She invented apparatus to exercise and strengthen arm and hand muscles, she encouraged the wonder and love of nature by providing a 'garden School'; she was always available to converse with children who needed the impetus and stimulation of adult companionship . . .

Miss McMillan gave us the occasional lecture. Her mind was so richly furnished that she couldn't confine herself to one subject. So a lecture headed 'School Building' would comprise some interesting aspects of Greek Education and scathing comments on the iniquities of provincial School Boards. It was a privilege to be in contact with her wise compassionate mind, a privilege I'll never forget nor minimise.[44]

Writing from Wales, G. Williams reported:

An enthusiastic party consisting of Miss Evans, Principal [of Barry Training College], several headmistresses, together with a few assistant teachers, set out from Barry to visit the Rachel McMillan Nursery School and the Training College at Deptford. It was my good fortune to be one of this party . . . Everywhere one was conscious of an atmosphere of happiness and well-being resulting from the loving care given to each individual . . . The little ones were happy and carefree for they were well and suitably dressed, they were properly fed and rested . . .

Miss McMillan and the late Miss Rachel McMillan, have both carried far the lighted torch of progress. It now remains for us, who are leaving College full of enthusiasm, new ideas and high ideals to snatch up the torch, so nobly lighted . . .

Miss McMillan's ideal is far beyond the reach of one generation, for as one aim is attained, another grows out of it to appear far away in the distance.[45]

As the new College neared completion the builders worked overtime to finish it. Eventually on 21 April 1930, *The Times* announced that Queen Mary would open the new building on 8 May and explained:

This event marks an epoch in the development of the nurture of young children . . . Henceforward it will be possible for 80 students to receive training instead of 40 in both the theory and practice of dealing with young children. This may seem to some to be but an episode in the unfolding story of education in England but it is more than that – it is a creative act.[46]

When the great day came there was an air of expectation at the Stowage and in the surrounding streets. In reporting the event the *Evening Standard* mentioned the pleasure the Queen's visit gave the crowds, and declared that she must have heard 'many announcements that in her light-coloured coat and flowery toque she looked "lovely"'. The reporter hoped she also heard 'an impulsive cry of "She's just like Princess Elizabeth."'[47]

Behind the scenes the students were excitedly trying to fulfil a number of roles. One of them recalled:

The number of students was still small so we all had several tasks to do – firstly we had to form a guard of honour . . . As soon as Queen Mary had entered the building we had to run round to the back so that we could sing outside the Hall where the ceremony was taking place. Then we were divided into three groups:

a) to 'wait' on Her Majesty and other guests,
b) to be on duty with the children in the Nursery School,
c) to form a guard of honour when Queen Mary and the other guests accompanied Margaret McMillan from the College to the Nursery School.[48]

Margaret's welcome to the Queen included:

I must express my gratitude, Madam, not only for your presence here to-day but for the wonderful strength you gave me in my hour of great distress, difficulty and fear, when you bridged for me a terrible chasm . . . You were with us in the hours of distress, and we are happy now to have you with us in the moment of fulfilment and joy.[49]

After the official opening, the Queen inspected the building. It had a common room, a lecture room, 16 bedsitting rooms and 14 cubicles, all of them centrally heated and simply but attractively furnished. Having admired the College the Queen went on to the School. As she watched the children play, Her Majesty exclaimed to Margaret, 'What a lot of lovely toys all the children have. It is splendid work you are doing.'

Recalling this day some years later, an old student wrote:

What a day it was (May 8th, 1930) with a feeling of Spring. All the children wore clean overalls and a shoe firm provided new sandals . . . Margaret McMillan was so happy about the college 'where my students will learn and go out to open up nursery schools'.[50]

In the new College, the staff, aims and curriculum were as in the Centre; the furniture, apparatus and equipment were much improved and gave the trainers better conditions in which to continue their task of developing teachers of quality – teachers with a positive approach to children and flexible views of teaching methods and curricula.

One of Margaret's creative insights into the training of teachers was that a three-year course was required. At this time most other colleges offered two-year courses – three-year courses only became standard procedure in 1960. Another area where Margaret's College was ahead of others was in its school-based courses. Practical training was concurrent with theoretical, and the Nursery School staff played a major part in training students.

The first Principal of the new College was Miss Emma Stevinson who for the previous eleven years had been Head of the Nursery School, and prior to that had had a wide experience of teaching young children. Speaking of her, Margaret declared that she had been utterly faithful to Rachel's tradition, then commented:

> These years have not been years of calm security and easy fulfilment. It would have been impossible to live through them except as one who guards a hidden treasure. I am thankful to know that Miss Stevinson will be the first Principal of the Rachel McMillan College.[51]

The Rachel McMillan College was the last of a series of interlocking experiments which Margaret, with Rachel's help, had created in Deptford. It was not only the last but it was the crowning achievement of her life.

Pointing to what she felt lay behind all of Margaret's institutions, one of her close acquaintances said that her schemes for children were 'more than stunts or isolated parts of reform – they were part of a plan which unfolded as she obeyed her inner directions'.[52]

Chapter twenty-three

Bowing Out from the World Stage 1930–1

In 1930, Margaret was made a Member of the Companions of Honour 'for services to the Nursery School Movement'. One of her students recollected: 'I remember her showing us her dress as she was about to attend the Investiture at Buckingham Palace; her heel caught in her dress and it was torn. She simply borrowed a safety pin.'[1] Mansbridge recalled seeing her in 1930, 'sitting alone at the Buckingham Palace Garden Party – neatly but poorly dressed – looking dreamily at the brilliant crowd, entirely unassertive of her presence'.[2]

Sir Charles Trevelyan – President of the Board of Education – in congratulating Margaret on her honour wrote:

> Of all the people in the world you deserve it. The greater
> honour which I hope to help you in attaining, and which you will
> eventually I know appreciate most, is the spread of your
> example throughout the country. It is undoubtedly coming.[3]

Once the Rachel McMillan College opened, applications for places flooded in from many different parts of the United Kingdom; others arrived from Germany, Russia, Sweden, Poland, China, Malta, Egypt, Canada and America. Margaret offered students a thorough professional training along with a vision of the better future teachers could help shape. One student recalled that in her lectures, Margaret 'often spoke to us . . . of the Deptford that is to be, when all shall be fair as in the Nursery School garden, and all the children straight limbed and beautiful'.[4] She fully expected students to innovate and take on a catalyst role.

Within a short time the demand for places at the College was so great that towards the end of 1930 Margaret began to plan an extension to the premises. Although plunged again into lengthy discussions with architects, she retained her keen interest in College life and continually encouraged students to take initiatives. In the autumn term she consented to be President of a newly-formed Dramatic Society. Soon plays were performed, including dramatised incidents from Victor Hugo's *Les Misérables*. Then, at a meeting where she presided, a Student Christian Movement group was formed. Margaret hoped too that students would gain vision and purpose from the religious assemblies held in the College each morning, where John Bunyan's hymn, 'Who would true valour see' was often sung. In addition, she wanted there to be a religious element in the whole day so that in their lectures and practical work students might develop useful skills and positive attitudes to others.

She was rarely happier than when participating in student activities, but her health which had declined during the previous year increasingly impeded her. One student wrote: 'During her last years, Miss McMillan was far from well and suffered much pain from arthritis. Helped considerably by Lady Astor's generosity she regularly visited a clever osteopath in Wigmore Street . . . Late in 1930 Miss McMillan's health deteriorated still further.'[5]

Mansbridge reported that in December 1930 Margaret was so ill that she had to ask one of her students to fulfil two public engagements for her. The student observed:

> Although in bed at the time, and seemingly very tired, both mentally and physically, she spared no effort to help me in preparing my speeches, and wrote down part of them herself. When she became too tired to write, she dictated the rest to me, and with such eloquence and rapid flow of words that I had to stop her once or twice as I could not keep up . . . This effort so exhausted her that she turned over in bed, and lay quite still for a minute or two, and then asked me to come back after lunch and read it over to her. When I returned . . . I started to read over the lecture, but she soon stopped me. 'You're going too fast, and remember never begin a speech too loudly. You get people's attention far better by talking quietly to start with.' One of her last pieces of advice to me was: 'If you're going to get on never be afraid of criticism. If you think a thing is right say it, and never mind what people say about you.'[6]

By January 1931 she had been persuaded by Lady Astor to go into a nursing home – Bowden House in Harrow-on-the-Hill. While she was resting there Nancy Astor proved to be a true friend – she both provided for Margaret's physical needs and tried to help her find peace of heart. Writing to her from Plymouth on 8 January, Nancy said:

> I have got to take my son, Bill, on Saturday to Switzerland for

ten days. I wish that I could take you with us . . . but I know that for all our sakes, you will be very patient and take care of your thoughts and soon be well. I hope you are no longer quarrelling with God!!! That did make me laugh. You are bound to get your healing as you are so honest. Just put in gratitude for all that He has allowed you to do, and that is a great deal. Best love, Nancy.[7]

Once it became generally known that Margaret was unwell, she became the recipient of a stream of letters, cards and flowers from old friends and colleagues. Members of the Deptford Borough Council sent a message expressing the hope that she would 'quickly be restored to health and be able to continue her magnificent work for children'. The Mayor said they were proud 'that Deptford should possess such a noble character', while Councillor J. Grenfell Hicks called her 'one of our most noble citizens'.[8]

Although physically exhausted, illness did not have the last word with Margaret; she kept up lively conversations about the Nursery School and College with the many visitors who went to see her. The Senior Student wrote: 'It was one of my duties to send her flowers every week-end with a note telling her about activities at the College and the Camp School. She always replied to these . . . most graciously.'[9]

As the weeks went by, Margaret's condition appreciably grew worse; soon it became apparent to her close friends that though she had planned the new extension to the College she was unlikely to see it built; the end was in sight. Even so all those who visited her during this time bore testimony to her relentless concern for her various experiments. Speaking of his visit to the nursing home with Hugh Railton Dent, who in 1931 became chairman of the Camp School, Mansbridge reported: 'On her death-bed Margaret McMillan begged him and myself to see that the work of the School went forward.'[10]

She died on 29 March, aged 70, and was buried in the same grave as Rachel at Brockley Cemetery, London, on 31 March. Her last words, a message to Nancy Astor, were, 'Tell her I have no fear. I am happy.'[11]

Margaret achieved in death the same prominence as she did in life. Speaking of her funeral, one who knew her well wrote:

The Queen sent tribute to her burying, the titled and the learned stood around her bier, a bishop pronounced the benediction on her life, her sorrowing staff and her body-guard of blue-robed students told of her inspiration, and the tear-dimmed eyes of the multitude of humble Deptford folk, who crowded church and streets for her last passing, told of the devotion she had evoked.[12]

The Times said: 'She died in the firm faith that the students of the college will carry onwards the torch she has dropped, and that the schools of her heart's desire will multiply and the children be comforted.'[13]

The Times Educational Supplement reported:

The death of Miss Margaret McMillan, the pioneer of nursery schools, comes at a moment when her cherished goal is not only blessed by all educationists but when active measures are being taken by the Board of Education to secure such schools as a universal part of our national education . . . Yet the fact remains that one-fifth of the children who enter the schools are in ill-health . . . The opening of this [College] . . . brought the work of Margaret McMillan to completion.[14]

The Scotsman, The Telegraph, The Labour Magazine, The Labour Woman and *The New Leader* were among the numerous national papers which paid tribute to her. Her local paper, *The Kentish Mercury*, reporting the speech of Councillor W. H. Green at a meeting of the Deptford Borough Council, said:

He described Miss McMillan as one of the greatest personalities of the age, and said her services were international in their effect. Her life, which was one of singular charm, was devoted almost exclusively to the higher interests of the children . . . Fortunately she lived long enough to inspire an army of young women teachers with her own ideals, and to place her work on a firm foundation.

The Mayor said, 'Deptford has lost a distinguished lady and a great personality.'[15]

H. B. Lees-Smith, President of the Board of Education, speaking in the House of Commons shortly after her death said: 'It is already quite evident that the life of Miss Margaret McMillan will leave a permanent mark upon the health of the children of our land.'[16]

In Australia, *The Sydney Morning Herald* – a paper which had previously reported Margaret's activities – published a letter which read:

I know her, not only as a great educationist, but as a great-hearted and lovable woman who has literally given her life for the children of the world. Though Margaret McMillan has left us, her work and her noble spirit belong to eternity.[17]

Margaret's beloved Miss Stevinson, the College Principal, giving her own personal tribute to a much-loved friend, declared to the students:

Margaret McMillan was a fighter. Her enemies were ignorance, prejudice, dirt and disease. She said, 'To be weak is to be wicked: to stand still is to go back.' Her last message to her students was 'Tell my girls to stick to the slums. Many teachers can be found for the schools set in pleasant places. The bravest and best are needed for the slums.' . . . Margaret McMillan's name will never die. Everywhere, in this country, and across the seas, men honour her for her chivalry. She needs no memorial. Her work will always go forward for it is God's work. She succoured the helpless, fed the hungry, clothed the naked. She brought light into the dark places of the earth.[18]

There are many memorials to Margaret. One of the earlier ones in the grounds of the Rachel McMillan Nursery School in Deptford was an ornamental lamp which symbolised the illumination she brought to dark places. One of the later ones was the Margaret McMillan Memorial College of Education in Bradford, officially opened in 1956. When the Memorial Fund for this was launched Queen Mary, as a token of her admiration for Margaret's work, was the first to make a donation.

Perhaps the commemoration which would have meant most to Margaret was the continuation of her work – the expansion of nursery education by her students together with the impact they made on the neighbourhoods they served. 'News of Old Girls' – a regular feature in the *Rachel McMillan Training College News Sheets* – shows the diverse range of work in Britain and further afield that her students undertook. Typical of the many entries in the 1928 edition and those which appeared long after Margaret's death, were:

J. T. is working for the Leeds Board of Guardians, teaching the children of nursery school age.
D. P. T. has just left England to take up work in a convent in Gibraltar.
G. M. is teaching in an Orthopaedic Hospital in Doncaster.
M. A. is in charge of a private nursery school in Kilburn.
I. B. is Nursery Governess in Southampton.
P. P. is still in New Zealand as Nursery Governess.

N. T. is teaching in an elementary school in S. Elmsall, near Pontefract.

M. L. is an assistant at the Magdalen College Nursery School in Somers Town.

H. O. has been studying social work in Dresden and Berlin.

B. A. is at present living in S. America.

J. L. is teaching at a school for English children in Hong Kong.

When Miriam Lord, one of her old students, died in 1968 a friend referred to her as 'a devoted disciple of Margaret McMillan who kept the vision bright and held aloft the torch to light the way'. Thinking of this student's 'shining example of selfless service' he added:

A younger generation would make a great mistake if it took for granted the many reforms for which she worked . . . We saw the struggles sometimes against heavy odds – indeed occasionally the entire establishment – and the gradual emergence of mutual respect and partnership with local authority and press . . . Her many acts of kindness and concern for others and especially for mothers and children cannot be counted . . . Her eyes saw the boundless possibilities for good in the life of a tiny child, however humble the arms in which it lay. Those of us who were close to her in recent years saw the unstinted outpouring of herself and her property and substance, often unknown to others, in service of the community.[19]

Chapter twenty-four

Some Personal Observations

'I was born in July, the month of storms, and so my life has been.'[1]
Such was Margaret McMillan's brief comment on her life. But
behind it lies the story of an energetic pioneer who, in the eye of
many storms, initiated several educational establishments and
found deep fulfilment in the creation of them.

Education apart, it would be possible to evaluate Margaret
McMillan's pioneering from many different angles. One could, for
instance, look at her achievements on the industrial front,[2] where
in her fight against child labour and the harsh treatment of children
she walked in the wake of Richard Oastler and Lord Shaftesbury.[3]
Or one might consider the political scene and assess her struggle
against injustice, through the Labour Movement and the ILP. But
perhaps it is in the field of education where she made her indelible
mark.

In trying to assess her work in that sphere, one could place her
contributions alongside those of numerous other pioneers. In her
involvement in nursery/infant education one could link her with
such early practitioners as Robert Owen[4] and Samuel Wilderspin.[5]
One could examine her educational principles, as Mellor[6] and
Curtis have done,[7] and consider how far she was influenced by the
work of Pestalozzi, Froebel, Séguin, Dewey, Susan Isaacs and
others, and how far she initiated her own novel approaches to
teaching.

Again, in looking at the part she played in the professional
training of nursery/infant teachers, one might set her work
alongside that of some of her contemporaries – Lillian De Lissa at
the Gipsy Hill College, London, Grace Owen at the Mather
Training College, Manchester and Dr Montessori in her various
Training Centres.[8]

Then one might consider her as a writer among many writers,
such as Elsie R. Murray[9] of the Maria Grey Teachers' College in
London who, in the 1920s, influenced teachers' thinking about

kindergarten methods, the curriculum, school organisation and resources through her books and articles.

Thinking of her distinctive contribution to educational thought and practice Curtis and Boultwood claimed her main achievement was: 'to convince England that it must free its children from dirt, disease, malnutrition, and fatigue before any educational process could succeed.'[10] The psychologist, Cyril Burt, maintained that she 'managed to integrate in a kind of synoptic vision a practical synthesis of child psychology, child medicine and child training in an inspired educational plan'.[11]

These are only a few ways of assessing her life's work. But I believe that to think of her exclusively as a pioneer in any one of these areas would be to miss the full scope and grandeur of her endeavours, and possibly to mistake the stage for the journey's end. For behind all her different activities, including her schemes for young children, stand her vision of a more just, equitable and caring society, and her unswerving commitment to the creation of it. In recent years this goal has rarely been given sufficient recognition. It appears to have been lost, amidst the paeans of praise for her pioneer nursery school, but it offers a wider perspective on all her innovations, and merits further examination. The emphasis I have placed on this long-term objective is one essential difference between this and other biographies of Margaret. I believe her innovations are seen best in the context of her commitment to the creation of a new society.

Unlike either Mansbridge or Lowndes, I derived my picture of her mainly from a study of her own articles and pamphlets. Although I was greatly helped by the biographers who preceded me and many of her old students, it was her newspaper articles and pamphlets which gave me a clearer idea of her political involvements and shed more light on certain periods of her life (such as her part in the struggle for school meals) which hitherto have always been hazy.

As indicated in the Preface, my special concern throughout the initial enquiry was to discover the real woman behind her many innovations and offer my findings to a new generation of students. I wanted to produce more of a human document than a factual analysis of her educational ideas, though I believe that there may be a fruitful field for further research there.

While my primary concern in this book has been to provide a faithful record of what Margaret said and did, based on historical evidence, I feel that here I would like to mention certain impressions of Margaret which I have gained over the years.

It is my opinion, and it is only an opinion, for which I accept sole responsibility, that Margaret was first a sincere Christian, possessed of a living faith which had personal, social and political dimensions, then a socialist and later an educational pioneer who devoted the second half of her life to uplifting her fellow citizens through education. I believe that her Christianity and her socialism dictated her principles of education and her attitudes to ethical questions.

After thinking about how Margaret came to espouse the values she lived by, I found it impossible to evade the conclusion that, apart from Rachel's influence on her, something happened to Margaret at Ludlow which set her life on a completely new course, and that the key to a fuller understanding of her work lies in the radical change of heart she experienced there. Unfortunately her own report of what happened during and immediately after this decisive event is fragmentary; it is more implicit than explicit. Many would dearly like to have known more about this crucial event from her own pen. Nevertheless, her own short account of it, together with that of her friends, add greatly to our understanding of the effect of this on her later.

It looks to me from what she did say, that something took place at Ludlow which is explicable only in religious terms: that there the barriers between her and her Maker were broken down and the faith in which she had been reared came alive. From this time onwards God seems to have flooded into her life, transformed it and given her a new selfless love for people which increased with age. When she said she got tuned 'to be the Instrument of the Unseen', she probably meant that she had yielded her own strong will to God and begun to let Him control her. When she spoke of 'the voices' she heard she was possibly referring to a direction which came to her from beyond herself.

It would be difficult to spend several years in a close study of this remarkable woman without at times having one's own conscience pricked and being profoundly challenged by her life. I was struck, for instance, by her religiously grounded vision of a new world society and her blazing passion to see it born. I was stirred by her unflagging determination to try to create the 'nobler human race in the new and nobler social order' she talked about.

Time and time again I looked wistfully at her charity, humanity and compassion. Even when engaged in demanding ventures herself she was acutely sensitive to the needs of people around her. Typical of the many examples of this was the occasion in Bradford, when in the heat of her own election campaign she noticed the look on the face of the bellman helping her and said enquiringly 'Charlie you look sad.' Then after his explanation she took action to relieve his anxiety. It was this same sympathy and unlimited love which she brought to Deptford's dirty, diseased children. Active love was her Christianity and her socialism.

I was gripped, too, by her disregard of material things, her ability to turn aside from personal ambition, comfort and financial security to become intelligently responsible for the restructuring of society. On several occasions, as I worked on the material I looked with envy at her ready forgiveness of those who deserved her severest censure. I see her now not just as a great personality to be revered, but as one to be emulated.

Margaret's character and approach to problems have, I believe, enormous relevance for us today. Her life kindles fresh hope that individuals and nations can be re-created and find new orientation. Her way of bringing innovative solutions to long-established and seemingly intractable problems challenges us to initiate the obvious changes needed in present society and be ready, just as she was, to work with people of all political and religious persuasions to do this.

Much of today's despair and apathy appear to stem from what I hold to be a fallacy, that ordinary people can do nothing to turn the tide of history. To me Margaret's life and those of other pioneers give the lie to that; they show that what individuals are and do can make an appreciable difference to the body politic and that one need not merely sit back and wait for governments to take constructive action.

Many who read Margaret's story may not be either Christian or socialist, but could not all of us whose privilege it is to care for the young make the bold decision to face the dilemmas and opportunities of our age with her zest and resoluteness? Could we not set out on the same adventure as she of pioneering an alternative society where our future citizens would be nurtured in sound homes, given access to an education of quality and offered a firm moral basis for their lives? Will we let Margaret McMillan's mantle fall on us?

Chapter twenty-five

Afterword – Some Unfinished Tasks

Today many of the things Margaret McMillan fought for, such as
school meals, medical inspection and school clinics, have been
incorporated into the British education system. Some, like open-
air schools and school baths, have been rendered less necessary
because of better housing, increased social services and improved
treatment of childhood ailments. Other aspects of her work, for
instance parent education and community schools, still await
further interpretation and implementation. But her dreams of
nursery education for all pre-school children whose parents wish
them to receive it, together with the related issue of adequate
training for all intending nursery school teachers, have never been
realised. These are major unfinished tasks which merit the serious
attention of today's educators, especially of those concerned with
the welfare of deprived children.

Nursery education has long remained the Cinderella of the
education system. The nursery clauses in the 1918 Fisher Act have
never been fully implemented; the more recent recommendations
for nursery provision included in the 1967 Plowden Report,
'Children and their Primary Schools' and the 1972 Department of
Education and Science Report, 'Education: A Framework for
Expansion', have never received the wholehearted support of
governments.

The increasingly long waiting lists most nursery schools have
indicate that many parents want pre-school education for their
children. The long-term benefits of it for those from low-income
families can be seen in the recent research findings of Dr Richard
Darlington and his colleagues at Cornell University, USA. After
examining groups of older children they reported that there was a
significant difference between children who had had pre-school
education and those who had not.[1] But despite the desire of
parents for pre-schooling for their children, and reliable evidence

229

of the beneficial long-term effects of it, provision remains inadequate and unequally scattered across the country.

In 1985 only 21 per cent of pre-school children in England and Wales were attending nursery schools or classes in the maintained sector on either a full-time or part-time basis. Those not attending these establishments were probably either at home with relatives, in private kindergartens, in day-nurseries, with registered or unregistered child minders, in pre-school playgroups or in primary schools. A recent report of the qualifications and training of those working with pre-school children – 'The Continuing Under Fives Muddle! An Investigation of Current Training Opportunities'[2] – shows how diverse the quality of training is and this gives cause for anxiety.

Lack of trained personnel, unfortunately, hampers those local authorities eager to expand their nursery provision. Although Margaret McMillan convinced many some 60 years ago that children under five need trained teachers as much as children over five years, initial courses of training for intending teachers who want to take up this specialised work with the under-fives, and in-service courses for infant teachers who wish to transfer to it, have gradually diminished. Consequently there is now a shortage of well-trained adults in nursery schools and classes.

A recent DES report on initial training courses for teachers in Colleges of Education highlights the paucity of provision for intending nursery school teachers. Many of the courses offered cannot be said to be appropriately related to the work of nursery school teachers, as the following extract from the report indicates:

> A quarter of the institutions offered a primary course which included a nursery component covering the 3 to 5 age range. Only a minority of these courses provided adequate training for nursery teachers. In those institutions which focused on the 3 to 8 age range, the emphasis with few exceptions was on the 5 to 8 year olds. A common pattern was to provide an option on 'nursery education' or 'nursery-infant curriculum' in the third or fourth year, with too little attention being paid to the specific needs of nursery children in the first two years of the course.[3]

In addition the survey showed the difficulty training institutions have in placing students in nursery schools staffed by trained teachers, during their teaching practice periods. Unless the number of courses on nursery education for students and qualified teachers is increased, and extra resources provided by central government for the expansion of this sector of the educational system, then the future of nursery education looks grim. If the quality of existing training courses is not improved then teachers are not likely to develop the new curricular strengths that nursery education will require as it moves into a new century.

Another issue crying out for attention today is how best to provide for the under-fives attending infant classes in primary schools, many of which have poor facilities and higher teacher/pupil ratios than nursery schools.

Recent research in Britain suggests that 'pre-school attendance can lead to lasting improvements in school performance, job prospects and self esteem . . . but not all programmes lead to lasting gains'. Only those described as 'high quality' appear to do so.[4]

Unless provision is made immediately for more and better nursery education, the reforms proposed by the Department of Education and Science in other parts of the education system may fall short because of the poor foundations primary and secondary school teachers have to build on. This matter requires urgent attention.

Margaret employed many methods which could be used again to promote nursery schools and increase public awareness of their value. She tackled the establishment of the day with skill and resolution. She knew senior civil servants personally, and through her work on committees, her writing, and the example of her own school, she helped shape their thinking about society's responsibility for children below school age and the benefits of good nursery education.

To goad sometimes less-than-eager local and national politicians into action, Margaret and her allies roused and enlisted public opinion. But her most powerful argument was the school of excellence she founded in one of London's poorest inner-city areas on a do-it-yourself basis. Her buildings were cheap to erect, her equipment was inexpensive, but her teachers were persons of quality. When young people heard of the way she was trying to help losers in society they applied in numbers to join her. Then visitors came from all corners of the globe to see her work and learn from it.

Realising that the quality of life for children is linked to the quality of their home life, she worked with and for her parents and then expected them to further the cause of nursery education and work for others less fortunate than themselves – which many did. Margaret believed that no Minister of Education would take nursery school provision seriously 'till the mothers of England take it seriously', and so she encouraged her parents to become vocal and use their votes wisely.

Through the Nursery School Association (now the British Association of Early Childhood Education) she battled with others for children to have access through nursery schools to a better start in life. At the age of 63 she became the Association's first President and never retired from the fight for the advancement and expansion of nursery education.

She was an early user of radio for propaganda purposes, and doubtless today would have seen television as a powerful educational force and probably monitored its use. Furthermore, she knew those who were seeking to mould public opinion through the arts, such as George Bernard Shaw, and interested them in nursery education.

One can speculate that, if alive today, Margaret would have been striving to help children living in inner-city areas, large impersonal housing estates, high-rise flats and rural areas, where children still have no access to nursery schools. The Commission on Urban Priority Areas, set up in 1985 by the Archbishop of Canterbury, described the appalling physical environment in which many children are still reared and the sense of hopelessness of many of their parents. The committee stated at the end of its exhaustive enquiry:

> We have to report that we have been deeply disturbed by what we have seen and heard. We have been confronted with the human consequences of unemployment, which in some urban areas may be over 50% of the labour force, and which occasionally reaches a level as high as 80% – consequences which may be compounded by the effects of racial discrimination. We have seen physical decay, whether of older Victorian terraced housing or of inferior system-built blocks of flats, which has in places created an environment so degrading that some people have set fire to their own homes rather than be condemned to living in them indefinitely. Social disintegration has reached a point in some areas that shop windows are boarded up, cars cannot be left on the street, residents are afraid either to go out themselves or to ask others in, and there is a pervading sense of powerlessness and despair.[5]

The decline in the community spirit in these areas, and in Deptford now, would have troubled Margaret; the under-achievement of children, especially black children, would have captured her attention and made her seek ways of rectifying it. It is more than likely that she would have been drawn into the debate about the role of schools in bringing about the change of attitudes called for in the Swann Report;[6] she would also have recognised the need for a core of values to maintain social cohesion amidst cultural diversity.

With her international outlook and limitless compassion Margaret would indubitably have been campaigning now for help for refugees and for the betterment of children and communities throughout the Third World where the young are the helpless victims of poverty and politics. Their needs are greater than any voluntary aid could ever meet, as was the case in Britain when Margaret first began to agitate for state provision of school meals.

The Committee of the United Nations' Children's Fund reported in 1986:

> Ninety eight per cent of all infant and child deaths in the world are in the developing countries. One in eight dies before reaching the age of five, compared with one in fifty six in the industrialized countries. Every year about nine and a quarter million infants die and nine million of them are in the developing world; others who survive are often hungry and diseased.[7]

When Margaret first went to work in Deptford approximately one-fifth of the children in the East Ward died in their first year. In her pamphlet – 'Infant Mortality'[8] – she wrote despairingly about the high number of children who died in infancy in 1903 in England and compared the figures with the lower ones of those in Western Australia, Switzerland, Denmark, Sweden, Norway and other nations.

In the developing world today, babies are dying in their thousands because of the interaction of malnutrition, diarrhoeal dehydration, measles and other childhood ailments. As in Margaret's day, the means to avoid these deaths exist; what is lacking is the political will to tackle the relevant issues realistically.

Barnes in his book, *200 Million Hungry Children*, says:

> At least 200 million children suffer from malnutrition. Of these 10 million are in danger of dying and 90 million are in a frail state of health and could not withstand a serious illness. Many of the children who survive are destined to be robbed by hunger of the chance of normal mental and physical development. People living in poverty pay scant attention to the protein needs of infants and most governments are far more concerned with financial aspects of food procurement and distribution than with the nutritional needs of children.[9]

Margaret found in Deptford that much misery could be prevented by nursery schools, which she regarded as preventive medicine. Seventy-five per cent of the deaths in the Third World could be prevented at low cost, but three-quarters of the medical budgets usually have to be spent on curative rather than preventive measures.

It has been recognised for many years in Britain that the free meals Margaret fought for can improve school children's physical well-being and intellectual performance, but this kind of help is not yet available for many children overseas. If alive today it is highly likely that she would be battling for a more caring, sharing world and for politicians of all parties to implement generous aid and development policies.

Margaret was both a woman of her day and a woman of the future. She firmly believed in man's ability to rise above his hereditary nature and shape a better world for coming generations. Shortly after her death a journalist wrote:

> Margaret McMillan was one of the greatest women of her time, and her true greatness will become more apparent as the years pass. For she was at once a reformer of the present world, and a builder of the future.[10]

Just as she took bold initiatives which brought a new direction to many in Deptford she would today have tackled the ills of this society with the same determination. The unstable family life of children, the child abuse, spiritual starvation, pornography, environmental pollution and other features of this era, would have made her yearn to get the nation on a new course.

Looking around Britain now she would have been gladdened by the improved health of most pre-school children and the decline in the infant mortality rate. Yet she would have been forced to admit that the Welfare State she helped to promote, and the better standard of living presently enjoyed by many, have not of themselves fostered more upright, unselfish citizens. She would probably have been busy today nurturing children and at the same time nurturing the values in people which raise society's moral tone. She possibly had something of this in mind when she wrote about teachers of tomorrow having as their goal 'the perfecting of the race'.

Just as she envisaged the nobler aspirations of man being cultivated and enhanced through education, so she saw civilisation not as something static but in the process of continually advancing or retreating. She might have said with Arnold Toynbee, 'Civilisation is a movement . . . a voyage and not a harbour.'[11]

She expected teachers to have their eyes on the future and be part of a continuous upward movement in society. She remarked:

The classroom of to-day is not the classroom of yesterday. It is full of new light – and of new shadows. As time goes on, some will make strange discoveries. And some, for the sake of comfort, may pull down the blinds. But the brave will not pull down the blinds. They will go on fearlessly to note conditions – to unearth the causes of defect, disease, suffering, and failure, to set these open to the sunshine of an enlightened public opinion, and to lay the foundations of a happier order of social life, and a new era of human progress.[12]

Notes

(Margaret McMillan has been abbreviated to MM.)

1 Introduction

1 M. Crosbie, 'Women Who Made History', *John O'London's Weekly*, 16 April 1932.
2 G. A. N. Lowndes, *Margaret McMillan 'The Children's Champion'*, Museum Press, 1960, p. 17.
3 C. Gore, *Reflections on the Litany*, Mowbray, 1932, pp. 76, 77.
4 A. Mansbridge, *Fellowmen*, Dent, 1948, p. 83.
5 Lady N. Astor, private letter to G. A. N. Lowndes, n.d. (*c.* 1960).
6 M. Sadler, in E. Stevinson, *The Open-air Nursery School*, Dent, 1927, pp. VII, VIII.
7 W. Whitman, 'Pioneers! O Pioneers', in *Songs of Praise*, OUP, 1943, p. 365.

2 Childhood Influences

1 MM, *The Life of Rachel McMillan*, Dent, 1927, p. 2.
2 Ibid., pp. 3, 4.
3 Ibid., p. 4.
4 A. Mansbridge, *Margaret McMillan Prophet and Pioneer*, Dent, 1932, p. 3.
5 J. McMillan, private letter to E. Cameron, 1858, in MM, *Life of Rachel*, p. 4.
6 MM, *Life of Rachel*, p. 4.
7 Ibid., p. 7.
8 MM, 'The Innkeeper's Daughter', *The Clarion*, 18 December 1897.
9 M. Cameron, private letters to J. McMillan, in Mansbridge, *Margaret McMillan*, p. 5.
10 MM, *Life of Rachel*, pp. 8, 9.
11 Mansbridge, *Margaret McMillan*, pp. 3, 4.
12 MM, *Life of Rachel*, p. 10.
13 Ibid., p. 11.
14 Ibid., p. 15.

15 MM, *Labour and Childhood*, Swan Sonnenschein, 1907.
16 MM, *Life of Rachel*, p. 15.
17 Ibid., p. 16.
18 Ibid., p. 20.
19 MM, 'How I Became a Socialist', *The Labour Leader*, 11 July 1912.
20 MM, *Life of Rachel*, p. 19.
21 MM, 'How I Became a Socialist', *The Labour Leader*, 11 July 1912.
22 MM, *Life of Rachel*, p. 18.
23 Ibid., p. 17.
24 MM, letter to Rev. J. MacKenzie, 7 July 1930, in Mansbridge, *Margaret McMillan*, p. 9.
25 Mansbridge, *Margaret McMillan*, p. 8.
26 MM, private letter to Lady Astor, 13 December 1930.
27 M. Stuart, 'Margaret McMillan', *The Post*, 17 April 1937.
28 MM, *Life of Rachel*, p. 21.
29 'The Labour Candidates', *The Bradford Observer*, 11 November 1897.
30 Mansbridge, *Margaret McMillan*, p. 10.
31 A. Grant, 'An Inverness School', *Highland News*, 1937, pp. 56, 58.
32 MM, *Life of Rachel*, p. 23.
33 MM, private letter to W. Blatchford, 20 July 1913.

3 Embarking on a Career 1878–89

1 A. Mansbridge, *Margaret McMillan Prophet and Pioneer*, Dent, 1932, p. 12.
2 MM, private letter to Robert Cameron (*c.* 1880).
3 Mansbridge, *Margaret McMillan*, pp. 166, 167.
4 K. Bruce Glasier, *Margaret McMillan and Her Life Work*, The Workers' Northern Publishing, n.d., p. 2.
5 MM, 'Women of the Russian Revolution', *The Labour Leader*, 5 May 1905.
6 MM, 'How I Became a Socialist', *The Labour Leader*, 11 July 1912.
7 MM, *The Life of Rachel McMillan*, Dent, 1927, p. 25.
8 MM, private letter to Mrs. Sutcliffe, 1922.
9 Ibid.
10 *In Memoriam – E. ff. Clayton*, privately printed, 1907.
11 MM, private letter to Mrs. Sutcliffe, 1922.
12 Mansbridge, *Margaret McMillan*, pp. 160, 161.

4 From Ludlow to Bloomsbury 1889–92

1 MM, *The Life of Rachel McMillan*, Dent, 1927, p. 24.
2 Ibid., pp. 24, 25.
3 A. Stafford, *The Age of Consent*, Hodder and Stoughton, 1964, p. 102.
4 C. Pearl, *Victorian Patchwork*, Heinemann, 1972, p. 197.
5 W. T. Stead, 'The Maiden Tribute of Modern Babylon', *Pall Mall Gazette*, 1885.

6 MM, *Life of Rachel*, pp. 27–9.
7 R. McMillan, private letter to a cousin, in MM, *Life of Rachel*, pp. 30, 31.
8 MM, *Life of Rachel*, p. 32.
9 Ibid., pp. 34, 35.
10 Ibid., p. 58.
11 MM, 'A Sign of the Times', *The Christian Socialist*, October 1889.
12 C. Booth, *Life and Labour of the People in London*, Macmillan, 1892–1903.
13 MM, *Life of Rachel*, pp. 38–41.
14 B. S. Rowntree, *Poverty: A Study of Town Life*, Macmillan, 1901.
15 MM, *Life of Rachel*, pp. 41, 42.

5 Park Lane Decision 1892

1 MM, 'A Sign of the Times', *The Christian Socialist*, October 1889; 'The Church and Socialism', ibid., December 1889; 'Liberty', ibid., April 1890; 'Evolution and Revolution', ibid., August 1890.
2 MM, *The Life of Rachel McMillan*, Dent, 1927, pp. 44, 45.
3 Ibid., p. 44.
4 Ibid.
5 C. Pearl, *Victorian Patchwork*, Heinemann, 1972, p. 144.
6 K. Chesney, *The Victorian Underworld*, Temple Smith, 1970, pp. 310, 311.
7 MM, *Life of Rachel*, pp. 48, 49.
8 Ibid., pp. 45–8.
9 Ibid., p. 50.
10 Ibid., p. 64.
11 A. Mansbridge, *Margaret McMillan Prophet and Pioneer*, Dent, 1932, p. 16.
12 MM, *Life of Rachel*, p. 64.
13 Ibid., pp. 71, 72.
14 Lord G. Elton, *England, Arise! – A Study of the Pioneering Days of the Labour Movement*, Cape, 1931, pp. 216, 217.
15 G. Lean, *Brave Men Choose*, Blandford, 1961, Ch. 7.
16 F. Brockway, *Socialism Over Sixty Years, The Life of Jowett of Bradford*, George Allen and Unwin, 1946, p. 409.
17 MM, *Life of Rachel*, p. 130.
18 Mansbridge, *Margaret McMillan*, p. 19.

6 A New Political Party 1892–3

1 F. Brockway, *Socialism Over Sixty Years, The Life of Jowett of Bradford*, George Allen and Unwin, 1946, p. 42.
2 K. B. Glasier, 'The Part Women Played in Founding the I.L.P.', *The Labour Leader*, 9 April 1914.
3 MM, *The Life of Rachel McMillan*, Dent, 1927, p. 73.

4 A. Mansbridge, *Margaret McMillan Prophet and Pioneer*, Dent, 1927, p. 20.
5 C. Cross, *Philip Snowden*, Barrie and Rockliff, 1966, p. 30.
6 B. Villiers, in C. Cross, *Philip Snowden*, Barrie and Rockliff, 1966, p. 40.
7 F. C. Price, 'Pioneer Work of Margaret McMillan', *Telegraph and Argus*, 30 June 1960.
8 Mansbridge, *Margaret McMillan*, p. 22.
9 MM, 'How I Became a Socialist', *The Labour Leader*, 11 July 1912.

7 Bradford 1893–4

1 J. B. Priestley, in F. Brockway, *Socialism Over Sixty Years, The Life of Jowett of Bradford*, George Allen and Unwin, 1946, pp. 9, 10.
2 MM, *The Life of Rachel McMillan*, Dent, 1927, pp. 73, 74.
3 F. Williams, *Fifty Years' March*, Odhams, n.d., pp. 102–5.
4 Lord H. Snell, in Williams, *Fifty Years' March*, p. 102.
5 F. Snowden, in Williams, *Fifty Years' March*, p. 103.
6 J. Coe, in Williams, *Fifty Years' March*, p. 105.
7 C. Cross, *Philip Snowden*, Barrie and Rockliff, 1966, p. 41.
8 Ibid.
9 MM, *Life of Rachel*, pp. 76–8.
10 K. B. Glasier, 'Enid Stacy: In Memoriam', *The Labour Leader*, 12 September 1903.
11 F. W. Jowett, 'Margaret McMillan', *Bradford I.L.P. News*, 3 June 1938.
12 A. Mansbridge, *Margaret McMillan Prophet and Pioneer*, Dent, 1932, pp. 26–7.
13 MM, *Life of Rachel*, pp. 81, 82.
14 K. B. Glasier, 'Margaret McMillan', *The Labour Leader*, 10 April 1931.
15 MM, *Life of Rachel*, p. 82.
16 Ibid., p. 83.
17 F. W. Jowett, 'Margaret McMillan', *Bradford I.L.P. News*, 3 June 1938.
18 MM, private letter to W. Blatchford, 30 May 1930.
19 MM, 'Drink in Labour Clubs', *The Clarion*, 24 February 1894.
20 MM, 'Music in Labour Clubs and Elsewhere', *The Clarion*, 3 March 1894.
21 MM, 'Women of the I.L.P.', *The Clarion*, 10 March 1894.
22 J. B. Priestley, in W.D'A.C. Cresswell, *Margaret McMillan A Memoir*, Hutchinson, 1948, p. 10.
23 MM, 'To All Overworked Mothers', *The Clarion*, 29 September 1894.
24 'Miss McMillan on Education', *The Labour Leader*, 3 November 1894.
25 G. A. N. Lowndes, *Margaret McMillan 'The Children's Champion'*, Museum Press, 1960, p. 54.
26 MM, 'How I Became a Socialist', *The Labour Leader*, 11 July 1912.

27 F. Brockway, *Socialism Over Sixty Years, The Life of Jowett of Bradford*, George Allen and Unwin, 1946, p. 60.

8 On the Bradford School Board 1894–1901

1 MM, 'My Experiences on the School Board', *The Labour Prophet*, November 1895.
2 Ibid.
3 MM, *Early Childhood*, Swan Sonnenschein, 1901, p. 6.
4 MM, *The Child and the State*, National Labour Press, 1911, p. 41.
5 MM, 'My Experiences on the School Board', *The Labour Prophet*, November 1895.
6 L. Thompson, *Robert Blatchford*, Gollancz, 1951, p. 141.
7 M. Lord, *Margaret McMillan in Bradford*, University of London Press, pp. 11, 16.
8 A. Mansbridge, *Margaret McMillan Prophet and Pioneer*, Dent, 1932, p. 16.
9 MM, *Early Childhood*, p. 6.
10 G. A. N. Lowndes, *Margaret McMillan 'The Children's Champion'*, Museum Press, 1960, p. 54.
11 MM, 'Child Labour and the Half-time System', *Clarion*, production 1896.
12 J. Glyde, private letter to M. Lord, 21 November 1955.
13 Lord, *Margaret McMillan in Bradford*, p. 22.
14 Mansbridge, *Margaret McMillan*, p. 26.
15 MM, *Early Childhood*, p. 2.
16 MM, 'Bradford', *The Labour Leader*, 15 June 1895.
17 MM, 'Bradford', *The Labour Leader*, 17 August 1895.
18 Ibid.
19 MM, 'Bradford', *The Labour Prophet*, May 1896.
20 MM, 'Conference Report', *The Labour Leader*, 18 April 1900.
21 *The Labour Leader*, 21 September 1900.
22 MM, 'Bradford', *The Labour Leader*, 28 April 1900.
23 MM, 'Bradford', *The Labour Leader*, 21 October 1900.
24 MM, 'The Coming Woman', *The Clarion*, 23 June 1894.
25 J. B. Glasier, 'Margaret McMillan's Book on "Early Childhood"', *The Labour Leader*, 22 December 1900.
26 MM, 'Bradford', *The Labour Leader*, 28 April 1900.
27 MM, 'Tom Maguire – A Remembrance', *The Labour Leader*, 26 October 1895.
28 MM, 'Education in the Primary School', *The Labour Leader*, 6 May, 13 May, 20 May, 27 May, 10 June, 17 June, 24 June, 1 July, 8 July, 15 July, 22 July 1899.
29 MM, 'An English Kindergarten', *The Labour Leader*, 15 April 1899.
30 MM, 'Voice Production in Board Schools', *The Clarion*, 28 November 1896.
31 MM, private letter in Mansbridge, *Margaret McMillan*, pp. 27, 28.

32 MM, 'The "New" Education', *The Highway*, June 1913, pp. 165, 166, 167.
33 MM, 'The March of Socialism in Bradford', *The Labour Leader*, 5 March 1898.

9 Leaving Bradford 1901–2

1 A. Mansbridge, *Margaret McMillan Prophet and Pioneer*, Dent, 1932, p. 47.
2 MM, 'A Priest of Eriskay', *The Labour Leader*, 24 November 1905.
3 Ibid.
4 Ibid.
5 Ibid.
6 J. K. Hardie, in H. Addison, *Contrast in Philosophies*, Educational Productions, 1982, p. 53.
7 M. Sutcliffe, *The Legend of Margaret McMillan*, manuscript of unpublished play, n.d. (*c.* 1924).
8 Bradford School Board, *11th Triennial Report, 1900–1903*, 1903.
9 Mansbridge, *Margaret McMillan*, p. 47.
10 MM, 'The Fight for the Schools', *The Yorkshire Daily Observer*, 22 September 1902.
11 'Yorkshire's Protest Against the Education Bill', *The Leeds Mercury*, 22 September 1902.
12 Bradford School Board, *11th Triennial Report, 1900–1903*, 1903.
13 W. Claridge, in Mansbridge, *Margaret McMillan*, p. 48.
14 M. Gosse, in Mansbridge, *Margaret McMillan*, p. 49.
15 G. Kekewich, in Mansbridge, *Margaret McMillan*, p. 52.
16 M. Fels, *Joseph Fels: His Life-Work*, George Allen and Unwin, 1920, p. 2.
17 Ibid., p. 208.
18 MM, *The Life of Rachel McMillan*, Dent, 1927, p. 141.

10 The Years Between 1902–5

1 D. Read, *Edwardian England*, Historical Association pamphlet No. 79, 1972, pp. 3, 4.
2 S. J. Curtis and M. E. A. Boultwood, *An Introductory History of English Education Since 1800*, University Tutorial Press, 1964, p. 164.
3 MM, *The Life of Rachel McMillan*, Dent, 1927, p. 98.
4 Ibid., p. 99.
5 A. P. Dudden, *Joseph Fels*, Temple University Press, 1971, p. 118.
6 MM, *Life of Rachel*, p. 98.
7 Ibid., p. 96.
8 Ibid., p. 94.
9 A. Mansbridge, *Margaret McMillan Prophet and Pioneer*, Dent, 1932, p. 54.

10 Ibid.
11 *The Labour Leader*, 21 March 1903.
12 'Scots in London', *The Inverness Courier*, 27 February 1903.
13 'Socialist Sunday Schools' Work', *The Leeds Weekly Citizen*, 2 September 1911.
14 MM, *Education Through the Imagination*, Dent, 1904; *Infant Mortality*, ILP pamphlet, 1906; 'Women of the Russian Revolution', *The Labour Leader*, 5 May 1905.
15 MM, *Life of Rachel*, p. 103.
16 MM, *Citizens of Tomorrow*, ILP pamphlet, 1906.
17 G. D. H. Cole and R. Postgate, *The Common People*, Methuen, 1963, p. 423.
18 R. E. Dowse, *Society and the Victorians*, Harvester Press, 1974, pp. VII–XXXI.
19 MM, *Report of the Thirteenth Annual Conference*, ILP, May 1905, p. 48.
20 MM, *Life of Rachel*, p. 108.
21 Ibid., pp. 108–10.
22 Ibid., pp. 111, 112.
23 MM, *The Camp School*, George Allen and Unwin, 1919, pp. 41, 42.
24 LCC, Day Schools Sub-committee Minutes, 26 July 1905 to September 1906.
25 MM, extract from private letter to F. W. Jowett, 1905.
26 Interview with Margaret McMillan, 'Proposed Experiment in Deptford', *The Kentish Mercury*, 15 December 1905.
27 C. Birchenough, *History of Elementary Education in England and Wales*, University Tutorial Press, 1938, p. 319.
28 Dudden, *Fels*, pp. 121, 122.

11 School Meals Victory 1906

1 Bentley B. Gilbert, *The Evolution of National Insurance in Great Britain*, Michael Joseph, 1973, p. 103.
2 MM, *Early Childhood*, Swan Sonnenschein, 1901, pp. 152, 153.
3 MM, *Education Through the Imagination*, Dent, 1904, p. 49.
4 The Inter-departmental Committee on the Employment of School Children Report, HMSO, 1902, Appendix 39.
5 The Royal Commission on Physical Training (Scotland) Report, HMSO, 1903.
6 The Inter-departmental Committee on Physical Deterioration Report, HMSO, 1904.
7 The Inter-departmental Committee on Medical Inspection and Feeding of Children Attending Public Elementary Schools Report, HMSO, 1905.
8 Ministry of Education, Report on Education 1900–1950, HMSO, 1950, p. 67.

9 F. Le Gros Clark, *Social History of the School Meals Service*, London Council of Social Service, 1948, p. 7.
10 'Socialism and the Question of the Hour', *The Labour Leader*, 1 July 1904.
11 A. Mansbridge, *Margaret McMillan Prophet and Pioneer*, Dent, 1932, p. 53.
12 Ibid., p. 67.
13 Countess of Warwick, *Life's Ebb and Flow*, Hutchinson, 1929, p. 276.
14 A. Leslie, 'Edwardians in Love', *The Sunday Telegraph*, 27 August 1972.
15 Warwick, *Life's Ebb and Flow*, pp. 227, 228.
16 Gilbert, *Evolution of National Insurance*, pp. 108, 109.
17 Clark, *History of the School Meals Service*, pp. 6, 7.
18 Gilbert, *Evolution of National Insurance*, p. 112.
19 Board of Education, 1908 Annual Report of Chief Medical Officer, HMSO, 1910, p. 68.
20 A. M. McBriar, *Fabian Socialism and English Politics 1884–1918*, Cambridge University Press, 1962, p. 335.
21 R. Barker, *Education and Politics 1900–1951. A Study of the Labour Party*, Oxford University Press, 1972, p. 9.
22 F. W. Jowett, in D. J. Mytum, thesis on 'Labour and the school feeding issue', 1985, p. 46.
23 Mansbridge, *Margaret McMillan*, pp. 42–3.
24 J. H. Palin, *Bradford and Its Children, How They are Fed*, ILP publication, 1908, p. 1.
25 Ibid., p. 12.
26 Clark, *History of the School Meals Service*, p. 7.
27 A. V. Dicey, in Gilbert, *Evolution of National Insurance*, p. 113.
28 MM, 'Free Meals. How the Bill Works', *The Labour Leader*, 22 March 1907.
29 MM, 'School Dinners To-Day', *The Labour Leader*, 29 November 1907.
30 MM, 'A Scholarship Child', *The Labour Leader*, 23 August 1907.
31 MM, and A. Cobden Sanderson, *London's Children: How to Feed them and How not to Feed Them*, ILP pamphlet, 1909, pp. 1–10.
32 MM, *The Child and the State*, National Labour Press, 1911,
33 W. G. Wilkins, 'School Meals at Derby', *The Municipal Journal*, 22 February 1907.
34 Gilbert, *The Evolution of National Insurance*, p. 103.

12 Mother of School Medical Inspection 1907

1 MM, 'Citizens of To-morrow', *The Independent Review*, August 1906, p. 173.
2 A. Mansbridge, *Margaret McMillan Prophet and Pioneer*, Dent, 1932, p. 61.

3 A. S. Arkle, *Supplement to the School Government Chronicle*, 12 January 1907, p. 77.
4 R. H. Crowley, *Supplement to the School Government Chronicle*, 12 January 1907, p. 79.
5 MM, *Supplement to the School Government Chronicle*, 12 January 1907, p. 81.
6 T. P. Sykes, *Supplement to the School Government Chronicle*, 12 January 1907, p. 82.
7 Report of the Annual Conference of the ILP, 1907, pp. 69, 70.
8 Bentley B. Gilbert, *The Evolution of National Insurance in Great Britain*, Michael Joseph, 1973, pp. 128, 129.
9 MM, 'A Coming Conference', *The Labour Leader*, 21 July 1907.
10 MM, 'After Echoes of the Congress of School Hygiene', *The Labour Leader*, 30 August 1907.
11 M. Fels, *Joseph Fels: His Life-Work*, George Allen and Unwin, 1920, pp. 210, 211.
12 MM, *The Life of Rachel McMillan*, Dent, 1927, pp. 114–16.
13 'The Children's Charter', *The Labour Leader*, 20 September 1907.
14 A. Mansbridge, *Dictionary of National Biography, 1931–1940*, pp. 587, 588.
15 G. A. N. Lowndes, *Margaret McMillan 'The Children's Champion'*, Museum Press, 1960, p. 96.
16 Gilbert, *Evolution of National Insurance*, pp. 118, 119.
17 G. Newman, 'The Evolution of a School Medical Service', *The Year Book of Education*, Evans, 1933, pp. 399, 400.
18 Mansbridge, *Margaret McMillan*, p. 65.
19 Lowndes, *Margaret McMillan*, p. 96.
20 Report of the Annual Conference of the ILP, 1908, pp. 60, 61.
21 No name given, private letter to A. Mansbridge, in Mansbridge, *Margaret McMillan*, pp. 123–5.

13 Starting a Health Centre in Bow 1908–10

1 MM, 'The Beginning That May Have to Halt', *The Labour Leader*, 17 May 1907.
2 Circular 576, Board of Education, HMSO, November 1907.
3 MM, 'New Report of the Education Board', *The Labour Leader*, 10 January 1908; 'Bradford Leads Again', ibid., 7 February 1908; 'The Food Depot "At Home" ', ibid., 13 March 1908.
4 MM, 'The London Council and the I.L.P.', *The Labour Leader*, 7 August 1908.
5 Ibid.
6 MM, *What the Open-Air Nursery School is*, Joint Labour Production, n.d., p. 1.
7 C. E. Grant, *Farthing Bundles*, privately published by the author, n.d., p. 75.
8 Ibid.
9 Ibid., p. 102.

10 Ibid., pp. 106, 107.
11 MM, 'A London Treatment Centre', *The Labour Leader*, 11 December 1908.
12 Grant, *Farthing Bundles*, p. 84.
13 Ibid., pp. 83, 84, 110.
14 MM, 'Clouds and the Rain', *The Woman Worker*, 17 July 1908.
15 MM, 'School Clinics: Their First Fruits', *The Labour Leader*, 9 July 1909.
16 M. D. Eder and R. Tribe, in A. Mansbridge, *Margaret McMillan Prophet and Pioneer*, Dent, 1932, pp. 76, 77, 78.
17 MM, 'Ten Hundred Thousand Philips', *The Christian Commonwealth*, 24 March 1909.
18 E. G. Rice, 'Bedales School and Children from Bow', *The Christian Commonwealth*, 26 October 1910.
19 MM, 'The Medical Treatment Bill', *The Labour Leader*, 6 August 1909.
20 M. D. Eder and R. Tribe, 'Are Children's Diseases to be Cured?', *The Labour Leader*, 30 July 1909.
21 MM, private letter to the Countess of Warwick, 23 August 1909, in Countess of Warwick, *Life's Ebb and Flow*, Hutchinson, 1929, p. 264.
22 G. A. N. Lowndes, *Margaret McMillan 'The Children's Champion'*, Museum Press, 1960, p. 96.
23 MM, *The Life of Rachel McMillan*, Dent, 1927, p. 118.
24 A. Mansbridge, *Fellowmen: A Gallery of England, 1876–1946*, Dent, 1948, p. 64.
25 MM, 'Schools and Hospitals', *The Labour Leader*, 8 January 1909.
26 M. D. Eder, in 'A Visit to A School Clinic', *The Christian Commonwealth*, 27 October 1909.
27 Bentley B. Gilbert, *The Evolution of National Insurance in Great Britain*, Michael Joseph, 1973, p. 127.

14 Nothing Less than a New Crusade 1910

1 E. Chase, *Tenant Friends in Old Deptford*, Williams and Norgate, 1929, pp. 32, 33.
2 A. E. Boyce, 'Through Fifty Years', *Deptford and Greenwich Wesleyan Golden Jubilee Report*, 1954.
3 MM, 'A Flower in the Slum', *The Christian Commonwealth*, 14 September 1910.
4 'Child Life Peril in Deptford', *The Daily Chronicle*, 5 October 1911.
5 Ibid.
6 B. S. Rowntree, *Poverty: A Study of Town Life*, Macmillan, 1901.
7 Ibid., p. 137.
8 *Deptford and Greenwich Wesleyan Mission Annual Report*, 1905, p. 19.
9 E. Bradburn, *Margaret McMillan Framework and Expansion of Nursery Education*, Denholm House Press, 1976, Ch. 3.
10 MM, *The Camp School*, George Allen and Unwin, 1919, p. 43.

11 MM, 'Faith and Fear', *The Labour Leader*, 27 January 1911.
12 MM, 'Deptford and Her Children', *The Labour Leader*, 4 November 1910.
13 G. A. N. Lowndes, *Margaret McMillan 'The Children's Champion'*, Museum Press, 1960, p. 63.
14 MM, 'Deptford's Health Centre', *The Clarion*, 4 November 1910.
15 MM, in Lowndes, *Margaret McMillan*, p. 63.
16 MM, *The Nursery School*, Dent, 1930, p. 8.
17 MM, 'Deptford's Health Centre'.
18 MM, 'Deptford and Her Children'.
19 MM, 'Johnny and Me', *The Christian Commonwealth*, 2 November 1910.
20 A. F. B., 'A Child Programme', *The Labour Leader*, 31 March 1911.
21 MM, 'The Doctor in the School', *The Staffordshire Sentinel*, 12 September 1910.
22 J. Gorst, 'School Clinics in London', *The Kentish Mercury*, 22 July 1910.
23 MM, 'The Tooth-Clinic and Kindred Matters', *The Christian Commonwealth*, 13 July 1910.
24 A. F. B., 'A Child Programme'.
25 MM, 'Save the Children', *The Labour Leader*, 17 November 1911.
26 K. B. Glasier, *Margaret McMillan and Her Life Work*, Co-operative Printing Society, n.d., p. 5.

15 Night Camps and a Camp School 1911–13

1 MM, *The Camp School*, George Allen and Unwin, 1919, p. 5.
2 Ibid., p. 80.
3 MM, 'In Our Garden', *The Highway*, July 1911, p. 148.
4 MM, 'The Child of the Future', *The Labour Leader*, 26 December 1912.
5 'The Schools of To-morrow', *The Christian Commonwealth*, 21 January 1914.
6 MM, 'Marigold – An English Mignon', *The Highway*, September 1911, p. 187.
7 MM, 'In Our Garden', *The Highway*, April 1912, p. 107.
8 'Churchyard as Dormitory', *The Daily Mirror*, 11 June 1912.
9 MM, *The Camp School*, p. 95.
10 'Churchyard as Dormitory'.
11 MM, *The Camp School*, p. 94.
12 Ibid., pp. 95, 96.
13 MM, in 'School Clinics', *The Derby Mercury*, 5 April 1912.
14 MM, 'In Our Garden', *The Highway*, September 1912, pp. 181, 182.
15 MM, *The Camp School*, pp. 97, 98.
16 MM, 'In our Garden – V', *The Highway*, August 1912, p. 168.
17 MM, 'On Reports and Other Things', *The Common Cause*, 25 April 1913.
18 MM, *The Camp School*, p. 88.

19 MM, in 'The Schools of To-morrow', *The Christian Commonwealth*, 21 January 1914.
20 Ibid.
21 MM, 'In Our Garden – IV', *The Highway*, July 1912, p. 157.
22 Ibid.
23 MM, 'In Our Garden – V', p. 169.
24 MM, in 'The Schools of To-morrow'.
25 D. Lob and G. Woodhams, personal letters to G. A. N. Lowndes, n.d. (*c.* 1960).
26 A. Mansbridge, *Fellowmen: A Gallery of England, 1876–1946*, Dent, 1948, p. 85.
27 Ibid., p. 68.
28 'The Schools of To-morrow'.
29 P. B. Ballard, *Margaret McMillan – An Appreciation*, privately printed, n.d., pp. 6, 7.
30 MM, *The Life of Rachel McMillan*, Dent, 1927, p. 132.
31 MM, in 'The Schools of To-morrow'.
32 P. Snowden, 'A Year's Working of the Insurance Act', *The Christian Commonwealth*, 21 January 1914.
33 G. Lansbury, 'After the Battle', *The Labour Leader*, 16 December 1910.
34 MM, 'On Reports and Other Things'.
35 Ibid.

16 A Camp for Pre-school Children 1911–14

1 MM, in A. Mansbridge, *Margaret McMillan Prophet and Pioneer*, Dent, 1932, p. 103.
2 E. Stevinson, *Margaret McMillan Prophet and Pioneer*, University of London Press, 1954, p. 8.
3 W. H., 'An Educational Pioneer', *Time and Tide*, 14 May 1932.
4 'The Schools of To-morrow', *The Christian Commonwealth*, 21 January 1914.
5 MM, *The Life of Rachel McMillan*, Dent, 1927, pp. 139, 140.
6 Ibid., pp. 142, 143.
7 Ibid.
8 Ibid., pp. 143, 144.
9 W. Gillespie, private letter to E. Bradburn, 7 October 1968.
10 MM, *The Camp School*, George Allen and Unwin, 1919, p. 52.
11 Ibid., p. 54.
12 MM, 'Life and Health', *Daily News and Leader*, 17 June 1914.
13 'The Cost of a Baby Camp', *The Crèche News*, November 1917.
14 MM, 'At the foot of the Rainbow', *The Christian Commonwealth*, 10 February 1915.
15 MM, *The Camp School*, p. 60.
16 Ibid., pp. 62, 63.
17 Ibid., pp. 63, 64.
18 Ibid., p. 61.

19 Ibid., pp. 67, 68.
20 Ibid., p. 76.
21 MM, in A. P. Dudden, *Joseph Fels*, Temple University Press, Philadelphia, 1917, pp. 116, 117.
22 MM, 'The Case for the Industrial Women', *The Men's League Handbook*, Men's League for Women's Suffrage, 1912, pp. 95–9.
23 J. K. Hardie, ILP Annual Conference Report, 1907, p. 47.
24 MM, in ibid., p. 48.
25 MM, *Life of Rachel*, pp. 137, 138.
26 'How Militants are Made', *The Christian Commonwealth*, 30 July 1913.
27 R. West, 'Militant Men', *The Christian Commonwealth*, 6 August 1913.
28 MM, *Life of Rachel*, p. 138.
29 G. A. N. Lowndes, *Margaret McMillan 'The Children's Champion'*, Museum Press, 1960, pp. 67, 68.
30 MM, 'A Pioneer', *The Labour Leader*, 5 September 1912.
31 Lord H. Sanderson, *Memories of Sixty Years,* Methuen, 1931, p. 128.
32 Mansbridge, *Margaret McMillan*, p. 153.

17 With Rachel in the War Years 1914–17

1 MM, *The Life of Rachel McMillan*, Dent, 1927, pp. 145–7.
2 Ibid., pp. 148, 149.
3 Ibid., pp. 150, 152.
4 W. Gillespie, private letter to E. Bradburn, 11 October 1968.
5 MM, *Life of Rachel*, p. 153.
6 Ibid., p. 154.
7 Ibid., p. 162.
8 J. R. Clynes, 'Trade Unionism's Debt to Keir Hardie', *The Labour Leader*, 30 September 1915.
9 MM, 'Reconstruction After the War', *The Teacher's World*, 1 March 1916.
10 MM, *Life of Rachel*, p. 164.
11 Ibid.
12 Ibid., p. 167.
13 E. Stevinson, *The Open-air Nursery School*, Dent, 1927, p. 57.
14 MM, *Life of Rachel*, p. 168.
15 Ibid., pp. 171, 172.
16 Ibid., pp. 172, 173.
17 Ibid., pp. 176, 177.
18 Ibid., p. 185.
19 Ibid., p. 186.

18 State Provision of Nursery Schools 1917–19

1 MM, *The Life of Rachel McMillan*, Dent, 1927, pp. 186, 187.
2 A. Mansbridge, *Margaret McMillan Prophet and Pioneer*, Dent, 1932, p. 163.

3 M. Sutcliffe, *Anthroposophic News Sheet* 41/42, October 1959.
4 Mansbridge, *Margaret McMillan*, p. 135.
5 MM, 'The Musician', *The Daily News and Leader*, 27 August 1918.
6 MM, *Life of Rachel*, p. 200.
7 H. A. L. Fisher, in 'Education Minister at Deptford', *The Kentish Mercury*, 10 August 1917.
8 MM, in ibid.
9 Sir R. Morant, in ibid.
10 H. A. L. Fisher, in ibid.
11 'Nursery Schools – A Deptford Experiment', *The Kentish Mercury*, 17 August 1917.
12 'The Imperial Orders', *The Kentish Mercury*, 31 August 1917.
13 MM, private letter to Cousin Elizabeth, 16 October 1917.
14 MM, 'The Nursery Schools of To-morrow and Their Effect on Education in Schools', Address given to Association of University Women Teachers, 12 January 1918, privately printed report.
15 MM, 'The Open-Air Nursery School', *The Labour Leader*, 30 May 1918.
16 MM, 'Some Boys', *The Daily News and Leader*, 21 September 1917.
17 J. King, in *Parliamentary Debates 1918*, vol. 106, pp. 1028, 1029.
18 MM, in 'Dawn of the Women's Day in Politics', *The Labour Leader*, 31 October 1918.

19 Our Maggie

1 H. Edwards, 'Margaret McMillan Reminiscences', Rachel McMillan Training College Old Students' Association, unpublished pamphlet, n.d., p. 13.
2 W. de la Mare, in M. Stuart, 'Margaret McMillan', *The Post*, 17 April 1937.
3 J. Robertshaw, in M. Lord, *Margaret McMillan in Bradford*, University of London Press, 1957, p. 19.
4 A. Mansbridge, *Margaret McMillan Prophet and Pioneer*, Dent, 1932, p. 136.
5 M. Bondfield, in M. Stuart, 'Margaret McMillan', *The Post*, 17 April 1937.
6 A. Mansbridge, *The Kingdom of the Mind*, Dent, 1944, p. 191.
7 G. A. N. Lowndes, *Margaret McMillan 'The Children's Champion'*, Museum Press, 1960, p. 37.
8 P. B. Ballard, *Margaret McMillan – An Appreciation*, printed for the Rachel McMillan Training College, n.d., pp. 8–10.
9 J. J. Mallon, 'The Portrait Gallery', *The Woman Worker*, 5 June 1908.
10 'Margaret McMillan', *The Times*, 18 March 1932.
11 J. B. Priestley, 'The Nuisance Who Worked Miracles', *The Daily Herald*, 27 June 1947.
12 M. Drummond, 'Margaret McMillan', *The Scottish Educational Journal*, 3 April 1931.
13 H. W., 'An Educational Pioneer', *Time and Tide*, 14 May 1932.

14 R. Blatchford, in Mansbridge, *Margaret McMillan*, pp. 131, 159.
15 G. B. Shaw, in Mansbridge, *Margaret McMillan*, p. 131.
16 G. B. Shaw, in Lowndes, *Margaret McMillan*, p. 98.
17 A. Mansbridge, *The Trodden Road*, Dent, 1940, p. 153.
18 Lady Norman, in 'A Terrible Nuisance', BBC Radio 4, 29 March 1981.
19 G. Harris, private letter to E. Bradburn, 19 November 1968.
20 K. Chambers, in M. Lord, *Margaret McMillan in Bradford*, University of London Press, 1957, p. 24.
21 H. Danby, private letter to G. A. N. Lowndes, 19 April 1960.
22 MM, private letter to Mrs R. Blatchford in Mansbridge, *Margaret McMillan*, pp. 143, 144.
23 E. M. Williamson, private letter to E. Bradburn, 19 November 1976.
24 A. Campbell, in 'Margaret McMillan Reminiscences', p. 9.
25 R. B. Phillips, in Mansbridge, *Margaret McMillan*, pp. 109–11.
26 MM, 'The Dream of Iona', *The Labour Leader*, 29 December 1905.
27 R. Brain, in 'Margaret McMillan Reminiscences', p. 5.
28 J. Burley, private letter to M. Davies, 31 January 1960.
29 I. Barnes, private letter to E. Bradburn, 18 May 1973.
30 Lowndes, *Margaret McMillan*, p. 42.
31 Mansbridge, *Margaret McMillan*, p. 133.
32 MM, in Mansbridge, *Margaret McMillan*, pp. 162, 163.
33 Ibid., pp. 160, 161, 163.
34 East Ham Borough Labour Party and Trades Council, 'Margaret McMillan', in *Pioneers of Social Progress*, May 1954 (no page given).
35 MM, *The Nursery School*, Dent, 1930, p. 139.

20 The Rachel McMillan Open-air Nursery School 1918–19

1 'New Books', *The Times Educational Supplement*, 11 December 1919.
2 MM, *Labour and Childhood*, Swan Sonnenschein, 1907, p. 205.
3 MM, *The Beginnings of Education*, ILP pamphlet, n.d. (*c.* 1906), p. 19.
4 MM, *The Child and the State*, National Labour Press, 1911, pp. 203, 204.
5 MM, *The Nursery School*, Dent, 1919, p. 21.
6 MM, 'Nursery Schools and the Pre-school Child', *Labour Magazine*, vol. 3, May 1924, p. 17.
7 MM, *The Nursery School*, pp. 173, 174.
8 MM, *Nursery Schools and the Pre-school Child*, Nursery Schools Association pamphlet, n.d. (*c.* 1925), pp. 5, 6.
9 A. F. B., 'A Child Programme', *The Labour Leader*, 31 March 1911.
10 MM, *The Nursery School*, p. 351.
11 MM, *Nursery Schools and the Pre-school Child*, pp. 4, 5.
12 MM, unpublished handwritten document, Rachel McMillan College, London, n.d.
13 MM, *The Nursery School*, Dent, 1930, pp. 55, 56.
14 Ibid., Dent, 1930, pp. 64–7.

15 Ibid., Dent, 1919, pp. 130, 131.
16 Ibid., Dent, 1930, p. 80.
17 MM, in G. A. N. Lowndes, *Margaret McMillan 'The Children's Champion'*, Museum Press, 1960, pp. 107, 108.
18 MM, *The Nursery School*, Dent, 1919, pp. 41, 42.
19 MM, 'To Lead Civilization', *Bolton Evening News*, 28 July 1930.
20 MM, in Lowndes, *Margaret McMillan*, pp. 107, 108.
21 MM, *What the Open-air Nursery School Is*, Labour Party pamphlet, 1930, p. 4.
22 MM, *The Nursery School*, Dent, 1930, p. 124.
23 MM, unpublished handwritten document, Rachel McMillan College, London, n.d.
24 MM, *The Nursery School*, Dent, 1919, p. 175.
25 Ibid.
26 M. Sutcliffe, 'Margaret McMillan and Rudolph Steiner', *Anthroposophic News Sheet* 41/42, October 1959.
27 MM, 'Nursery Schools and the Pre-school Child', *Labour Magazine*, vol. 3, May 1924, p. 17.
28 H. Edwards, 'Margaret McMillan Reminiscences', Rachel McMillan Training College Old Students' Association, unpublished pamphlet, n.d., pp. 13, 14.
29 G. Harvey, 'Margaret McMillan Reminiscences', pp. 2, 3, 4.

21 Developing the Nursery School and Training Centre 1919–25

 1 MM, in G. A. N. Lowndes, *Margaret McMillan 'The Children's Champion'*, Museum Press, 1960, p. 48.
 2 A. Campbell, recorded interview with E. Bradburn, 1978.
 3 J. M. Dent, private letter to Margaret McMillan, 1 March 1919.
 4 J. M. Dent, private letter to Margaret McMillan, 1 January 1923.
 5 A. Mansbridge, *Fellowmen: A Gallery of England, 1876–1946*, Dent, 1948, p. 84.
 6 MM, private letter to J. M. Dent, 22 September 1923.
 7 P. B. Ballard, T. M. Morton and C. J. Thomas, LCC Inspectors' Report on Rachel McMillan Nursery School, 23 May 1919.
 8 MM, *The Nursery School*, Dent, 1930, pp. 23, 24.
 9 Ibid., p. 25.
10 Ibid., pp. 25, 26.
11 Ibid., p. 28.
12 Ibid., p. 29.
13 Ibid., p. 41.
14 J. Snowden, private letter to E. Bradburn, 3 December 1976.
15 MM, *The Nursery School*, Dent, 1930, p. 78.
16 Ibid., Dent, 1919, pp. 228, 229.
17 MM, in A. Mansbridge, *Margaret McMillan Prophet and Pioneer*, Dent, 1932, pp. 101, 102.
18 MM, 'Some Boys', *The Daily News and Leader*, 21 September 1917.

19 MM, 'College and Cloister', *The Daily News and Leader*, 18 October 1918.
20 E. Stevinson, *The Open-air Nursery School*, Dent, 1927, p. 58.
21 MM, *The Nursery School*, Dent, 1930, p. 127.
22 'New Books', *The Times Educational Supplement*, 11 December 1919.
23 MM, *The Nursery School*, Dent, 1930, pp. 131–3.
24 G. Yorath, private letter to E. Bradburn, 7 December 1972.
25 I. Barnes, private letter to E. Bradburn, 18 May 1973.
26 A. Campbell, recorded interview with E. Bradburn, 1980.
27 Stevinson, *The Open-air Nursery School*, p. 60.
28 MM, *The Nursery School*, Dent, 1930, p. 89.
29 Ibid., 1919, p. 330.
30 Stevinson, *The Open-air Nursery School*, p. 48.
31 MM, *The Nursery School*, Dent, 1930, pp. 90–2.
32 MM, 'Housing and Homemaking', *The Times Educational Supplement*, 3 April 1919.
33 Stevinson, *The Open-air Nursery School*, pp. 12, 13.
34 Ibid., pp. 10, 11.
35 MM, *The Nursery School*, Dent, 1930, p. 134.
36 A. Campbell, recorded interview with E. Bradburn, 1980.
37 MM, Minutes of LCC Education Meeting, 24 February 1920, p. 113.
38 P. B. Ballard, 'Margaret McMillan – An Appreciation', printed for the Rachel McMillan Training College, n.d., p. 6.
39 Stevinson, *The Open-air Nursery School*, p. 59.
40 M. Sutcliffe, 'Margaret McMillan and Rudolph Steiner', *Anthroposophic News Sheet* 41/42, October 1959.
41 G. Yorath, private letter to E. Bradburn, 7 December 1972.
42 M. Davies, private letter to G. A. N. Lowndes, 1959.
43 MM, *What the Open-air Nursery School Is*, Labour Party pamphlet, 1930, p. 2.
44 K. Freeman, *If Any Man Build*, Hodder and Stoughton, 1965, p. 44.
45 'Miss Margaret McMillan', *The Daily News*, 25 September 1924.
46 F. J. Bryer and A. Purkis, Address of Appreciation by the Mayor, Aldermen and Citizens of Deptford, 10 November 1924, in Lowndes, *Margaret McMillan*, Appendix B.
47 J. Pearse, 'Memories of Margaret McMillan', *News from British Association for Early Childhood Education*, Diamond Jubilee issue, 1983, p. 5.

22 A Dream College 1925–30

1 MM, 'Those that are Sent Away', *Anthroposophy*, vol. II, no. II, 1923, p. 152.
2 D. E. M. Gardner, private letter to G. A. N. Lowndes, 1960.
3 MM, '*The Clarion* And Children', *The Clarion*, 5 February 1926.
4 MM, 'Education And *The Clarion*', *The Clarion*, 21 May 1926.
5 MM, private letter to J. M. Dent, 2 November 1925.

6 MM, private letter to J. M. Dent, 25 April 1926.
7 MM, handwritten document 'President's Address to the Froebel Society in Bradford', 1926.
8 MM, 'Education And *The Clarion*', *The Clarion*, 28 May 1926.
9 MM, 'Education And *The Clarion*', *The Clarion*, 23 April 1926.
10 MM, 'Education And *The Clarion*', *The Clarion*, 9 April 1926.
11 W. Bonny, 'Margaret McMillan Reminiscences', Rachel McMillan Training College Old Students' Association, unpublished pamphlet, n.d., p. 1.
12 J. Pearse, recorded interview with BBC, 1980.
13 Viscountess N. Astor, private letter to G. A. N. Lowndes, 1960.
14 C. Sykes, *Nancy (the life of Lady Astor)*, Collins, 1972, pp. 283, 284.
15 MM, private letter to Lady Astor, 10 November 1926.
16 MM, private letter to Lady Astor, 20 November 1926.
17 Sykes, *Nancy*, p. 284.
18 A. Mansbridge, *Fellowmen: A Gallery of England, 1876–1946*, Dent, 1948, p. 68.
19 'Lady Astor At Deptford', *The Times*, 7 November 1929.
20 Lady Astor, in 'Margaret McMillan Memorial', *The Kentish Mercury*, 28 October 1932.
21 MM, private letter to K. B. Glasier, 8 July 1927.
22 'Training Fund for Girls', *The Yorkshire Post*, 5 February 1929.
23 MM, 'Nursery Schools: the Base of Education', *Royal Sanitary Institute Journal*, October 1928, p. 186.
24 K. B. Glasier, 'The End of Child Suffering', *The New Leader*, 8 July 1927.
25 M. Tai, private letter to M. McMillan, 20 April 1927.
26 P. B. Ballard, 'Margaret McMillan – An Appreciation', printed for the Rachel McMillan Training College, Temple Press, n.d. (*c.* 1937), p. 1.
27 L. Middleton, private letter to E. Bradburn, 22 September 1969.
28 S. Baldwin, in '20 Years Work for Children in London Slums', *Evening Standard*, 19 April 1929.
29 MM, in ibid.
30 'Old Timer', letter to E. Bradburn, 1973.
31 W. Llewellyn Jones, 'Margaret McMillan Reminiscences', p. 22.
32 M. Collis, *Nancy Astor*, Faber, 1960, p. 143.
33 Deptford Mother, in 'Nursery Schools: the Base of Education', *Royal Sanitary Institute Journal*, October 1928, p. 186.
34 MM, 'The Schools of To-morrow', *The Christian Commonwealth*, 21 January 1914.
35 MM, from 'Letter to Students', printed in *Rachel McMillan News Sheet*, 1929, p. 1.
36 J. K. Hardie, *From Serfdom to Socialism*, Harvester Press, 1974, pp. 101, 102.
37 Prudentia, in 'It was a Famous Victory', *The Clarion*, March 1929.
38 R. Blatchford, 'It was a Famous Victory', *The Clarion*, March 1929.
39 MM, private letter to R. Blatchford in A. Greenwood, 'All Children Are Mine', University of London Press, n.d., p. 15.

40 MM, from 'Leaflet for the Visitors present at the Stone-Laying Ceremony', at the Rachel McMillan College, 6 November 1929.
41 Lady Astor, in 'Current News Among Friends', *The Friend*, 15 November 1929.
42 'Current News Among Friends', *The Friend*, 15 November 1929.
43 MM, in 'Margaret McMillan', *Times Literary Supplement*, 7 April 1932.
44 H. G. Bannan, 'Brave Beginnings', unpublished document, n.d., pp. 1–3.
45 G. Williams, 'My Visit to the Rachel McMillan Nursery School', *Under the Red Dragon*, no. 16, June 1931, pp. 36–8.
46 'Helping the Slum Child', *The Times*, 21 April 1930.
47 'Queen in Deptford', *The Evening Standard*, 9 May 1930.
48 D. E. Brown, private letter to E. Bradburn, 29 January 1973.
49 MM, in 'Miss McMillan's Speech at the Opening', *Rachel McMillan Students' News Sheet*, July 1931, p. 4.
50 M. Wilson, 'Margaret McMillan Reminiscences', p. 12.
51 MM, *The Nursery School*, Dent, 1930, p. 139.
52 M. Sutcliffe, 'Margaret McMillan and Rudolph Steiner', *Anthroposophic News Sheet* 41/42, October 1959.

23 Bowing Out from the World Stage 1930–1

1 W. Llewellyn Jones, private letter to E. Bradburn, 25 January 1973.
2 A. Mansbridge, *Fellowmen: A Gallery of England, 1876–1946*, Dent, 1948, p. 67.
3 C. Trevelyan, private letter to M. McMillan, 3 June 1930.
4 M. Peet, 'A Prophet and Pioneer', *The Friend*, 15 April 1932.
5 H. Edwards, 'Margaret McMillan Reminiscences', Rachel McMillan Training College Old Students' Association, unpublished pamphlet, n.d., pp. 14, 15.
6 A. Mansbridge, *Margaret McMillan Prophet and Pioneer*, Dent, 1932, pp. 118–20.
7 Lady N. Astor, private letter to M. McMillan, 8 January 1931.
8 'Miss Margaret McMillan', *The Kentish Mercury*, 16 January 1931.
9 W. Llewellyn Jones, private letter to E. Bradburn, 25 January 1973.
10 Mansbridge, *Fellowmen*, p. 85.
11 C. Sykes, *Nancy (the life of Lady Astor)*, Collins, 1972, p. 284.
12 J. P., 'In Memoriam: Margaret McMillan', *The Friend*, 17 April 1931.
13 'Miss Margaret McMillan', *The Times*, 30 March 1931.
14 'Rachel and Margaret McMillan: Nursery School Pioneers', *The Times Educational Supplement*, 4 April 1931.
15 'The Late Miss Margaret McMillan', *The Kentish Mercury*, 24 April 1931.
16 H. B. Lees-Smith, 'Mother-Wit', *Everyman*, 7 April 1932.
17 J. B. Webb, 'Margaret McMillan', *The Sydney Morning Herald*, 23 May 1931.

18 E. Stevinson, letter in *Rachel McMillan Training College News Sheet*, July 1931.
19 D. Steele, unprinted appreciation of life and work of Miriam Lord, July 1968.

24 Some Personal Observations

1 MM, in M. Lord, *Margaret McMillan in Bradford*, University of London Press, 1956, p. 5.
2 R. Rees, *Social and Political Change in England 1880–1914, Margaret McMillan and the Battle for the Slum Child*, Longman, 1986, pp. 20–8.
3 J. Wesley Bready, *Lord Shaftesbury and Social Industrial Progress*, Allen and Unwin, 1926.
4 E. Bradburn, 'Britain's First Nursery-Infant School', in K. B. Spodek, *Early Childhood Education*, Prentice-Hall, New Jersey, 1973, pp. 153–62.
5 P. McCann and F. A. Young, *Samuel Wilderspin and the Infant School Movement*, Croom Helm, 1982.
6 E. Mellor, *Education through Experience in the Infant School Years*, Blackwell, 1966.
7 A. Curtis, *A Curriculum for the Pre-school Child*, NFER-Nelson, 1986.
8 S. Phillips, 'Maria Montessori and Contemporary Cognitive Psychology', *British Journal of Teacher Education*, vol. 3, no. 1, January 1977, pp. 55–68.
9 E. R. Murray and H. Brown Smith, *The Child Under Eight*, Arnold, 1919.
10 S. J. Curtis and M. E. A. Boultwood, *A Short History of Educational Ideas*, University Tutorial Press, 1953, p. 482.
11 C. Burt, in G. A. N. Lowndes, *Margaret McMillan 'The Children's Champion'*, Museum Press, 1960, p. 97.

25 Afterword – Some Unfinished Tasks

1 R. B. Darlington, 'Pre-school Programs and Later School Competence of Children from Low-Income Families', *Science*, vol. 208, 11 April 1980.
2 D. Hevey, *The Continuing Under Fives Muddle! An Investigation of Current Training Opportunities*, VOLCUF, 1986.
3 'Quality in Schools: the Initial Training of Teachers', DES Report, HMSO, 1987, p. 97.
4 S. Jowett and K. Sylvia, 'Does kind of pre-school matter?' *Educational Research*, vol. 28, no. 1, February 1986, pp. 21–30.
5 Report of the Archbishop of Canterbury's Commission on Urban Priority Areas, 'Faith in the City', Church House Publishing, 1985, p. xiv.
6 The Committee of Inquiry into the Education of Children from Ethnic Minority Groups, 'Education for All', HMSO, 1985. Cmnd 9453.

7 UNICEF Report, 'Statistical Review of the Situation of Children in the World', 1986, p. 3.

8 MM, *Infant Mortality*, ILP pamphlet, n.d., p. 6.

9 S. Barnes, *200 Million Hungry Children*, Grosvenor Books, 1980, p. 18.

10 T. W. Mercer, 'Margaret McMillan: Prophet and Pioneer', *The Millgate Monthly*, June 1932, p. 542.

11 A. Toynbee, *Civilization on Trial and The World and the West*, Meridian Books, World Publishing Co., 1958, p. 50.

12 MM, *Labour and Childhood*, Swan Sonnenschein, 1907, p. 205.

Index